FLORIDA'S
BEST BEACH
VACATIONS

◎　　◎　　◎

OTHER BOOKS CO-AUTHORED BY ROBERT TOLF AND RUSSELL BUCHAN

Florida: A Guide to the Best Restaurants, Resorts, and Hotels
Florida Weekends: 52 Great Getaways Throughout Florida and the Keys

FLORIDA'S
BEST BEACH
VACATIONS

GREAT GETAWAYS FOR FUN
IN THE SUN ALL YEAR ROUND

ROBERT TOLF AND
RUSSELL BUCHAN

CLARKSON POTTER/PUBLISHERS
NEW YORK

Copyright © 1992 by Robert Tolf and Russell Buchan
Map copyright © 1992 by David Lindroth

Published by Clarkson N. Potter, Inc., 201 East 50th Street, New York,
New York 10022. Member of the Crown Publishing Group.

CLARKSON N. POTTER, POTTER and colophon are trademarks of Clarkson N. Potter, Inc.

Manufactured in the United States of America

Library of Congress Cataloging-in-Publication Data
Tolf, Robert W.
    Florida's best beach vacations : great getaways for fun in the sun
all year round / by Robert Tolf and Russell Buchan.
        p. cm.
    Includes index.
    1. Florida—Guidebooks. 2. Beaches—Florida—Guidebooks.
I. Buchan, Russell. II. Title.
F309.3.T67 1992
917.5904'63—dc20
92-8428
CIP

ISBN 0-517-58599-5

10 9 8 7 6 5 4 3 2 1

First Edition

CONTENTS

INTRODUCTION   ix

SOUTHEASTERN FLORIDA:
THE GOLD COAST AND THE KEYS

THE MIAMI AREA
Miami Beach   3
Key Biscayne   19

THE KEYS
Key Largo   30
Middle Keys   38
Key West   46

HOLLYWOOD TO VERO BEACH AREA
Hollywood Beach   59
Fort Lauderdale Beach   73
Boca Raton and Delray Beach   86
Vero Beach   100

CENTRAL FLORIDA AND THE
SPACE COAST
Cocoa Beach   113
Daytona Beach   125

NORTHERN FLORIDA: PENSACOLA TO JACKSONVILLE TO ST. AUGUSTINE

Pensacola   141
Okaloosa and Walton Counties   154
Panama City Beach   170
Sandy Shangri-las: Dog Island and St. Joseph Peninsula
   State Park   184
Amelia Island and Fernandina Beach   188
St. Augustine Beach   197

SOUTHWESTERN FLORIDA: TAMPA BAY TO FORT MYERS BEACH

Clearwater Beach   213
St. Petersburg Beach and Fort DeSoto Park   223
Longboat Key and Lido Beach   237
Sanibel and Captiva Islands   247
Fort Myers Beach   264

INDEX   277

INTRODUCTION

L ife's a Beach!"
So say Florida T-shirts and bumper stickers.

And if a beach vacation is your dream, there's no better place to come than Florida, according to several surveys that name Florida beaches as the best in the world.

A recent rating by the Maryland-based Laboratory for Coastal Research ranked fifteen of Florida's beaches among the top twenty in the country, evaluating them on the basis of water and air temperatures, number of sunny days, currents, land and water pests, softness of sand, cleanliness, ease of access, crowds, and crime rate.

The best of Florida's beaches dot both its coasts—on the Atlantic Ocean from Amelia Island in the north, down the Space Coast to Miami Beach, then around the Florida Keys and up the coast of the Gulf of Mexico to Sanibel and Captiva islands, Tampa Bay, and the northern Panhandle.

Florida has more beaches and barrier islands than any other state in the nation; some 1,200 miles of coastline, 8,000 miles counting islands and islets. There are beaches for basking and bronzing or for swimming and surfing, for lazing under palm trees or for surf casting, for boating or for snorkeling and scuba diving. You can toss a Frisbee, spike a volleyball, build sand castles, glide along in a sailboat, or roar over the waves with engines at full throttle.

Our favorite beaches were selected after years and years of dedicated beach-going, from the tan and broken-shell strips on the northeast coast and the hard-packed surfaces of Daytona and Ormond beaches to the many crowded and compact stretches of the Gold Coast in the southeast, the hard-to-find sites in the Keys, and the family-oriented spots on the Gulf of Mexico where the sand is as pristine as fresh-fallen snow.

The beaches included in this book run the gamut from the sands fronting the Art Deco masterpiece that is the heart of the National Historic District of South Miami Beach to the expanse of sand by one of Florida's classic 1920s hotels in St. Petersburg; from a National Seashore where jets whiz overhead to a sunny shoreline watched over by a solid-as-Gibraltar fortress built before the Civil War.

The beaches of Florida are sensational for shell collectors of all ages and degrees of experience and expertise. Most famous, as well as one of the top three shelling sites in the world, is Sanibel-Captiva, but on many other beaches there are thousands of shells for conchologists to collect; for example, more than 200 species can be found on Tampa Bay beaches alone.

And Florida cares for its beaches, supporting and funding all levels of renourishment projects including the most ambitious in the United States, which brought Miami Beach back to life in the 1980s. Recent projects pumping sea-bottom sand revitalized the Boca Raton beach, as well as the beaches of Fort Lauderdale, Hollywood, Hallandale, and the John U. Lloyd Beach State Recreation Area—a total 875,000 cubic yards of sand at a cost of $9 million.

Florida and its beach communities also care about the safety of their beach vacationers. Flag systems in use where there are lifeguards are simple to decipher:

Green—Good Conditions
Yellow—Caution
Red—No Swimming
Orange—No Surfing
Blue—Portuguese Man-of-war Present

The Portuguese man-of-war jellyfish arrive sporadically as blue-and-purple diaphanous blobs, which are found in shallow water or marooned on the sand. Do not touch or probe at the bags, which contain a toxic gas that could harm your eyes as seriously as the tentacles of the noxious beastie can sting your skin.

Obey the yellow flag warning of riptides, those powerful, speedy rushes of water that occur when high winds blow in the kinds of waves surfers love. But when the water crashes onto a sloping shoreline, gravity forces it back into the sea, creating outgoing currents and an undertow that can become supercharged as the water roars through gaps or depressions in the sandbar. The resulting riptide can seriously affect swimmers—even strong, experienced ones—as much as a hundred yards out in the water.

Don't ignore these warnings. If there is a question about beach conditions, check with your hotel or contact the local chamber of commerce or beach information bureau.

So, come and enjoy some of the best beaches in the country—all year round. In the winter, sun worshipers favor the beaches in the southern part of the state, where warm days still threaten sunburn. In summer, beaches throughout Florida draw vacationers, depending on the beach lover's degree of tolerance for sun and heat. This is a booming season for beaches in northern Florida, where summer temperatures are a bit cooler.

But no matter what the season, the beaches statewide offer countless choices of recreational activities—opportunities for fun in the sun.

HOW TO USE THIS GUIDE

We have separated the twenty-two different beach vacations in this book into four geographical sections:

Southeastern Florida: The Gold Coast and the Keys—Miami, Key Biscayne, Hollywood, Fort Lauderdale, Boca Raton, Delray Beach, Vero Beach, and the Keys.

Central Florida and the Space Coast—Cocoa Beach and Daytona Beach.

Northern Florida—Pensacola, Okaloosa and Walton counties, Panama City Beach, Dog Island and St. Joseph Peninsula State Park, Amelia Island and Fernandina Beach (north of Jacksonville), and St. Augustine Beach.

Southwestern Florida—Clearwater Beach, St. Petersburg Beach and Fort De Soto Park, Longboat Key and Lido Beach (near Sarasota/Bradenton), Fort Myers Beach, and Sanibel and Captiva islands.

*   *   *

Each beach vacation focuses on a specific geographical area. In describing each vacation, we tell you about the special qualities and features of that beach area that make it different from others. We also tell you about special sights and other recreational activities to help you make your day-to-day plans.

At the end of each vacation write-up, we provide additional information such as the following:

Where It Is

This will tell you where the beach area is located, including highway and mileage information.

Where to Stay

For accommodations, we offer a range of choices—from deluxe resorts and hotels to motels, beach cottages, and condominium rentals, where available—so you can choose what is appropriate for your beach vacation. The where-to-stay listings include our review, the address, telephone number (including an 800 number if available), and price range.

Because of the current proliferation of credit cards, we have not listed all the individual cards accepted by an establishment. Unless we have noted that a hotel, motel, or restaurant does not take credit cards, you can plan on at least one major credit card being accepted.

Where to Eat

We provide a variety of restaurant choices—so you may choose from the ones in keeping with your preference of beach vacation, whether it be a luxurious, high-style escape; a budget-oriented family vacation; or a bathing-suit-and-sandals, sandwich-and-burger-type getaway with friends. The where-to-eat listings include the type of cuisine featured, our review, address, telephone number, price range, days open, and meals served (breakfast, lunch, dinner).

We have not included holiday closings (Thanksgiving, Christmas, or New Year's Day) or specific hours of operation in the restaurant listings. In such a seasonal state, consistency seldom prevails in these matters and we advise you to inquire concerning hours and holidays. We have, however, noted those restaurants that close during certain months of the year or seasonally.

Where to Shop

In this section, we direct you to places for beach accessories and beachwear, sunglasses and T-shirts, tanning oils and souvenirs. For necessities, we cover drugstores, delis, pharmacies, and grocery stores. Most of the stores listed are open daily, but hours and days can change with season and locale.

More Fun in the Sun

For those who don't want to spend every moment on the beach, we've suggested other recreational activities, including parasailing, snorkeling and scuba diving, boat cruises and shelling expeditions, beach trolley sight-seeing, nature trips, moped and bicycle outings, fishing and miniature golf, and more. Where applicable, names, addresses, and phone numbers are included to help you make plans before you arrive.

Where to Write

In this section you'll find the addresses and phone numbers of chambers of commerce, visitor bureaus, attractions, and state and national parks in your beach vacation area so that you can obtain more information before you go.

PRICES

We have used three categories of prices for accommodations and restaurants: inexpensive, moderate, and expensive. For accommodations, prices are based on a double occupancy room, but not tax or tips. For restaurants, prices are based on dinner, including appetizer, entree, and dessert, but not tax, tip, or drinks.

Inexpensive: Under $15 for dinner
                 Under $75 for a double occupancy room
Moderate: Between $15 and $30 for dinner
                 Between $75 and $125 for a double occupancy room

Expensive: $30 and up for dinner

                       $125 and up for a double occupancy room

    Room prices are general and, of course, subject to change, and there are great variations between high-season and low-season rates. So, during the off-season, inquire about special rates and budget-stretching deals.

    High season in the Panhandle section of Florida (beaches in northern Florida on the Gulf of Mexico) is from Memorial Day to Labor Day. In most of Southeastern, Southwestern, and Central Florida, high season is from December to mid-April.

SOUTHEASTERN FLORIDA: THE GOLD COAST AND THE KEYS

◎　　◎　　◎

THE MIAMI AREA
MIAMI BEACH

Miami Beach was mightily blessed in the late 1970s when the U.S. Army Corps of Engineers launched the greatest beach restoration project in the country's history—the pouring of 13.5 million cubic yards of sand on a little more than nine miles of shoreline that created a brand-new beach 300 feet wide with some 211,000 cubic yards needing to be refed annually. The $62 million investment was a real boon to Miami Beach, which was undergoing its own renascence on land, including the restoration and refurbishment of such giant superluxe resorts as the Fontainbleau Hilton and an infusion of sufficient capital and talent on South Beach to make over a fair portion of the square mile of the Art Deco District, in the National Register of Historic Places since 1979. That was only sixty-four years after the visionary Carl Fisher, the automobile baron who built the Indianapolis Speedway, first bridged the mangrove swamps of the island to the mainland, convinced that he could inspire another Riviera, a new tourist Mecca for all those seeking June in January.

We have nothing against the spreads of sand to the north of that district, the miles that go all the way to the 172 acres of Haulover Park and its fine beach. The Art Deco District is simply far more fascinating, especially the stretch along the oceanfront from Fifth Street in the south to 23rd Street in the north. We terminate our favorite strip at 15th Street, and start it at the southernmost tip of the island, at South Pointe Park, with its wonderful

3

boardwalk along Government Cut, overlooking Fisher Island and providing grand sentry posts for watching the giant tankers, container ships, and cruise ships glide past. Boat-watchers and old salts can while away many an hour keeping track of that traffic or taking the short trip over to the Port of Miami, Cruise Capital of the World, where millions of passengers take to the waters around the Caribbean and beyond.

At South Pointe Park you can also get a good look at the stables of the Miami Beach Mounted Police and take the younger set on Friday nights to the petting zoo and on weekends to the outdoor theater for free concerts and shows. Scattered around the plantation plantings of palms are plenty of picnic tables, grills, and playgrounds to keep the kids occupied while the hamburgers and hot dogs are getting ready.

Pier Park, at the intersection of Ocean Drive and Biscayne Street, just north of South Pointe, has more than four acres of developed beach. The area is the best spot for surfing, but only the best of the hang-ten bunch should brave the waves during the high seas of the tropical storm season. It's safer to join the crowds, especially on the weekends, at South Pointe, with its good-size parking lots, rest rooms, and outdoor showers; or the mobs that congregate— *sardine* is a better word—at First Street to watch the nonstop volleyball games. Penrod's Beach Club, a pink-and-blue oasis of pool parties, dancing, and people mingling, is smack in the center of all the action. Across the street are buildings awaiting the Art Deco decorators and restorers: the Pizza Playhouse, with raw bar and foot-long hoagies; Rolo's, Home of the Best Burger, next door; and the unique Leonard Beach Hotel.

The mix is more than coincidental; it's an introduction to the cultural carousel coursing all along the ten blocks of Art Deco delights, in themselves a crash course in the unique style that flowed from the French Arts Decoratifs in the 1920s, modified by Art Moderne, the world's fairs of the time, and luxury ocean liner themes.

Cubism, Expressionism, and Futurism were somehow merged into a peculiarly American statement of style, incongruously popping out of the sand in subtropical Miami Beach. Familiar to fans of TV's "Miami Vice," it's a style of curvilinear dimensions, of smooth-line nudes and flora twisting out of the Art Nouveau complexities, placing their accents as relief on the predominately vertical low-rise structures—seldom taller than the palm trees planted all along the beach and streets.

There are no Art Deco monuments on the beach to compete with Chicago's

Board of Trade, New York's Rockefeller Center, Radio City Music Hall, or the Waldorf Astoria; in fact, none of the twenty Art Deco masterpieces of the style still existing in the United States are in Florida. But some of the architects who designed them and many who copied them did their work in Miami Beach, adding eyebrows (technically known as cantilevered window shades), portholes, Mayan-Aztec-inspired tile treatments, and in recent years, painting them in a candy store array of sherbet colors and softly subdued pastels. In the Art Deco District some 650 of the 800 buildings reflect in one way or another such emphasis and excess, and that's why we like to stroll the pinkish promenade along Ocean Drive, finding such Spanish and Mediterranean Revival interruptions as the old Amsterdam Palace at number 116, modeled after Casa Colon, the Christopher Columbus home in Santo Domingo. If you can gain entrance into the courtyard, take a peek at the bas-reliefs of Columbus caravels, Queen Isabella and King Ferdinand, and much else.

Across the street is Lummus Park, a forty-eight-acre spread of developed beach that runs from Fifth Street to 14th Street, with playgrounds, rest rooms, volleyball nets, benches for resting and watching, chickee huts for finding shade and snacking on picnic fare, and a variety of entrepreneurs renting water sports gear and selling sustenance—our favorite is the van that is painted as beautifully pastel as the Miami Beach water towers. During one wonderful weekend a year, the first or second in January, Lummus is jammed with concertgoers gathered in front of two stages, one in northern Lummus and one in the south, attracting the likes of Dizzy Gillespie and Dixieland greats. The weekend kicks off with a Moon over Miami Ball at the Miami Beach Auditorium; black-tie or vintage 1930s dress and reservations are required (305-672-2014). The street fair is free and it's in full swing on Friday, Saturday, and Sunday. With the best backdrop in the world, various vendors, artists, and antiques dealers peddle and promote their Art Deco treasures—clothing, jewelry, furnishings, doo-dads, and enough flamingos to block the sun.

There are special Art Deco exhibits at the Bass Museum of Art, 2100 Park Avenue, close to the 21st Street branch library, which sponsors Art Deco lectures and seminars. Foot and tram tours are organized by members of the Miami Design Preservation League, which has a large booth in the center of the street fair, and is the only official outlet for Art Deco Weekend products, posters, books, postcards, and T-shirts, the sale of which benefits its active preservation programs. After the hectic happenings of the weekend, the league returns to its regularly scheduled ninety-minute Saturday-morning guided bus tours through the square mile of pastels, incised ornamentation, aluminum, chrome, and glass blocks. If you want to do some homework before taking the tour, buy the 192-page *Miami Beach Art Deco Guide* at the departure point, the league's welcome center in the Promenade Building at 661 Washington Avenue (305-672-2014). There are half a dozen self-guided walking tours outlined in the book.

You'll see a good many familiar buildings and locations as you take your stroll through Crockett's and Tubbs's turf—"Miami Vice" was filmed all over the Art Deco District. And thousands, literally, of models, photographers, and other TV crews have used the district extensively in their movie, fashion, and food shoots. And that's another reason we like this particular portion of South Beach. There are some three dozen restaurants that are among the most exciting to be found—not only in Florida but in the nation. They cater to artists, cameramen, and models from around the world; to yuppies and yuccas (young upper-class Cuban-Americans); and to Europeans and South Americans who find the Miamamerican cuisine as stimulating as memories of the Jazz Age.

Where It Is
South Miami Beach, with its Art Deco District, is three miles from downtown Miami, five from the Port of Miami, ten from the Miami International Airport, and is easily reached by well-marked roads and Interstate 395, which leads directly to the MacArthur Causeway (U.S. 41) and Fifth Street, the beginning of the Art Deco District.

Where to Stay

BEACON
Hotel/Miami Beach
The Beacon sign beckons brightly at the entrance to this four-story, free-standing Art Deco delight, not quite as elaborate—or as expensive—as the leaders of the Ocean Drive pack, but a pleasant place with lobby lounge, steak

house restaurant, and free parking for registered guests. In addition, there's
the fun simply of staying in a Jazz Age home with all the abstract ornamentation.

720 Ocean Drive, Miami Beach 33139. 305-531-5891. Inexpensive.

THE BENTLEY
Hotel/Miami Beach
Near the southern flank of the South Beach Art Deco District and not in the
same sensational league as its big brothers up the promenade, but the rooms
are clean and have private baths and there are various shops alongside selling
the necessaries for your holiday in the sun.

510 Ocean Drive, Miami Beach 33139. 305-538-1700. Inexpensive.

THE BETSY ROSS HOTEL
Hotel/Miami Beach
The newest rebirth on South Beach, at the northern flank of the stretch of Art
Deco magic we regard as best, is this mixed-metaphor kind of a place with
Southern plantation house pillars, federal crowns, a colonial doorway, and a
clapboard facade—truly an example of all-American architecture. Of course,
they call their café the Stars and Stripes (see page 15) and the menu is
all-American in the most modern sense. To make the transition from the café
to the elegance of restrained Art Deco in their A Mano restaurant (see page
11) there's the beautifully appointed lobby with silk flower arrangements
dramatically flowing from oversize Art Deco vases in shades of blushing
burgundy and teal.

1440 Ocean Drive, Miami Beach 33139. 305-531-3310. Moderate.

BREAKWATER/EDISON
Hotel/Miami Beach
Not one but two Art Deco hotels (described by the new owners as "the greatest of all time 1940s resorts") with all the modern conveniences in the 66 single and double rooms and the 4 one- and two-bedroom suites with kitchen. The Edison is home to the Tropics International Café of fun and good food, while the Breakwater houses I Paparazzi, a northern Italian retreat overlooking the handsome courtyard and fountain. In between the two hotels is a swimming pool served by an artistically designed terrace bar.

940/960 Ocean Drive, Miami Beach 33139. 305-531-0461; toll-free: 1-800-237-3522. Inexpensive to moderate.

THE CARDOZO
Hotel/Miami Beach
One of the two anchors of the Art Deco hotel revival of the 1980s, the other being the Carlyle, across the street—both painstakingly reborn, after several false starts, in all their neon-pastel beauty, and both now on the National Register of Historic Places. The hotels were built in 1939 by trend-setting Art Deco architect Henry Hohauser, who named this one for Supreme Court Justice Benjamin Nathan Cardozo, whose portrait graces the lobby lounge-café area. Just as it was in its first life, this 70-room hotel is popular with visiting celebrities—Frank Sinatra and crew filmed *A Hole in the Head* here. Complimentary continental breakfast is served on the top floor facing the ocean, but there's no registration desk; guests discreetly sign in next door at the Hotel Leslie.

1300 Ocean Drive, Miami Beach 33139. 305-531-6424; toll-free (outside Florida): 1-800-327-6306. Expensive.

THE CARLYLE
Hotel/Miami Beach
Kissin' cousin to the Cardozo, by the same architect, and with 76 rooms that serve as total immersion tributes to the spirit and substance of Art Deco, with

all kinds of curvilinear forms and accent pieces. The front porch is great for lunch, the lobby grill for dinner, and the neon bar for anytime.

1250 Ocean Drive, Miami Beach 33139. 305-534-2135; toll-free (outside Florida): 1-800-327-6306. Moderate to expensive.

CAVALIER HOTEL AND CABANA CLUB
Hotel/Miami Beach

Built in 1936 during the heart of the Great Depression, and thoroughly restored and reopened half a century later, this four-story 48-room monument strives to live up to its claim of being "a home for the well traveled," those who expect an emphasis on personal service and such added amenities as morning papers at the door and complimentary breakfast in the lobby, fresh flowers and Evian in the room, and turndown service.

1320 Ocean Drive, Miami Beach 33139. 305-534-2135; toll-free (outside Florida): 1-800-338-9076. Expensive.

CLEVELANDER
Hotel/Miami Beach

The most popular bar on the beach, with nightly entertainment featuring reggae, blues, and jazz; there's also an indoor-outdoor spread of Art Deco pastels. We like the fresh-air section, all glass brick and pink lights, and a sign that says it all: DRINK. Oh yes, there is a hotel—with mod-furnished guest rooms, a busy lobby, and a souvenir gift shop with Art Deco mementos.

1020 Ocean Drive, Miami Beach 33139. 305-531-3485. Moderate.

THE NEW LEONARD BEACH HOTEL
Hotel/Miami Beach

Southernmost of all the reborn hostelries and a real stunner, sensationally restored (local artists were handed keys and given *carte blanche* to decorate the rooms in whatever style or fantasy they wanted—and they really had fun), there's no hotel like it in the country. This oldest of all the so-called continuing hotels on the beach takes the art-in-public-places idea to its logical, maybe absurd, extreme. What a choice of settings you have, with everything from paintings of homoerotic nude dancers, flamingos against a Florida backdrop, Dubuffet-like landscapes, to giant tropical plantings—something for every whim and fancy. Each room does have a private, also decorated bathroom, but there's no air-conditioning, only ceiling fans. Originally opened in 1925, the 50-room hotel is more or less Mediterranean, with all rooms opening onto a tiled outdoor courtyard, which also serves as the lobby.

54 Ocean Drive, Miami Beach. 305-532-2412. Inexpensive.

PARK CENTRAL
Hotel/Miami Beach
This 1937 rebirth has a café, Barocco Beach, in the ground-floor lobby, which at night is magically transformed with candlelight and some formal fuss (see page 11). The rooms are decorated in hues of blue, mint, and lavender as soft as the balmy ocean breezes, and there's a proud attention to maintenance, with the hotel team working hard to live up to the pledge: "Our mission is to insure that your time with us will be all you want it to be; a time you'll always remember!"

640 Ocean Drive, Miami Beach 33139. 305-538-1611. Moderate.

Where to Eat

AL AMIR
Lebanese/Miami Beach
The ethnic exotica immediately accessible to South Beach-goers includes hummos and tabouli, keema and kafta, in this elegant and well-served enclave. A transplant from New York City, like so many other restaurants on

South Beach, this Lebanese gem reminds us of something special in Paris or from the good old days in Beirut. Small, select wine list.

1131 Washington Avenue, Miami Beach. 305-534-0022. Moderate to expensive. Dinner daily.

A MANO
Nouvelle American/Miami Beach

An Art Deco dining room hiding behind an eye-popping, strangely out of place Neo–New England facade. *Feast of Sunlight* cookbook author Norman Van Aken is in residence, as he is in the far less formal and expensive Stars and Stripes café a few feet away. Here, he makes such marvels as crab cakes with an orange béarnaise sauce, black beans, and a salsa sporting grilled corn, and grouper carefully grilled and presented with a colorful arrangement of plantains, mango relish, and those devilishly purple wild Peruvian potatoes—like a Joan Miró painting, Van Aken is proud to point out in his pixielike manner.

Betsy Ross Hotel, 1440 Ocean Drive, Miami Beach. 305-531-6266. Moderate to expensive. Dinner Tuesday to Sunday.

BAROCCO BEACH
Italian/Miami Beach

Spread out in the lobby of a classic Art Deco hotel of the 1930s, this tribute to the nuances of Northern Italian cuisine is a spinoff of a restaurant of the same name in Manhattan—as was Lucky's, its predecessor on the premises. The setting is not as smashing or serene as the competition's, but we like the friendliness of the staff and the honesty of the kitchen, where fresh fish is handled with respect, and the mesquite-fired grill with care and competence.

Park Central Hotel, 640 Ocean Drive, Miami Beach. 305-538-7700. Moderate. Lunch and dinner daily.

CARLYLE GRILL
Continental/Miami Beach

Occupying the lobby level of one of the first of the Art Deco onetime dumps to be modernized, the Carlyle provides a terrifically nostalgic look back to the age of neon and peculiarly patterned tile/terrazzo floors. We like the porch for lunch, while the bar off to one side is a great place to kick off an evening in the lobby-filling grill, straight from the set, it seems, of a Charles Coburn movie. It's a class act featuring such specialties as roast duck cassis, fresh swordfish, and tuna steak saluted with a macadamia-honey-pesto sauce. Good wine selection.

Carlyle Hotel, 1250 Ocean Drive, Miami Beach. 305-534-2135. Moderate to expensive. Lunch and dinner daily.

CRAWDADDY'S
American/Miami Beach

What counterpoint! At the foot of a sky-scraping condominium stands a rustic ragamuffin of a rugged fish camp, a two-story assemblage of weathered planking sheltering an ole-timey front parlor kind of setting, complete with fireplace and staff in period dress. Stick with the theme and order cornmeal-coated catfish, 'gator tail, grilled barbecue shrimp embraced by bacon, and fish camp fry. On Sundays there's brunch.

South Pointe Park, 1 Washington Avenue, Miami Beach. 305-673-1708. Moderate to expensive. Lunch and dinner daily.

FAIRMONT GARDENS BAR & GRILLE
American/Miami Beach

Housed in the carefully restored Fairmont, winner of the best hotel rehabilitation award in 1988, these are indeed gardens, magically lighted at night and featuring live entertainment and a groaning-table champagne brunch on Sundays with made-before-your-very-eyes omelets, smoked and poached salmon, steamship round of beef, and all kinds of fruits and salads—precisely what one finds on a cruise ship, but that should come as no surprise. The owners supply the food to several cruise lines, including the *Discovery* and *Dolphin.*

The Fairmont Hotel, 1000 Collins Avenue, Miami Beach. 305-531-0050. Moderate. Lunch and dinner daily.

IL PAPARAZZI
Italian/Miami Beach
Black, pink, and green are the colors blending so reassuringly in this Art Deco hotel, and there's splendid alfresco dining on the front porch and in the back garden. Service is skilled and the chef works wonders with his al dente pastas, his fresh seafood, and scallops of veal. He also takes full advantage of the porcinis, mingling them with a fine risotto Milanese or heightening their boskiness with marsala to complement the red snapper. The fried calamari fra diavolo is terrific. This is northern Italian food at its Florida finest.

Breakwater Hotel, 940 Ocean Drive, Miami Beach. 305-531-3500. Moderate. Dinner daily.

JOE'S STONE CRAB
Seafood/Miami Beach
The origins of this place date back to 1915, and almost from the beginning it became known as a reliable provider of those most marvelous of all of Florida's natural resources, stone crabs. During the crab-trapping season, from mid-October to mid-May, the boats—including Joe's sizable fleet—haul up the treasure, remove one claw only (and never from a female with eggs), and toss the hapless creature back into the deep. Joe's is also a provider of great fried oysters and potatoes, creamed spinach, and other noncrab fare. But there are no reservations and in the season the wait is too long—so do lunch or arrive early for dinner.

227 Biscayne Street, Miami Beach. 305-673-0362. Expensive. Lunch Tuesday to Saturday. Dinner daily. Closed mid-May to mid-October.

LULU'S

American/Miami Beach

An upscale setting with budget-pleasing, solid Southern fare—as in collard greens, corn-and-okra fritters, fingerlings of those little snow-white catfish, and, of course, fried chicken.

1035 Washington Avenue, Miami Beach. 305-532-6147. Inexpensive. Lunch Monday to Friday; dinner daily.

MEZZANOTTE

Italian/Miami Beach

Northern Italian mission to the waterfront by the owner of Cafe Tanino in Coral Gables, Piero Filpi, who has put together a thoroughly mod, happy retreat with concerned waiters and a fine menu. Start with some pappardelle or fettuccine Dolce Vita, then proceed to some veal or shrimp scampi, while not forgetting the desserts—all sinful. Late in the evening—and we mean "Latino late," past *mezzanotte*—this place jumps with high-decibel rockin' rhythms and patrons dancing on chairs and tables.

1200 Washington Avenue, Miami Beach. 305-673-4343. Moderate to expensive. Dinner daily.

NEWS CAFE

American/Miami Beach

The place to be seen, and to do the seeing, of the fashion models sliding into barely comfortable chairs or gliding past or going to the newsstand for out-of-town press and fashion magazines. A great place for breakfast—they start serving at 8 A.M., except on Friday and Saturday, when they're open around the clock. The food is nothing to put in the paper, but it's more than acceptable and with the quintessential South Beach crowd all around you, who cares?

Boulevard Hotel, 800 Ocean Drive, Miami Beach. 305-538-6397. Inexpensive to moderate. Breakfast, lunch, and dinner daily.

STARS AND STRIPES CAFE
Nouvelle American/Miami Beach

The same Norman Van Aken who's responsible for A Mano in the faux colonial New England Betsy Ross hotel (see page 7) holds forth here in this aptly named café. The tropical treats he's discovered since his long hegira from Chicago to Florida—cheffing at Jupiter in Boca Raton, and most notably at Louie's Backyard in Key West—are all on offer at this hotel. To name a few, that means calamari and onions sautéed with garlic and chilies splashed with lime juice, fresh Norwegian salmon stir-fried with equally fresh veggies, and desserts highlighting the harvest of the citrus capital of the world.

Betsy Ross Hotel, 1440 Ocean Drive, Miami Beach. 305-531-3310. Expensive. Lunch and dinner daily.

STUART'S AT THE CARDOZO
American/Miami Beach

At this indoor/outdoor soda shop/café, which winds around the porch and takes over the lobby, management does its best to live up to its promise to serve "Good Comfortable Food at Good Comfortable Prices." That translates to beautiful burgers and salads for lunch; all-American seafood, chops, and steaks for dinner.

Cardozo Hotel, 1300 Ocean Drive, Miami Beach. 305-534-0858. Moderate. Lunch and dinner daily.

THAI TONI
Thai/Miami Beach

When the irresistible urge strikes for some do-it-yourself satay, a ginger-scallion shrimp salad, coconut milk–gentled curries, and a crisped, palate-tingling whole fish—snapper is best—all of it complemented by beer from Bangkok, then head for Thai Toni. In a handsome setting harmonious with all the Art Deco surroundings, Toni is running one of the best Thai restaurants in South Florida.

890 Washington Avenue, Miami Beach. 305-538-8424. Moderate. Lunch Tuesday to Sunday; dinner daily.

TIJUANA JOE'S
Mexican/Miami Beach

For those who have not yet discovered the kinetic joy of fajitas, this is the place. They're fabulous! Prize-winners from El Paso's annual Fajita Cookoff, brought to the beach by the Garcias from Juarez, along with such Tex-Mex standbys as chimichangas stuffed with chopped vegetables, chicken, or beef; cheese-filled enchiladas; and the usual platemates: Spanish rice, refried beans, sour cream, and guacamole.

1580 Washington Avenue, Miami Beach. 305-531-9082. Inexpensive. Lunch and dinner daily.

TONI'S
Japanese/Miami Beach

The same Toni (otherwise known as Hiromi Takarada) who brought us all the triumphs of the Thai kitchen at Thai Toni, performs similar service here with his cross-cultural menu of Japanese and continental cuisines. Except for the desserts—the orange cake is a worthy testament to the citrus capital of the world—we stick with the Oriental side of the menu, elbowing into the sushi bar to work over all the freshness of the rice-rolled headliners brought to life with the zing of that special horseradish known as wasabi.

1208 Washington Avenue, Miami Beach. 305-673-9368. Moderate. Lunch Tuesday to Sunday; dinner daily.

TROPICS INTERNATIONAL
American/Miami Beach

A bright and breezy spot designed to live up to the name, and blaring with jazz and blues groups; a fun spot with a youthful look and youthful delivery of solidly packed noontime veggie omelets, great French toast with real maple syrup, and nighttime grilled fish, steaks, shrimp fresh off the barbecue, and duckling.

Edison Hotel, 960 Ocean Drive, Miami Beach. 305-531-5335. Moderate. Breakfast, lunch, and dinner daily.

Where to Shop

There are nifty little discoveries all along Ocean Drive, and a lot more on Washington Street, many of them offering discount merchandise. An easy walk, past a good deal of the history of this richly cross-cultural section of the state, is the **Lincoln Road Mall,** located between 16th and 17th streets, from Alton Road to Collins Avenue. The line of boutiques on Lincoln, seemingly still struggling for a place in the sun, if not survival, is joined by several galleries and a gaggle of snackeries.

On Ocean Drive look for the **Too Cool O.D. Beach Swimwear Shop** (305-538-5101), located at 510 Ocean Drive, next door to the Bentley Hotel; at number 800, adjacent to the Boulevard Hotel, is **Beach Bun** (305-532-2866) a funky outlet for beachwear; and at number 500, **Tommy on the Beach** (305-538-5717) provides the necessaries for body-bronzing.

Pharmacies, florists, liquor and convenience stores are located on Washington and on Lincoln Road.

More Fun in the Sun

When you want to continue your Southern sunning and are thinking of cruising to the Florida Keys or the Bahamas, contact **Florida Yacht Charters and Sales** at the Miami Beach Marina, 1290 Fifth Street (305-532-8600; toll-free 1-800-537-0050).

For less strenuous exercise, indulge in some of the cultural benefits of the beach:

Acord Theater, 2100 Washington Avenue (305-673-7735)
Colony Theater, 1040 Lincoln Road (305-675-1040)

Concert Association of Greater Miami, 555 17th Street (305-532-3491)

Miami Beach Community Theater, 2231 Prairie Avenue (305-532-4515)

Miami City Ballet, 905 Lincoln Road (305-532-4880)

New World Symphony, 541 Lincoln Road (305-673-3330)

Theater of the Performing Arts, 1700 Washington Avenue (1-800-937-3721)

Where to Write

Miami Beach Chamber of Commerce, 1920 Meridian Avenue, Miami Beach, Florida 33139. 305-672-1270.

Miami Design Preservation League, 1201 Washington Avenue, P.O. Bin L, Miami Beach, Florida 33139. 305-672-2014.

KEY BISCAYNE

The spiritual ancestor of too many present-day developers is Sam Lincoln, the contractor who built what is now the oldest existing structure in South Florida, a 95-foot-tall exclamation point at the tip of Miami's very own Caribbean getaway, Key Biscayne. Lincoln doubled his profit when constructing the Cape Florida Lighthouse in 1825 by using engineering common sense and only half of the brick required by contract. Instead of solid walls five feet thick at the base and two feet thick at the top, he reduced the thickness and left the walls hollow.

That was four years after the United States acquired the territory of Florida from Spain and eleven years before the territory came under siege by the Seminole Indians, who attacked the lighthouse, setting fire to wooden structures with 225 gallons of oil. The keeper and his assistant barricaded themselves at the top of the tower but were wounded, one fatally, by Seminole rifle fire. The dramatic story is related during tours of the sturdy survivor by a guide who explains that the only other times the lighthouse was dark were during the War Between the States and again in 1878 when the Fowey Rock Light two miles south went into service. A century later, in July 1979, the lamp was again lit as a glowing aid to navigators and the fleets of pleasure craft that call Key Biscayne and South Florida home.

The lighthouse is the most prominent attraction of the jut of land at the end of the boulevard that extends directly from the causeway leading from the mainland. There are 406 acres in the Bill Baggs Cape Florida State Recreation Area, named for a Miami newspaper editor who crusaded long and hard for just such a sanctuary. Today, it's the best picnic beach in the greater Miami area, with tables snuggled into a tranquil wooded setting. With a mile and a half of beach and a network of hiking and bicycle trails, a snack stand, and a seawall for trying your luck with snook, snapper, and grouper, it's a justly popular destination.

Crandon Park has another 698 acres of beach greenery, including a golf course, and there's more swimming and sunning space—145 acres—at Virginia Key Beach, where you'll find plenty of parking, excellent snorkeling sites near the breakwater rocks, plus picnic tables, bathhouses, showers, playgrounds, and concession stands. Virginia Key Park is a heavily wooded tropical jungle, just north of which is a wonderful refuge for walking in solitude on a carpet of pine needles or watching the water birds—gallinules and gulls; multicolored herons, plovers, and sandpipers; dowitchers; yellowlegs; and sanderlings.

On warm summer weekdays we like to flee to this area, park our lounge chairs out on a sandbar, and walk over to the ruins of an ole-timey fish camp a half mile from the northern tip of the key, directly across from the water treatment plant. We always get the feeling that we're on the set of a 1950s movie.

Our reaction is far different when approaching Key Biscayne via the causeway named for World War I flying ace Eddie Rickenbacker. There's a feeling of exhilaration in rising higher and higher on the long bridge, with its seemingly endless vistas of the sea and the modern marvels of the born-yesterday Miami skyline.

Silhouettes of the giant cruise ships, with smaller craft bobbing along everywhere, disappear from view only to be replaced by all kinds of other boats and ships.

Windsurfers with their colorful sails can be seen on both sides of the causeway as it lowers into Key Biscayne and Crandon Boulevard. Crandon is one of the loveliest boulevards in the world. Tropical vegetation, swaying palms, whispering pines, magnificently manicured lawns, and a few mansions here and there flash by as Cape Florida and its famous lighthouse get closer and closer.

There won't be too many hotels to look at—only two—and a single motel; and not too many restaurants—most of them are over in the Miami you just left. But that's the abiding appeal of Key Biscayne. It's not just a trip. It's an escape.

Where It Is

Key Biscayne is six miles from downtown Miami via Brickell Avenue, which is U.S. 1, leading directly to the Rickenbacker Causeway (toll). Interstate 95 terminates at U.S. 1 directly across from the entrance to the causeway.

Where to Stay

SHERATON ROYAL BISCAYNE BEACH RESORT & RACQUET CLUB

Resort/Key Biscayne

This 192-room beachfront resort offers everything imaginable for a family dream vacation: swimming pools, a playground, fitness programs, bike rentals, volleyball, shuffleboard, Ping-Pong, sailing, and a dozen tennis courts. Accommodations have private balconies and lanais with waterfront views, and there are four restaurants in this romantic tropical oasis, including the noteworthy Caribbean Room (see page 22). Entertainment nightly in the lounge.

555 Ocean Drive, Key Biscayne 33149. 305-361-5775; toll-free: 1-800-325-3535. Expensive.

SILVER SANDS MOTEL

Motel/Key Biscayne

With 300 feet of private beach and 54 deluxe efficiency apartments, this is a great place to romp with the family. Enjoy scuba diving and sailing, schedule a fishing trip on their 40-foot vessel, *Royal*, or just cool off with a refreshing swim in the Olympic-size pool. Then rest and recuperate in the lounge with one of their special tropical treats before charging into a great dinner at the Sandbar restaurant with its own spectacular view of the beach (see page 24).

300 Ocean Drive, Key Biscayne 33149. 305-361-1049. Moderate to expensive.

SONESTA BEACH HOTEL
Hotel/Key Biscayne

A sensational Mayan temple–like property bordering ten acres of spacious beachfront with 300 rooms and suites and 28 deluxe resort homes. On the grounds are a dozen tennis courts, a fitness center with aerobics classes, and a place to rent bikes, so even while vacationing you can stay in shape or go home with a new bod to match that great tan. Your offspring can do the same in the "Just Us Kids" programs, which run daily from 10:00 A.M until 10:00 P.M. There are also baby-sitting services to give parents the freedom to roam Key Biscayne and enjoy a second honeymoon in its romantic atmosphere. If shopping is your thing, there's the gift shop, the tennis pro shop, and the boutique with designer fashions for men and women. And to titillate your taste buds there's a trio of restaurants and the Sea Grape Bar, actually constructed of real sea grape logs. The Two Dragons is a beautifully designed room with Chinese stir-frying in action on one side and sword-flashing Japanese chefs going through their drills—in the best Benihana manner—on the other. Close by, alongside the Olympic-size swimming pool overlooking the ocean, are the Rib Room and the Rib Room Terrace. Prime rib is the specialty but don't overlook the seafood, especially the pompano and the Dover sole. And remember those desserts—baked out back daily. The setting is elegant with Lalique lamps, rich silk-covered chairs, and neon palm trees. There's live entertainment in the lounge and a granite dance floor.

350 Ocean Drive, Key Biscayne 33149. 305-361-2021; toll-free 1-800-343-7170. Expensive.

Where to Eat

CARIBBEAN ROOM
Seafood/Key Biscayne

The best seafood buffet in South Florida. It's an 80-foot-long extravaganza that features, on the surf side, Florida and Maine lobster, shrimp, and shucked oysters and clams, and on the turf side, carved roast beef—along with more than a dozen different salads and a belt-busting dessert table.

Sheraton Royal Biscayne Beach Resort & Racquet Club, 555 Ocean Drive, Key Biscayne. 305-361-5775. Expensive. Dinner daily.

ENGLISH PUB
English/Key Biscayne

We'll call it Pub II in honor of the first English Pub, which earned landmark status during its lifetime, from 1951 to 1989. That's where Richard Nixon and Bebe Rebozo used to hang out, along with flocks of the wealthy from everywhere. Memories are reborn in Pub II, with its old pubby prints, lots of pewter mugs, heavy wooden beams, and a time-honored menu—chicken pot pie for lunch; Caesar salad, prime rib, or veal chop for dinner. The upstairs lounge has a dance floor to help you burn off the calories.

Galleria, 320 Crandon Boulevard, Key Biscayne. 305-361-8877. Expensive. Lunch and dinner daily.

LA CHOZA
Nicaraguan/Key Biscayne

The best Nicaraguan food in the world is not found in Managua but in Miami. Lighter than the Cuban cuisine that has predominated in the local Hispanic market, traditional Nicaraguan cooking is based on the grill and an overwhelming love for beef, which here translates to *churrascos* and *brochetas* sauced with *chimichurri, marinera,* or *encurtido.* That means steaks or kabobs with garlic-oil-parsley, tomato-onion, or jalapeño-onion sauces. But don't sell the seafood short, especially the shrimp and *pargo,* the red snapper.

L'Esplanade Mall, 973 Crandon Boulevard, Key Biscayne. 305-361-0113. Moderate to expensive. Lunch and dinner daily.

NEW YORK PIZZA
Italian/Key Biscayne

"A little bit of New York and a whole lot of Italy . . . right here on Key Biscayne" is the come-on of these transplanted New Yorkers who whip out pizzas, calzones, stromboli, hot and cold subs, and dinners featuring lasagna, cannelloni, and baked ziti.

260 Crandon Boulevard, #35, Key Biscayne. 305-361-2111. Inexpensive. Lunch and dinner daily; delivery service evenings.

RUSTY PELICAN
American/Key Biscayne

The best indoor observation post for participating in the nightly sayonara to the sun—watching the red ball sink slowly into the Miami skyline, in itself a joy to look at any time of the day or night. So come here for the view and the tropical drinks in the lounge. The food is acceptable—more or less Americanized Polynesian—but it's nothing to write Trader Vic about.

3201 Rickenbacker Causeway, Key Biscayne. 305-361-3818. Expensive. Lunch and dinner daily.

THE SANDBAR
Seafood/Key Biscayne

Office types who lunch here risk reprimands for getting back late, but they find it hard to leave this wonderful stage-set with its beautiful ocean view, that deeper-than-deep suntanned parade of surf lovers, and the tempting array of seafood: scallops, prepared any way you wish; fillets of fish; and fresh lobster.

Silver Sands Motel, 300 Ocean Drive, Key Biscayne. 305-361-1049. Moderate to expensive. Lunch and dinner daily; breakfast on Saturday and Sunday.

STEFANO'S
Italian/Key Biscayne

Back-to-the-basics Italian food with homemade pasta, all the familiar veal variations, and fresh seafood. There's a surprisingly extensive wine list, their claim to fame in this area, and late-night entertainment. A deli and package store are attached.

24 Crandon Boulevard, Key Biscayne. 305-361-7007. Moderate to expensive. Dinner daily.

SUNDAYS ON THE BAY
American/Key Biscayne

The Sunday brunch is a beaut with its complimentary mimosas or Bloody Marys introducing an endless parade of goodies—everything from turkey, beef, and seafood to salads, sweets, Belgian waffles, and made-to-order omelets. During the week there's a variety of sandwiches and burgers for lunch, and seafood selections and all-American steaks for dinner. With a great waterfront setting, nightly live entertainment, and a casual atmosphere, this rustic-looking feedery is a must.

Crandon Park Marina, 5420 Crandon Boulevard, Key Biscayne. 305-361-6777. Moderate to expensive. Lunch and dinner daily.

VENTANA'S RESTAURANT ON THE GREEN
Continental/Key Biscayne

To harmonize with the South Florida scene they prepare their continental cuisine with a Latin flair, whether rack of lamb, veal, lobster, or any of their pastas. The service is all smiles and the view of the greens through the *ventanas* is inspiring.

6700 Crandon Boulevard, Key Biscayne. 305-361-0496. Moderate to expensive. Lunch and dinner daily.

Where to Shop

The **Key Biscayne Galleria,** 328 Crandon Boulevard, located next door to the English Pub, has boutiques, a yogurt shop, a drugstore, and most of the necessities you'll need on vacation.

The **Key Biscayne Shopping Center,** Crandon Boulevard, is the oldest on the island and houses **Burns Ltd.,** at number 624 (305-361-2568), a designers' paradise of men's clothing; **Key Bootery,** at number 632 (305-361-2131), for the latest in footwear; plus shops for swimsuits and beachwear, casual clothing, greeting cards, sundries, film developing, and groceries.

The **Square Shopping Center,** located at 260 Crandon Boulevard, offers a great variety of shops to choose from, including a hair salon; **Bristol's**

Camera, at number 11 (305-361-3686), with same-day film processing; and The Pretty Boutiques, at numbers 8, 9, 33, 39, 41, and 43 (305-361-2855, 9220, 5718, 2653, 8682). Take a break from shopping and grab a deli sandwich or salad at the Buffet Bazaar (305-361-1113), or browse through their gourmet gift section stocked with imported chocolates, wines, pastries, and caviar and ship a tasty delight to those you left behind.

More Fun in the Sun

Club Paradise (305-361-2021), on the waterfront of the Sonesta Beach Hotel, and Sailboards Miami (305-361-SAIL), at Windsurfer Beach just past the tollbooths, are the places for rentals of Windsurfers with or without lessons. Sailboards claims it has taught some 20,000 people this adventurous sport, and it guarantees success.

Miami Seaquarium, situated on 60 acres of prime oceanfront property at 4400 Rickenbacker Causeway (305-361-5703), is the home of television star Flipper and his several successors, and more than 10,000 species of marine life displayed in numerous viewing tanks. There are dolphin, killer whale, and sea lion shows as well as manatee exhibits, shark feedings, and underwater food frenzies in the giant tanks. Educational for the kids and fun for the whole family.

The annual Key Biscayne Art Festival is a two-day happening the last week in January and brings in art lovers from all corners of the world to view the works of some 185 nationally known artists including jewelers, potters, stained-glass artisans, photographers, sculptors, and wood carvers. Their creations are displayed on Crandon Boulevard between Knollwood Avenue and Bill Baggs State Park.

The annual Key Biscayne Bicycle Triumph, a two-day, 100-kilometer race held in October, attracts world-class cyclists as well as local enthusiasts. Bicyclists travel the route from Bill Baggs State Park through Key Biscayne and over Rickenbacker Causeway. Also scheduled are special activities for children.

The annual Fourth of July celebration, the oldest in Dade County, includes a parade, concerts, food and craft booths, and performances by the Key Biscayne Chowder Chompers, a 32-member marching band of musicians from ages 16 to 70.

The **Miss Budweiser Unlimited Hydroplane Regatta** in June, the Grand Prix of boat racing, fills Key Biscayne's Miami Marine Stadium, 3601 Rickenbacker Causeway (305-361-6730), with over 25,000 people who gather for this two-weekend event to get a glimpse of the world's fastest boats. Racers compete in a 1⅔-mile course at speeds up to 140 miles per hour. Grand prize is $120,000. The stadium has a floating stage where artists such as the Beach Boys perform in concert. Holiday fireworks displays, Easter Sunday Sunrise Services, water and ski shows, and various festivals are also held there. Extras are the great view of the moon-over-Miami skyline and the sunset. There are also Jet Ski rentals available.

Planet Ocean, 3979 Rickenbacker Causeway (305-361-5786), at the International Oceanographic Foundation, features nine theaters, twelve main exhibits, and over a hundred hands-on experiences of the wonders of the earth. You can walk through a hurricane and learn how such storms are born, "shrink" inside a drop of water and learn of the life that exists there, or get a glimpse of the past by viewing a replica of a 40-foot prehistoric shark. You can also experience the birth of the oceans and touch Florida's only iceberg while learning the properties of water. This is truly a tremendous educational experience for you and your children.

Bill Baggs Cape Florida State Park, located at the southernmost point of this island paradise, has a 1½-mile beach, campgrounds, nature trails, picnic and fishing areas, snack bars, and the famous Key Biscayne Lighthouse, which you can tour for a nominal fee.

The **International Tennis Center of Key Biscayne,** 7200 Crandon Boulevard (305-361-8633), home of the Lipton mid-March International Players Championship, the fourth richest tournament in the world, has 15 courts open to the public daily.

Crandon Marina, 4000 Crandon Boulevard (305-361-1281), is the home of at least nine deep-sea fishing vessels available for charter trips to pursue sailfish, marlin, wahoo, tuna, and shark. To list a few of the best: *Lisa L.* and *Si'l Vous Plait* (305-361-7600); *Carrie Ann* (305-361-0117); and *Ellen H.* (305-361-9318), which must be booked well in advance because it goes where the fish are running whether that is the waters of New Jersey, Mexico, or the Florida Panhandle. Also available are rental boats for cruising or waterskiing.

The **Key Biscayne Golf Course,** 6700 Crandon Boulevard (305-361-9129), is an 18-hole, par-72 course that is considered by some players one of the most challenging in the nation. It's certainly one of the most beautiful, with its tropical setting of lagoons, mangroves, and hammocks.

Where to Write

Key Biscayne Chamber of Commerce, 95 West McIntire Street, Key Biscayne, Florida 33149. 305-361-5207.

THE KEYS

The famous Florida Keys, that necklace of 700 islands and islets adorning more than a hundred miles of the aquamarine waters of ocean and gulf, are not noted for their beaches. But beaches do exist here and there, some in public parks and others in private resorts. In driving through and flying over islands large and small, causeways, and bridges, we have identified those worth recommending, dividing our findings into three sections: Key Largo, with its unique opportunities for snorkeling and diving; the Middle Keys, with the best of the beaches and superb resorts; and Key West, the end of the line.

◎　　◎　　◎

KEY LARGO

B ogie and Bacall are the best known of the stars who have shone in Key
Largo, the first of the islands stretching from the Everglades to the
Florida Straits. Memories of their presence in the early 1950s are played up,
but far more divers frequent the area today than movie buffs. They come to
dive the only living coral reefs in the continental United States, six to seven
miles out in the Gulf of Mexico and reaching all the way from Fort Lauderdale
to the Dry Tortugas, a distance of some two hundred miles.

For those with or without gear for excursions—everything necessary is
available for rent or charter—the center of all the waterborne fun and exploration is the John Pennekamp Coral Reef State Park, 178 nautical square
miles of swamp, sea grass, and coral reefs. All this can be explored from the
park's 2,640 feet of Largo land, replete with snorkeling and dive boats, large
and small, as well as a pair of vessels outfitted with glass bottoms for those
who don't want to get wet. There are more than 650 varieties of tropical fish
living in the park's underwater world of silence surrounded by 40 different
kinds of coral, including a couple of dozen splendid species of *Gorgonia,* the
primitive alcyonarian polyps the nonscientific world knows as sea fans. We
won't even mention the proper names of the brain and star corals, the elk and
staghorn, or the coral tunnels, ridges, and valleys.

Certified scuba divers have the opportunity of submerging themselves to
depths ranging from 30 to 50 feet to explore a German freighter from World
War II, a British warship, and other vessels, some dating from the era when
Florida was under Spanish rule.

For nondivers there are canoes, Hobie Cat catamarans, and powerboats along with a drift fishing boat equipped with all the necessary equipment including bait. And for beach bums there are a couple of man-made spreads of sand for sunning and walking into the water. Picnic sites abound, but before you settle into your salad or burger—you can buy them as well as grill your own—spend some time in the visitor center, the best possible introduction to the park and all its underwater creatures. A short video gives the history, and a series of aquariums, including a 12-sided, 50,000-gallon one, showcases the live creatures, those who await you out on the reef, fulfilling the promise of Captain Nemo to passengers boarding his *Nautilus* in *20,000 Leagues Under the Sea*: "You are about to take a journey into wonderland. You will find it hard to remain indifferent to the spectacle unrolling before your eyes."

There are regularly scheduled departures of the several boats, which are manned by pleasant, informed, and communicative park rangers. Reservations are strongly advised, especially in season.

Where It Is
Key Largo is 63 miles south of Miami via U.S. 1.

Where to Stay

JULES' UNDERSEA LODGE
Underwater Hotel/Key Largo
The ultimate overnight for properly certified scuba freaks is this 20-by-50-foot mini-house 20 feet underwater. Through the portholes you'll see all kinds of sea creatures at all hours of the day and night. And you can even swim out and greet them using the 100-foot hookah hose. The lodge has a completely stocked refrigerator, a microwave oven, and a VCR with a small library of videos (featuring *20,000 Leagues Under the Sea* and *Jaws,* of course). All you need, and are allowed to bring down with you, are toiletries and a few changes of clothes, just enough to fit into a small duffel bag. No aerosol spray cans, no plastic bottles, no alcoholic beverages, and no smoking!

P.O. Box 3330, Key Largo 33037. 305-451-2353. Expensive.

KEY LARGO HOLIDAY INN RESORT AND MARINA
Hotel/Key Largo

Here are 122 rooms, an easy-to-recommend restaurant, live entertainment in the lounge, a pool marina with glass-bottom and snorkeling boats, and lots of tropical landscaping, but the real appeal for us is the very same *African Queen* that was used in the Humphrey Bogart–Katharine Hepburn movie of the same name. This little vessel with the big reputation is at the Holiday Inn docks (as is the Chris Craft used in the film *On Golden Pond*). It's available for three-mile, 30-minute tours, and the resort's gift shop is filled with all kinds of *African Queen* memorabilia.

99701 Overseas Highway, Mile Marker 100, Key Largo 33037. 305-451-2121; toll-free: 1-800-THE KEYS. Moderate.

MARINA DEL MAR BAYSIDE
Hotel/Key Largo

This bayside hotel, sister to the resort of the same name, is picture-perfect with its peachy pink coloring and perky atmosphere—a prime choice for a great getaway vacation. Even the blooming hibiscus match the color of this newly constructed pastel wonderland, and there is a great little Japanese restaurant on the premises—also peachy pink. All the facilities at the ocean-side resort are open to Bayside guests.

P.O. Box 1050, Bayside Mile Marker 99.5, Key Largo 33037. 305-451-4450; toll-free: 1-800-242-5229. Moderate.

MARINA DEL MAR RESORT AND MARINA
Hotel/Key Largo

Each of the 32 rooms and 20 suites is equipped with a Jacuzzi and fridge, and has a view of water—whether it be the Atlantic, the tropical oversized-pool area, or the deep-water full-service marina, which accommodates up to 42 vessels. The suites also have fully equipped kitchens and microwaves. There are tennis courts, an exercise room, a nautical store, and a dive center. Visit

Doc's Galley Restaurant for a great waterfront breakfast while watching the sun rise or a lunchtime break from the action atop the Ocean Divers Building. For more serious dining there's Coconuts restaurant and lounge, also with a waterfront view and serving a feast of fresh seafood. Live entertainment nightly.

P.O. Box 1050, 527 Caribbean Drive, Mile Marker 100, Key Largo 33037. 305-451-4107; toll-free (in Florida): 1-800-253-3483, (outside Florida): 1-800-451-3483. Moderate.

SHERATON KEY LARGO RESORT
Hotel/Key Largo

This 200-room (44 of them suites) masterpiece of tropical design and landscaping was rebuilt in 1985 and is one of the Keys' most complete resorts, with a 21-slip marina, two large pools, a nature trail, and sailboat and parasailing rentals. There is a fine restaurant called Christina's, as well as Cafe Key Largo, with Sunday brunch, breakfast buffets, and an eye-popping salad bar. The lush tropical landscaping takes your breath away as you drive into the entrance to launch your vacation escape. This Sheraton is super, with wide-open breezeways, patios, atriums, tin roofs, and panoramas of Florida Bay.

97000 South Overseas Highway (U.S. 1 at Mile Marker 97), Key Largo 33037. 305-852-5553; toll-free: 1-800-325-3535. Expensive.

SUNSET COVE MOTEL
Motel/Key Largo

Located on the Gulf side, this simple, clean, and quiet motel is a good place for adults to get away from it all. Mary, the owner, keeps improving the property, which is located close to a supermarket (at the point where U.S. 1 splits into north and south lanes) with fresh produce, a good selection of wines, and friendly service.

Mile Marker 100, Key Largo 33037. 305-451-0705. Inexpensive. No children.

Where to Eat

BJ'S BAR-B-QUE
Barbecue/Key Largo

Look for the covered wagon pointing the way to mesquite-smoked barbecue cuisine, as well as fresh Florida seafood, conch fritters, and homemade soups and stews.

Mile Marker 102.5, Key Largo. 305-451-0900. Moderate. Lunch and dinner daily.

THE FISH HOUSE RESTAURANT AND FISH MARKET
Seafood/Key Largo

A restaurant with a fish market attached is a good bet for fresh seafood, and this place is no exception. It serves the catch of the day with a smile and—if you're lucky—a song from the owner and head waiter, who serenade with special selections of Keys-style music—a blend of Caribbean, country, and reggae. Landlubber dishes of steaks and burgers are also available.

102401 Overseas Highway, Mile Marker 102.4 (U.S. 1 northbound), Key Largo. 305-451-4665. Inexpensive to moderate. Lunch and dinner daily.

HARRIETTE'S RESTAURANT
American/Key Largo

Home-cooked meals at bargain prices in a homey little setting. There's usually a crowd on weekends, and that means lines and a wait.

Mile Marker 97.5, Key Largo. 305-852-8689. Inexpensive. Breakfast and lunch daily.

ITALIAN FISHERMAN
Seafood/Key Largo

This spacious restaurant, with its oversize statue of the namesake *paesano* standing watch out front, is hard to miss. It sits on the Gulf, which provides the stage for the nightly sunset spectacular. You can have a serious meal dining on the catch of the day simply broiled or prepared with Italian flair, or settle for a snack while you enjoy the scenery.

10400 Overseas Highway (Mile Marker 104), Key Largo. 305-451-4471. Inexpensive to moderate. Lunch and dinner daily.

THE QUAY RESTAURANT
Seafood/Key Largo

The class act of Key Largo, a Gulf-side surprise with a dazzling view of water and sunset. The rack of lamb and prime rib are excellent, the shrimp and fish impeccably fresh, the bananas Foster and the steak Diane a blast from the past. The oversize bar is a beaut.

102050 Overseas Highway (Mile Marker 102.5), Key Largo. 305-451-0943. Moderate to expensive. Lunch and dinner daily.

SNOOK'S BAYSIDE CLUB
Continental/Key Largo

The restaurant and patio face the Gulf and that means a prime position for sunset-watching. Brushed with pastels, the beautiful Mexican tiled rooms are bright and inviting, with sparkling glassware, handsome appointments, and a Cinemascope-size window. Whether dining indoors or out, you'll love the casual feeling and the excellent food. You can bring in your own catch and they will gladly prepare it to your specifications. As this is a club, there's a nominal cover charge or yearly membership fee.

Mile Marker 99.5, Key Largo. 305-451-3857. Moderate to expensive. Lunch and dinner daily; Sunday brunch.

SUNDOWNERS
Seafood/Key Largo

This waterfront eatery is located on Blackwater Sound and has a veranda where every seat is front-row quality for sunset-watching. The dock is only a few feet away and you can come by boat. There is a wide variety of seafood on the menu, with nightly specials featuring a catch of the day.

Mile Marker 104, Key Largo. 305-451-4502. Moderate. Lunch and dinner daily.

TOWER OF PIZZA
Italian/Key Largo

It's easy to tell what the specialty is, but the spaghetti is in the sauce major league. A great place to grab a snack or pig out on pizza.

Mile Marker 100.5, Key Largo. 305-451-1461. Inexpensive. Lunch and dinner daily.

Where to Shop
The **Center of Key Largo**, at Mile Marker 103.4, is a pink-and-blue shopping center with stores carrying tanning products, vacation necessities, T-shirts, swimwear, children's clothing, and casual wear for the older set.

Largo Cargo, at Mile Marker 103, 103101 Overseas Highway (305-451-4242), is a neat-as-a-pin shop for kites, T-shirts, great casual clothing and beachwear, swimsuits, and all types of gifts and souvenirs. But it is not a typical souvenir shop. It sells quality merchandise, including the Jimmy Buffett line.

More Fun in the Sun
John Pennekamp Coral Reef State Park, at Mile Marker 102.5 (305-451-1621 or 248-4300; toll-free [in Florida]: 1-800-432-2871), is the place for glass-bottom boat trips, rentals, snorkeling and diving excursions, camping, swimming, or sunning on the sandy beach. If you're prone to queasiness on

the water, before embarking on a boat tour of any kind be sure to take the motion sickness tablets provided at the ticket counters and check on weather and wave conditions to make sure the seas are calm.

Kimbell's Caribbean Shipwreck Museum, 102670 Highway U.S. 1 (305-451-6444), is loaded with dreams of wealth from the past, relics from royalty, gold and silver ingots, remnants of shipwrecks from the time of Columbus, and such exhibits as the original Taj Mahal rupee treasure, Chinese porcelains, and the rarest of all treasure taken from the waters of the Keys, the Haskins Capitana medallion. You can also learn something about salvage techniques to inspire your own dreams of treasure hunting.

Where to Write

John Pennekamp Coral Reef State Park, P.O. Box 487, Key Largo, Florida 33037. 305-451-1202.

Key Largo Chamber of Commerce, 103400 Overseas Highway, Key Largo, Florida 33037. 305-451-1414; toll-free: 1-800-822-1088.

◎   ◎   ◎

MIDDLE KEYS

A t the southern end of 27-mile-long Key Largo is Tavernier, a small settlement with 250 feet of Atlantic beach in the Harry Harris County Park. There are also a couple of hundred feet of beach in Upper Matecumbe, another county park, two keys and three bridges to the south. At Mile Marker 67 is Long Key State Recreation Area, a mile and a half of campsites and swimming, wading and bird-watching on the Atlantic; but before you settle into that site, cross the road to the Gulf and take the Layton Trail, a nature walk into the wilds of tropical vegetation—gumbo limbo and thatch palm trees; black, red, and white mangrove, whose tentacles reach out into the shallow flats; pigeon plum; and poisonwood. It's near the place where the exclusive Long Key Fishing Club thrived with such famous anglers as Zane Grey in command. The miniature railroad these fishermen rode from docks to camp is commemorated at the entrance to the area by a set of wheels from that line. The club, founded in 1906, disappeared in the great hurricane of 1935.

In the overbuilt town of Marathon, there's 1,500 feet of public beach at the Switlick County Park, which provides rest rooms and showers, a playground, and covered picnic shelters with grills. Not far south is the Seven Mile Bridge, an engineering marvel that leads to the Little Duck Key County Park and 1,400 feet of Atlantic shoreline. A few miles farther south on the Highway that Went to Sea is the best and most extensive beach in the Keys, the Bahia Honda State Recreation Area. Two and a half miles at its widest point, and consisting of 1,550 feet of white sand that slopes gradually to the sea and provides sensational snorkeling possibilities, this skeleton of an ancient coral reef is the geologic transition point from the upper and middle to the lower keys. For more than a century it has been a magnet for botanists the world over; they come to study the rare plants that have found their way to the key from lands far and near. There's a park snorkeling boat and the remnants of an old bridge (now a fine observation tower) from Flagler's Railroad that Went to Sea, a seven-year project that was completed in 1912 at a cost of $50 million and the lives of 700 workers, and was destroyed in the hurricane of 1935. Bahia Honda, which means "deep bay" in Spanish, is pronounced "Buy a Honda " by the locals.

Where It Is

The middle keys, as we define the area for our pursuit of the best beaches, extend from Islamorada at Mile Marker 84 to Big Pine Key at Mile Marker 33.5.

Where to Stay

THE BARNACLE
Inn/Big Pine Key

Located 15 miles south of Marathon, just off U.S. 1 at Mile Marker 33 on Longbeach Road, this bed-and-breakfast gem is the place to be for R and R. Total seclusion with splashes of tropical sophistication is what you get here. You will think you've gotten lost on the road out to the place, where you might catch a glimpse, or even see a slow show, of a small Key Deer—they're all small—crossing the road.

Route 1, Box 780A, Big Pine Key 33043. 305-872-3298. Moderate.

BUCCANEER LODGE
Resort/Marathon

On this ten-acre Gulfside resort you will find lush tropical landscaping with 50 cottages, each having two double beds and a bath, tucked under palms and pines. There are also 26 villas with two bedrooms, two baths, a Jacuzzi, a full kitchen with a dishwasher and microwave, and a living room with dining area. Some villas and rooms have views of the Gulf. Go swimming or snorkeling on the private sandy beach, where Windsurfer, sailboat, and Jet Ski rentals are available. At the marina, overnight docking is available, as are charter fishing trips to the many bridges in the area (where the big ones lurk), to the Gulf Stream, or out to the reef. The lodge also offers tennis, shuffleboard, volleyball, and badminton courts as well as table tennis. The Sunset Cafe is at water's edge and serves breakfast, lunch, and dinner. Sunset-watching is celebrated here with a complimentary cocktail.

2600 Overseas Highway, Marathon 33050. 305-743-9071; toll-free (in Florida): 1-800-843-1799, (outside Florida): 1-800-237-3329. Moderate to expensive.

CHEECA LODGE
Resort/Islamorada

With 49 rooms in the main lodge, 154 villa rooms and suites, and luxurious penthouse accommodations, this 27-acre resort has something for everyone. Each villa has one or two bedrooms, a fully equipped kitchen, a living room, and a screened porch. Most guest rooms have private balconies; all have a VCR and stocked mini-bar. The 525-foot lighted pier is the perfect spot to catch the big ones. For those who love to swim, there are 1,100 feet of private beach, two freshwater pools (one a 50-foot lap pool), and an ocean lagoon. Also, you can get a good workout on one of six lighted tennis courts or on the 9-hole, par-3 golf course designed by Jack Nicklaus. Afterward, you can relax and soothe those muscles in one of five Jacuzzis. Dine in luxury in the lodge's oceanfront restaurant or casually in the open-air grill or raw bar by the pool. The Sunday brunch, offers an infinite selection. The fun continues in the evening when the Light Tackle Lounge livens up with music and dancing. The Camp Cheeca children's program for 6- to 12-year-olds is not just busywork or baby-sitting but an education in environmental awareness and an excellent way for your children to get involved in a worthwhile venture while you take a break. The Aquatic Program, for children and adults, teaches both guests and employees about the fragility of the ecosystem of the Keys. There are also water sports programs, snorkel and scuba facilities, a sport shop, and a boutique.

P.O. Box 527, Mile Marker 82, U.S. 1, Islamorada 33036. 305-664-4651; toll-free: 1-800-327-2888. Expensive.

CHESAPEAKE OF WHALE HARBOR RESORT
Resort/Islamorada

The Sandry family has owned and operated this wonderful 65-unit resort for almost 32 years and recently put it through a $3 million expansion and renovation project. Oceanfront deluxe, luxury, and one-bedroom suites are available, as are garden view standard rooms, and on the deep-water lagoon are efficiencies and one- and two-bedroom villas with complete kitchens; all units have refrigerators. This waterfront resort features two freshwater pools, a tennis court, a Jacuzzi, and a gym. There is also a playground for the kids, as well as shuffleboard, barbecue grills, and a pearly white beach. The Hobie Shack on the beach has water sports rentals, and on the lagoon there are an observation deck, boat dock, and ramp. The restaurant showcases nightly all-you-can-eat seafood buffets with many of the dishes wok-ed before your very eyes. The grill is open all day, and the upstairs Harbor Bar offers a lunchtime menu, a raw bar, and cocktails, along with a great view.

Oceanside on U.S. 1, Mile Marker 83.5, Islamorada 33036. 305-664-4662; toll-free: 1-800-338-3395. Expensive.

HAWK'S CAY RESORT AND MARINA
Resort/Duck Key

On this 60-acre West Indies–style resort you can find the peace and tranquillity you want, or all the excitement of discovery while snorkeling, diving the coral reef, or landing that trophy fish. All rooms and suites, most with views of the Gulf or the Atlantic, have a separate dressing area, walk-in closets, and a private balcony. The Tennis Clinic will help you smooth out your game, and with eight lighted courts to choose from, you'll get plenty of time on the clay. If golf is your game you'll enjoy the use of the 18-hole private course nearby, with complimentary shuttle service to and from the greens. A large pool and two Jacuzzis are located at the tropical lagoon, where Windsurfers, tiki boats, and sailfish are available, as is a white sandy beach for swimming or sunning. At the 70-slip marina you can sign up for a deep-sea or back-country fishing excursion or rent a boat and venture out on your own. At the marina dive shop, glass-bottom boat tours and sunset cruises are available. A program for children ages 5 to 12 is offered throughout the summer, and during Christmas and Easter school breaks. Supervised activities change daily and include raft races, fishing, guided nature hikes, scavenger hunts, water balloon fights, and various contests. Three times daily the Dolphin Encounters program, which is part of the resident training program for sea lions and dolphins, allows guests to swim with newfound finned friends. Dining is a treat at this private island resort, with four restaurants to choose from and a variety of cuisines. The Cantina is great for snacks by the pool or a light meal. Ships Galley features prime beef and seafood; the Caribbean Room is all fine dining with an island atmosphere and seafood with a tropical flair. The complimentary 60-item breakfast buffet, served daily on the Palm Terrace, is a real knockout. We found evening excitement in the Ship's Pub Lounge, where there's live entertainment and a variety of tropical concoctions.

Mile Marker 61, Duck Key 33050. 305-743-7000; toll-free (in Florida): 1-800-327-7775. Expensive.

HOLIDAY ISLE RESORTS & MARINA
Resort/Islamorada

This island resort community has four separate hostelries with 180 rooms, including efficiencies and suites, a complete marina with water sports equipment, three swimming pools, a sandy beach, five restaurants, recreation areas, and the very popular Holiday Isle Tiki Bar. Kokomo Pool and Beach Bar also calls this resort isle home, as does Theater of the Sea, second oldest marine park in the world, junior only to Marineland in northern Florida. The lagoon where the dolphins perform is in its natural state, with its own ecosystem, which you can observe from a glass-bottom boat while touring the site. Tidal pools formed from native coral rock exhibit a stingray feeding area, a turtle observation point, a tame shark inlet, and an array of tropical reef fish. H. I. Parasailing and Watersports (305-664-5390, ext. 695) takes you 400 feet in the air above the action for an exhilarating view of the reefs, the beach line, and surrounding isles. Or get into the action by renting a sailboard, Hobie Cat, waverunner, aquacycle, or raft. For swimming and fishing oceanside, rent a 19-foot powerboat for a half or a full day (305-664-9425, ext. 646). Half-day reef-and-wreck scuba and snorkeling trips are available at the dive shop (305-664-4145), where you can sign up for a dive course to be fully certified. Gear rentals are available. For half-day, full-day, or night fishing excursions, either deep-sea or reef (305-664-8070 or 664-8498), try one of three vessels with tackle rental available. Charter your own boat (305-664-2321, ext. 642) or try back-country angling day or night trips (305-664-2321, ext. 654). Holiday Princess Cruises (305-664-2321, ext. 672) offers afternoon, sunset, morning, and evening cruises aboard the 45-foot, 49-passenger glass-bottom boat. Bimini Town Shops is an oceanfront, outdoor, nautical, boardwalk-style mini-mall, where you can buy unusual and original gifts, souvenirs, swim-wear, casual and beach clothing, shoes, art objects, and sweet treats. Guest laundries are also located on the premises, as are a children's playground and a volleyball and shuffleboard court. Okay—so they have it all!

84001 Overseas Highway, Mile Marker 84, U.S. 1, Islamorada 33036. 305-664-2321; toll-free: 1-800-327-7070. Moderate to expensive.

Where to Eat

ADVENTURE ISLAND
American/Marathon
Barbecue chicken and ribs with cole slaw, potato salad, and French fries are only some of their specials. Fresh-dough pizza is the big surprise here. It is absolutely delicious. Walk along the dock and see a variety of Florida's marine life. We even spotted a large lobster.

Mile Marker 54, Marathon. 305-743-8899. Inexpensive. Lunch and dinner daily.

LORELEI RESTAURANT
Seafood/Islamorada
At the entrance is a mounted replica of the mangrove snapper, 4 pounds 8 ounces, caught by Barbara Bush on January 4, 1991, and prepared by chef Tom Emerson, who makes terrific conch fritters and chowder. The Sunset Cabana Bar is great for sunset-watching. A portable bar has been stationed on the beach, where tables and chairs are conveniently positioned so close to the water you might want to bring a life preserver for this daily end-of-the-evening ritual. Wonderful island and romantic mood music begins at twilight at the cabana bar—complete with dance floor—to add to the atmosphere.

Mile Marker 82, Islamorada. 305-664-4656. Moderate to expensive. Lunch and dinner daily; Sunday brunch.

Where to Shop

Fenton's, 2357 Overseas Highway, Marathon (305-743-9307), is a small department store with the latest in name-brand swimwear, tennis shoes, and casual clothing, and the very popular diamond dust T-shirts, decorated with tropical scenes and lots of tasteful glitter designs.

Gulfside Village, at Mile Marker 51, Marathon, has a variety of small shops selling casual clothing for all ages and gifts for the folks back home.

Kmart Plaza, at Mile Marker 51, across from Gulfside Village, has a drugstore, a large grocery, and small shops where you can browse for gifts, souvenirs, and sundries.

More Fun in the Sun

Flipper's Sea School, at Mile Marker 59, Grassy Key (305-289-1121), is a great place for the little ones to get a firsthand lesson in dolphin training. Watch trainers teach the baby dolphins in their own natural habitat—they were born there. Also on view are alligators, tame deer, and sea turtles. Continuous shows daily.

Long Key State Recreation Area, at Mile Marker 67.5 (305-664-4815), is great for camping enthusiasts of all ages. Here you can swim, fish in shallow water, go canoeing, or tour the nature trails—on Wednesday morning there is a guided tour. There is also a campfire program on Friday afternoon and a lecture on Saturday. Reservations are recommended. You can bring your own boat and go snorkeling and scuba diving.

The **Museum of Natural History of the Florida Keys,** at Mile Marker 50, Marathon (305-743-9100), is located on Crane Point Hammock, a rare palm hammock covering 63½ acres. This is a trip through 5,000 years of the Keys' history, with many exhibits of the flora, fauna, and geography of the region. The museum opened in January 1990 after the Florida Keys Land & Sea Trust purchased the land to prevent its development. As a result, 10 endangered plant and animal species and 210 native and exotic plants have been preserved. You can travel back in time as you study pre-Columbian artifacts from shipwrecks and Caloosa Indian relics. In 1982, a jug from the late 1500s was discovered buried in the sand under more than 20 feet of water in Bahia Honda Channel. The jug is now one of the main attractions in the museum. Remnants from the Henry Flagler railroad, a hurricane-proof Indian-built home, and an ancient Bahamian village are on the grounds.

There's also a 20,000-gallon tropical lagoon and tidal basin filled with tropical fish native to the area, as well as rays and sharks. Marine touch tanks, a children's museum, a two-story walk-through reef exhibit, a Florida Keys wildlife display, and a natural sciences activity center are among the many attractions. This is a great learning experience as well as a very enjoyable way to entertain the family.

San Pedro Underwater Archaeological Preserve, one mile south of Islamorada, is Florida's second shipwreck park, created in hopes of relieving some of the pressure on the living coral reefs by the increasing number of divers.

Where to Write

Greater Marathon Chamber of Commerce, Marathon, Florida 33050. 305-743-5417.

Islamorada Chamber of Commerce, Overseas Highway Mile Marker 82, Islamorada, Florida 33036. 305-664-4503; toll-free: 1-800-322-5397.

Lower Keys Chamber of Commerce, Big Pine Key, Florida 33043. 305-872-2411.

◎   ◎   ◎

KEY WEST

The southernmost city in the continental United States is certainly not known for its beaches, but there are some. Most spacious—and with plenty of room for parking—is the spread of 3,950 feet of Smathers Beach on South Roosevelt Boulevard. The Clarence Higgs Memorial Beach is 300 feet long and is located at Atlantic Boulevard. South Beach is even smaller, only 200 feet at the southern end of Duval Street, alongside the Eatery, which is open for breakfast, lunch, and dinner.

Other beaches can be found on the hotel properties in town; the best of the bunch is at the Registry, former site of the well-known Sands Beach Club and the starting point for the annual Swim Around Key West, a twelve-and-a-half-mile mini-marathon that started in 1975. There's also a shortcut swim of a mile. The Casa Marina has its own small beach, as do the Holiday Inn near the entrance to the key on Roosevelt Boulevard, the Hyatt, and Pier House, where a section of the beach is topless.

Where It Is
Key West is the southernmost point in the continental United States, 155 miles south of Miami, where U.S. 1 terminates.

Where to Stay

BEST WESTERN KEY AMBASSADOR RESORT INN
Motel/Key West
This 100-room motel features private balconies facing the Atlantic, free HBO, a pool, complimentary continental breakfast, a café, and a cocktail bar. The food is above motel norm and the level of maintenance is high.

1000 South Roosevelt Boulevard, Key West 33040. 305-296-3500; toll-free (in Florida): 1-800-432-4315, (outside Florida): 1-800-528-1234. Moderate to expensive.

CURRY MANSION INN
Inn/Key West
This newly restored Victorian mansion-museum is the home of Al and Edith Amsterdam, who have filled the 16 rooms with period antiques and Tiffany glass, all against a backdrop of outstanding woodwork. The museum is open to the public during the day but the visitors do not detract from the tranquillity of the setting. Conveniently located two blocks from the Pier House, the inn has a widow's walk, which is great for viewing Old Town Key West.

511 Caroline Street, Key West. 305-294-5349. Expensive.

HOLIDAY INN BEACHSIDE
Motel/Key West
A better-than-average link in the chain, this motel sits on 600 feet of private beach with water sports rentals, an Olympic-size swimming pool, a Jacuzzi, and two lighted tennis courts. Seventy-nine of the 222 rooms are directly on the beach; the others face a tropical garden setting. The café is called Hemingway, and the poolside bar, Angler's Paradise, is a comforting retreat for those seeking a casual atmosphere. Also available are glass-bottom boat tours of the coral reefs.

3841 North Roosevelt Boulevard, Key West 33040. 305-294-2571; toll-free: 1-800-HOLIDAY. Moderate to expensive.

HYATT KEY WEST
Hotel/Key West

Decorated with Caribbean flair and flavor and designed to look as if it belongs in the 19th century, this hotel has open, airy rooms with private balconies great for viewing the famous Key West sunset. The location, fronting both Gulf and ocean, gives you the best of both possible worlds: a private beach and a marina for boating activities. The pool has a large deck area and an oversize Jacuzzi with a waterfront view. C. R. Provision Co. is the on-site boutique, making shopping easy for vacation extras, gear you left behind, or gifts and souvenirs for family and friends. Bicycle and motor scooter rentals are available at the hotel, as are sunset cruises aboard a 60-foot yacht, sportfishing charters with all the necessary gear, and catamaran rentals. Snorkeling and scuba excursions to coral reefs can be arranged through the concierge. Lunching, munching, and dining are outdoor-indoor, either on the Promenade deck or in Nicola Seafood, which offers a fine wine list and arguably the best conch fritters in town.

601 Front Street, Key West 33040. 305-296-9900. Expensive to very expensive.

LITTLE PALM ISLAND RESORT
Resort/Little Torch Key

Bring your boat or board the private launch service from the shore station at Mile Marker 28.5 in Little Torch Key and leave the cares of civilization behind. This five-acre island resort doesn't have phones, televisions, or children under nine. What it does have is swimming on a totally secluded beach or in a freshwater pool, diving and snorkeling, sailing and canoeing, bicycling and nature tours, and all sorts of water sports equipment and fishing gear on hand. You can schedule activities on other islands or the keys close by. If you absolutely must keep in touch with the real world you can find televisions and telephones inside the Great House lodge. There are two suites in each of the 14 thatched huts and two in the lodge, all with individual whirlpool bath, air-conditioning, stocked refrigerator, and private wraparound sun deck complete with hammock. The atmosphere is unbelievably tranquil, with no cars or boom-boxes, just the sound of palm fronds rustling in the gentle breeze.

The free-form swimming pool, which is surrounded by lush tropical land-scaping, has a waterfall and the Palapa bar. If you miss mingling with other folks, you can do so at lunch or dinner. The reputation of the dining room has reached the mainland and the restaurant is now open to the public. Breakfast, lunch, and dinner are available to guests.

Mile Marker 28.5, Route 4, Box 1036, Little Torch Key 33042. 305-872-2524; toll-free: 1-800-3-GET-LOST. Very expensive.

MARRIOTT'S CASA MARINA RESORT
Hotel/Key West

This oceanfront hostelry was the southernmost point of the Flagler hotel empire when it opened in 1921. It suffered the hard times of the Great Depression, and subsequently passed through the hands of numerous owners before being purchased by Marriott in the late 1970s, when it was totally renovated. A new wing was added followed by another wing of one- and two-bedroom suites in 1986, providing a total of 314 rooms. The lobby was beautifully restored to its reassuring sense of something special. The large free-form swimming pool faces 1,110 feet of private white sandy beach and a fishing pier stretching 600 feet out into the Atlantic. Start your day viewing the spectacular sunrise, then indulge in the fabulous breakfast buffet. Henry's, as in Henry Morrison Flagler, builder of the great railroad through the keys, is a magnificently decorated eatery and specializes in dinners of prime steak and fresh fillets of fish. After dinner, there's live entertainment and your favorite cocktails in the Calabash Lounge.

Reynolds Street on the Ocean, Key West 33040. 305-296-3535; toll-free (in Florida): 1-800-235-4837, (outside Florida): 1-800-228-9390. Expensive. Open year-round.

OCEAN KEY HOUSE SUITE RESORT & MARINA
Hotel/Key West

Located in Old Town, this historic hotel overlooks Mallory Square, famous magnet for many at sunset. The one- and two-bedroom suites feature a private Jacuzzi, full kitchen, and large private balcony. To find out what else is going on, check the What's Happening board out front. The Dockside Bar is a terrific outdoor waterfront oasis with live entertainment in the evenings. Sunset cruises are available at the adjacent marina, which has an extensive charter fleet.

Zero Duval Street, Key West 33040. 305-296-7701; toll-free: 1-800-328-9815. Expensive.

PIER HOUSE
Hotel/Key West

Each of the 129 rooms and 13 suites of this newly renovated hotel has a private balcony overlooking the private sandy beach (part of which is topless), the beautifully landscaped tropical gardens with Jacuzzi and pool, or downtown Old Key West. The Caribbean Spa has 22 rooms, including two one-bedroom suites, available to guests who want to be shamelessly pampered with the ultimate in decadence. Loofah rubs, European-style massage, one-on-one exercise, weight training and aerobics, along with full cosmetology services are just a few of the features. The Harbour View Cafe is open for breakfast, lunch, and dinner and you can come as you are. D.J.'s Raw Bar is great for snacking on clams, oysters, and shrimp, and the Beach Club Bar has frozen cocktails for keeping cool on or off the beach. The Pier House Restaurant is an award-winning establishment that caters to those who want the elegance of fine dining in a casual atmosphere. It specializes in American-Caribbean cuisine, working conch into salads, sensational fritters, bisque, and chowder; sautéeing yellowtail with key lime butter, and dressing fresh greenery with red raspberry vinaigrette There's an excellent wine list to complement such fare and the Wine Galley has a cruvinet. The Chart Room is very nautically casual, with TVs covering national sporting events.

One Duval Street, Key West 33040. 305-296-4600; toll-free (in Florida): 1-800-432-3414, (outside Florida): 1-800-327-8340. Expensive.

THE REACH
Hotel/Key West

This newest of Key West hotels sits on one of the best beaches of the island. The guest rooms, although not very roomy, have terraces, most with an ocean view. Two restaurants and five lounges make it easy to find dining and entertainment on the premises. Emma's Seafare is the hotel's Mediterranean-style indoor-outdoor oceanside restaurant. The piquant tropical cuisine utilizes locally caught seafood enhanced with the spices of the Bahamas, Cajun country, and Thailand. The best site for lunch is the Sand Bar, dangling over the water at the end of the private pier. There are a health spa for exercising your body and a library for exercising your mind, in case you want to do something besides veg out while on vacation.

1435 Simonton Street, Key West 33040. 305-296-5000; toll-free: 1-800-874-4118. Expensive.

SPINDRIFT TROPICAL RESORT
Motel/Key West

This 20-unit (two with kitchens), family-oriented, 1950s-style motel is two blocks from the beach in a secluded tropical atmosphere with a small pool set in a garden with fountains and waterfalls. Free coffee is served around the pool in the mornings, and the staff is friendly.

1212 Simonton Street, Key West 33040. 305-296-3432. Inexpensive to moderate.

Where to Eat

ANTONIA'S RESTAURANT
Italian/Key West

Antonia supervises the front while husband Phillip is out back doing his northern Italian thing using veal and fresh local seafood in a variety of ways, complementing them with excellent homemade pastas and a good selection of wines.

615 Duval Street, Key West. 305-294-6565. Moderate. Dinner daily.

AUNT ROSE'S
Italian/Key West

Pasta freshly assembled, veal treated to Parmesan and marsala magic, shrimp, either scampi or grilled, these are Rose's specialties, along with island libations in Rosario's Lounge.

1900 Flagler, Key West. 305-294-6214. Moderate. Lunch and dinner daily.

BILL'S KEY WEST FISH MARKET & RESTAURANT
American/Key West

With an on-the-premises fish market, this place serves the best seafood in Key West. There are schools of shrimp ("Key West gold") and sensational cole slaw—and portions are huge. Snapper Vera Cruz is our favorite.

2502 North Roosevelt Boulevard, Key West. 305-296-5891. Moderate. Lunch and dinner daily. Reservations requested for parties of five or more.

THE BUTTERY
Continental/Key West

A Cape Code kind of place with an array of original dishes, a full bar, an excellent wine list, and nightly specials. Its unique preparation of fresh local seafood has given it a reputation for excellence—and that's on an island that has some 200 restaurants, one for every 125 people.

1208 Simonton Street, Key West. 305-294-0717. Expensive. Dinner daily.

CAFE DES ARTISTE
French/Key West

Dine inside in a European-like setting or outdoors on the garden patio. Both are very French, very romantic, and the food is superb—snapper in a superior refined light sauce, scallops enhanced with curry and rum, lobster with mango, "raspberry-infused" duck, and filet mignon. The seafood is local and might include seasonal catches such as cobia and wahoo in addition to the usual grouper and yellowtail. The extensive wine list specializes in French labels, and the desserts, such as white chocolate mousse, are a must.

1007 Simonton Street, Key West. 305-294-7100. Expensive. Lunch and dinner daily.

EL SIBONEY
Cuban/Key West

Here's the best Cuban food in town. The headliners—our favorites—include melt-in-your-mouth roast pork, shrimp enchiladas spiced with a touch of the bayous, black bean soup, yellow rice, onion-smothered steaks, flaky pastry meat pies, and ham croquettes. For dessert what else than flan or guava and cream cheese?

900 Catherine Street, Key West. 305-296-4184. Moderate. Breakfast, lunch, and dinner daily.

HALF-SHELL RAW BAR
Seafood/Key West

This waterfront eatery is ultrasimple in decor, with crews from the local fishing fleet hunkered into the up-front bar and a back room with walls of windows overlooking the docks. Spiffy service and a blackboard menu. For starters order the cream-cheese-stuffed jalapeños and then a conch salad or fresh fish sandwich of the day. But only after you've indulged in the freshly shucked clams and oysters and maybe some peel-'em-yourself shrimp.

Number 1, Land's End Village, Key West. 305-294-7496. Inexpensive. Lunch and dinner daily. No credit cards.

LOUIE'S BACKYARD
American/Key West

If you want to eat in a National Historic landmark, find this Classic Revival–style house built on the water in 1909—it's close to the Casa Marina. Eat outside on the deck a few feet from the gently rolling surf, or in one of the interior rooms. Either way, you will be well served by a staff proud to bring forth such delights as omelets filled with Cajun creativity, a shrimp salad taken out of the ordinary by mayo spiked with bits of roasted peppers, a salad structured around strips of smoked duck with a zinger of a sauce straight from Sichuan, or a rack of lamb redolent to the *n*th degree with rosemary and roast garlic and Dijon mustard.

700 Waddell Avenue, Key West. 305-294-1061. Expensive. Lunch Monday to Saturday; dinner daily; Sunday brunch.

MAISON DE PEPE
Cuban/Key West

Cuban food in a very casual, laid-back setting. We start here with the caldo gallego, a brown bean soup, and then move onto boliche, stuffed eye of the round, or something with shrimp; anything, as long as we can have the black beans and white rice—commonly referred to as the Moors and the Christians—and fried plantains.

1215 Duval Street, Key West. 305-296-6922. Inexpensive. Breakfast, lunch, and dinner daily.

MANGIA MANGIA
Italian/Key West

For dinner on the run, indoors or in the garden, come to this café, noted for its large portions, hearty sauces, and homemade pastas. The conch sauce with pasta is rated the greatest by the islanders and you can bring your own wine or beer.

900 Southard Street, Key West. 305-294-2469. Expensive. Dinner daily. No reservations are accepted, so come early to avoid the wait.

MARGARITAVILLE CAFE
American/Key West

WELCOME PARROTHEADS! To Jimmy Buffett's downtown happening. His Key West home is ten minutes away (with a brass sign on the gate door that reads BEWARE OF OCCUPANT), but his words of wisdom are found here— "We are the people our parents warned us about," "If the phone doesn't ring, it's me," "Ain't life grand?" and "If God had meant for fish to taste like tofu, there would be no catch of the day." But here you can enjoy locally caught fish, golden fried, marinated, or grilled; fresh shrimp or conch burger; smoked fish with horseradish and mustard sauce. As well as grilled pork chops, barbecue chicken, baby-back ribs, and a "Cheeseburger in Paradise"—served like the song says.

500 Duval Street, Key West. 305-292-1435. Moderate. Lunch and dinner daily.

RUSTY ANCHOR RESTAURANT AND FISHERY
American/Stock Island

Owned by a fourth-generation Conch family, this restaurant is on the island where commercial fishermen unload their harvests. It serves seafood so fresh that it supplies many in-town eateries. Owner Patty is proud of the fact that they make "nothing fancy; just good, honest seafood pan-fried, deep-fried, or broiled." Choices include grouper, yellowtail, dolphin, and shrimp year-round; wahoo, golden tile, cobia, and triggerfish in season. They also serve steak and baby-back ribs to those who have not acquired their sea legs. This casual down-home eatery is removed from the tourist area and that's another reason locals love it.

5510 3rd Street, Stock Island. 305-294-5369. Inexpensive to moderate. Lunch and dinner Monday to Saturday.

Where to Shop

Key West Kite Co., 409 Greene Street (305-296-2535), for those who love to play in the wind with stunt kites, wind socks, and other flying toys.

Land's End Village, at the foot of Margaret Street, is filled with gift, clothing, and snack shops. With the name, you know it's located on the water at a marina.

Margaritaville, next to the café of the same name, is a shop where you can purchase anything associated with Jimmy Buffett, including greeting cards, T-shirts, casual clothing and beachwear, and souvenirs and gifts, along with Buffett's albums and tapes. Although Buffett's album output has decreased, he remains one of the music industry's most refreshing artists, with a cult of die-hard fans, which is obvious when you visit Key West. He still tours occasionally and you might catch him sitting in with local musicians.

Mallory Market, at 1 Whitehead Street in Mallory Square, has specialty shops for the adults and attractions to keep the little ones happy, all in a great waterfront location, so if you shop all day you will still be able to catch the brilliant sunset.

Shades of Key West is the place for those special name-brand sunglasses that seem made just for you. For a choice of hundreds of styles, shop any of their three locations: 306 Front Street, 335 Duval Street, and 121 Duval Street (305-294-0519).

More Fun in the Sun

The **Annual Key West Literary Seminar** (305-745-3640) is held every January. This four-day event, with lectures, seminars, receptions, and dinners, has covered such notables as Hemingway and Tennessee Williams, and topics such as mystery and travel writing.

The *Atlantic X* **dinner cruise,** Key West Bight (305-292-1777), provides a continental buffet, music, entertainment, and casino while you're gliding along the waterways.

Audubon House and Gardens, 205 Whitehead Street (305-294-2116), is a fine tribute to the Key West of the 1800s. Audubon visited the house, which was built by wrecker (a Key West boat salvage expert) and pilot Captain John H. Geiger, while painting the birds of the Keys.

Can't Miss, at the City Marina, Garrison Bight (305-296-3751), is a

75-foot yacht available for a fun day of fishing, sunset cruises, or excursions to the Dry Tortugas and Fort Jefferson.

Captains Corner, Zero Duval Street, Ocean Key Marina (305-296-8865), offer glass-bottom boat tours leaving every two hours, trips via seaplane to the Dry Tortugas, and scuba diving and snorkeling trips.

Conch Tour Train, 301 Front Street (305-294-5161), takes you on a 90-minute guided tour past 60 of the most popular and important sites of Key West's 400-year history.

Downtown Water Sports, 700 Front Street (305-292-9765), behind A & B Marina, rents single and double-rider Jet Skis.

The **Ernest Hemingway Home and Museum,** 907 Whitehead Street (305-294-1575), was the residence of the famous writer until 1961. It was here that he penned many of his best-sellers, built the town's first swimming pool, and raised six-toed cats.

Fireball Glass-Bottom Sight-seeing Boat, Two Duval Street (305-296-6293 and 294-7084), sails rain or shine because you view the waters below from the comfort of the enclosed cabin. A sun deck, a snack bar, and rest rooms are provided for your convenience.

Key West Rowing Club, Land's End Marina, Zero Margaret Street (305-292-7984), has small boat rentals for rowing, sailing, sculling, and windsurfing, with instructions if desired.

Little White House Museum, 111 Front Street (305-294-9911), is the painstakingly restored favorite vacation home of President Harry S. Truman, who called it the winter White House. As a close friend of the Truman family was quoted after touring the home: "You have the same feeling you had when he was there."

Mel Fisher's Maritime Heritage Society, 200 Greene Street (305-294-2633), displays some of the loot Fisher and his salvagers found off the shores of Key West. There's a hefty entrance fee.

Mosquito Coast, 1107 Duval Street (305-294-7178), schedules guided back-country wildlife tours via kayak through the shallow waters around the mangrove islands of Sugar Loaf and Geiger Key, stopping for a snorkeling excursion to study the complex environment that makes the keys so beautiful.

Nautical Excursions, Safe Harbor Marina, 528A Front Street (305-294-2911 or 296-1442), is a great place to schedule a fishing trip or get some time in sailing, snorkeling, or diving out at the living coral reef.

Old Town Trolley, 1910 North Roosevelt Boulevard (305-296-6688), offers a 90-minute town tour, making pickups at major hotels and four stops downtown at 30-minute intervals.

Schooner Wharf, Key West Seaport, 631 Greene Street (305-296-WOLF), is the home of the 19th-century topsail schooner *Wolf,* which has a daily schedule of Reef Adventure, Champagne Sunset, or Starlight Cruise sails. Charters for up to 44 passengers are also available anytime for groups and parties, weddings, or any special occasion.

Sunset Watersports, Inc., located at Smathers Beach, Higgs Beach, and Hilton Haven Motel (305-296-2554), rents everything from Windsurfers and Jet Skis to Hobie Cats and snorkeling equipment. It's also the place to sign up for parasailing.

Waterfront Playhouse, Mallory Square (305-294-5015), is open during the season, November through June, and features plays not only by Key Wester Tennessee Williams but Agatha Christie.

Why Not, at South and Simonton streets (305-296-0514), has scooter and bicycle rentals—great ways to see the island—and sells ice cream and sandwiches to refresh you before, during, or after your travels.

Where to Write

Florida Keys & Key West Visitors Bureau, P.O. Box 1147, Key West, Florida 33041. You can also call and order free brochures: 305-296-3811; toll-free: 1-800-FLA-KEYS.

Key West Chamber of Commerce, Key West, Florida 33041. 305-294-2587.

HOLLYWOOD TO

VERO BEACH AREA

HOLLYWOOD BEACH

Christened Hollywood-by-the-Sea when it was founded in 1921 by a Californian who might or might not have been thinking of Tinseltown, this stretch of land along the sand is a retro trip to the 1950s, to the days before the high-rises closed off ocean views and the glitz and glitter of the Gold Coast gobbled up almost everything and everyone in its grasp. Mom-and-pop motels, grungy bars, and semi-tatty restaurants are a part of the scene; but there are also more than five miles of developed, uninterrupted beachfront with a boardwalk to rival that of Atlantic City or any other resort, although it's only the width of a two-lane road and it's actually called the Broadwalk. Yes, "broad," because it was not built of boards but of asphalt on a coral rock foundation. You can stroll, walk, run, jog, or ride a bike on it for miles, all the way from North Beach Park to Georgia Street in the south. The bike lane begins at Azalea Street and goes to Balboa Street, passing through the busiest sections of the strip and through North Beach Park, some four miles. There are a few detours, but they are well marked and easy to follow. No bikes are allowed on the Broadwalk between 10 and 4.

The bike and foot paths are real people parades, so don't be surprised to see the body-bronzers sitting on their lounge chairs facing the Broadwalk instead of the ocean. Because the people, too, are an integral part of the seascape, as important and maybe even as interesting as the sea oats and dune plantings protected by real boardwalks leading from land to shore. The portion of the beach from Bougainvilla Terrace to Washington Street is especially attractive and it's where on several occasions we have found a fascinating variety of sea creatures—baby blue crabs and starfish, sea urchins, tiny shrimp, and hermit crabs—clinging for dear life to ocean vegetation washed ashore. When you wade out past the gentle surf and into the calm water, watch for more of the same, as well as schools of tiny fish that the kids will try to catch with their sand buckets, no doubt thinking of aquarium lodgings back home. But the darters are far too swift.

From Sherman Street in the north to Greenbrier in the south, there are no fewer than 51 access roads, 24 of them named after U.S. presidents.

Parks with a variety of facilities for family enjoyment can be found all along what the locals regard as the finest beachfront in Florida. Charnow Park at Garfield Street, the "muscle beach" of the area, has three pavilions, barbecue grills, playground equipment for the kids, and the Par Cours Fitness Circuit, and nearby are six three-wall paddleball courts. Local musicians occasionally put on impromptu concerts at the pavilions. There are regularly scheduled concerts every Friday at the Hollywood North Beach Park on A1A and Sheridan Street (305-926-2444), which also has a boardwalk to the beach, a watchtower, a pair of snack bars, and a playground, plus a turtle hatchery, volleyball nets, showers, water fountains, and rest rooms.

Across A1A on the Intracoastal Waterway at Sheridan Street is a newly opened vest-pocket park with barbecue grills, picnic tables, and metered parking. North of that, past the Moors Townhouses, is more metered parking in an idyllic setting shaded by palm trees and sporting a half-mile walkway on the breakwater. The landscaping of those lots is part of the city's ambitious beautification program: Hollywood is working to improve its image everywhere along the beach.

Appearances are as important as the safety of the citizens and that's guaranteed by the NICE squads—as in Neighbors Involved in Community Enforcement—with police cyclists garbed in blue shorts and white shirts. Not that the beach really gets rowdy or out of hand, despite the throngs that gather at strategic spots such as Johnson Street or Angelo's Corner, a pizzeria on Garfield Street.

The beach itself is what is special: a well-maintained, properly protected spread of sand with a strategic scattering of palm trees and a shoreline that beckons the walker to go on and on. If you do that on Hollywood Beach you can go beyond North Beach Park to the 1,000 feet of undeveloped Dania Beach, with its Sea Fair complex of shops and restaurants, marina and parking meters, and special entertainment events; and then onward to the 244 acres of barrier island wilderness, the John U. Lloyd State Recreation Area (6503 North Ocean Drive, Dania; 305-923-2833). In addition to plenty of parking, there are sites for picnics, places to fish from the rock jetties, and a nature trail through a coastal hammock with birds overhead and four-footed creatures on the ground. You might spot a manatee or two heading north for the warm waters by the power station at Port Everglades, a deep-water seaport that handles general cargo ships and luxury liners. The recreation area acreage backs into the eastern boundaries of the great cruise port, and if you're on the northern tip of the island at the right time, you can watch the giant ships glide through the cut. You'll be struck by the vivid contrast between those floating hotels with the high-rise condos of Fort Lauderdale in the background and the unspoiled beach and its aquatic and subtropical vegetation.

You'll find another study in contrasts in your fellow vacationers. Hollywood Beach is an international oasis filled with Europeans, including Scandinavians, Germans, and some French. But most of the French you'll hear on this beach is spoken by the more than 700,000 French-Canadians who visit Hollywood each year, and that's why the Canadian flag is flying from so many restaurants and hostelries and why so many cars have the *Je Me Souviens*—"I Remember"—license plates.

Where It Is

Hollywood Beach is on State Road A1A north of Miami and south of Fort Lauderdale, between Hallandale Beach Boulevard and Dania Beach Boulevard. The best approach to the beach is from U.S. 1 at Young Circle in Hollywood proper, along Hollywood Boulevard, State Road 820, as lovely a thoroughfare as you'll find in urban Florida. Six lanes lined with stately royal palms fronting an inventory of architectural achievement ranging from Spanish Mediterranean Revival to Art Deco to just plain Florida mansion, lead directly to A1A and the magnificent and massive Hollywood Beach Hotel, a castle from the Roaring Twenties.

Where to Stay

DAYS HOTEL GULFSTREAM BEACH RESORT
Hotel/Hollywood Beach

This oceanfront hotel sits on some of Hollywood's widest and most beautiful palm tree–dotted beachfront. The grounds are lushly landscaped with tropical plantings framing a large swimming pool with Jacuzzi, a tiki bar, and the Suntan Hut, which sells tanning products, T-shirts, and beachwear and rents beach umbrellas and chaise longues. You'll go bananas over Bananas, their restaurant that serves breakfast, light lunches, and dinner. The Bananas Lounge has nightly entertainment. Kids 12 and under eat free; kids 17 and under stay free with parents. Immediately south of the hotel you can rent Jet Skis, waverunners, and powerboats (see the "More Fun in the Sun" section for details).

2711 South Ocean Drive, Hollywood Beach 33019. 305-922-8200; toll-free: 1-800-221-5846. Moderate to expensive.

DRIFTWOOD ON THE OCEAN
Hotel/Hollywood Beach

This place looks like a little bit of heaven—the grounds are very well maintained with plush green vegetation, the rooms are decorated in cheery pastels, and the pool is fresh and clean. Our favorite accommodations are the two-bedroom, two-bath corner apartments and the executive two-bedroom apartments, which are spacious, attractively furnished, and reasonably priced. Special rates for weekly and monthly rentals.

2101 South Surf Road, Hollywood Beach 33019. 305-923-9520 or 305-927-1732. Moderate.

GREENBRIAR APARTMENT/MOTEL
Motel/Hollywood Beach

The owners here boast that the Greenbriar is "Set like a Gem between the Sun and Sea." And it's true; the place is unpretentious, quiet, clean; the beach is glistening white. Included among the amenities are temperature control, cable television, telephones, radios, and alarm clocks in the guest quarters, plus lounges, shuffleboard courts, and a large heated pool with a sheltered sun deck. Single and double rooms, studios, efficiencies, and one-bedroom apartments are available.

1900 South Surf Road, Hollywood Beach 33019. 305-922-2606. Inexpensive.

HOLLYWOOD BEACH HILTON
Hotel/Hollywood Beach
Renovated in 1986, this hotel has 306 rooms and 16 suites, many with terraces and ocean or Intracoastal views, a health club with exercise equipment and sauna, tennis courts, and a pool with Jacuzzi to help keep you in shape after you overindulge in any, or all, of the three on-site restaurants.

4000 South Ocean Drive, Hollywood Beach 33019. 305-458-1900; toll-free: 1-800-HILTONS. Moderate to expensive.

HOWARD JOHNSON HOLLYWOOD BEACH RESORT INN
Resort Hotel/Hollywood Beach
All 242 rooms are furnished in HoJo style, and each has an oceanview balcony. A HoJo restaurant serves three meals a day, snacks, and some of the chain's famous ice cream flavors in between. As an indication of the international clientele, staff members—at least some of them—speak Spanish, French, and German.

2501 North Ocean Drive, Hollywood Beach 33019. 305-925-1411; toll-free (in Florida): 1-800-643-3970, (U.S.A. and Canada): 1-800-423-9867. Moderate.

RUFFY'S INTRACOASTAL WATERWAY RESORT
Hotel/Hollywood Beach

This recently redecorated retreat is a mixture of Art Deco hotel and rustic sea shack, a schizophrenic with a pastel interior and a rugged raw bar/marina on the water—the Intracoastal, that is, not the ocean. But you can see the Atlantic across the street. The hotel rooms and efficiency suites have been newly and neatly decorated, and Ruffy's restaurant (see page 70) offers fine dining inside as well as "island casual" outside. You can schedule fishing trips or rent Jet Skis at the hotel's marina.

2300 North Ocean Drive, Hollywood Beach 33019. 305-920-0600. Moderate.

SHELDON OCEAN RESORT
Resort Hotel/Hollywood Beach

Newly renovated and beautifully decorated, this hotel sits on the Broadwalk, and most of its rooms have ocean views. They all have ceiling fans, temperature control, and cable TV, and each has been named after a super celebrity, so you can sleep among the stars in the Humphrey Bogart room, or in one of those named for Marilyn Monroe, James Dean, Elvis Presley, or Brigitte Bardot—to list a few. Hallways and rooms are decorated with pictures of the celebrities. That's the Sheldon gimmick, but this hotel doesn't need one. Although there's no pool, this is one of our favorite destinations because of the tropical, laid-back feel of the place. The beach is right out the door across the Broadwalk.

1000 North Surf Road, Hollywood Beach 33019. 305-922-6020; toll-free (outside Florida): 1-800-344-6020. Inexpensive to moderate.

SHORE VIEW APARTMENTS
Apartments/Hollywood Beach

This is the place for unbelievable beachfront accommodations at unbelievable prices! You can get a two-bedroom, two-bath apartment overlooking the ocean with maid service for the cost of a hotel room. And if you rent by the month you receive a considerable discount. The view from the two-bedroom corner apartment with the beach just a few feet away is sensational. Although we prefer soft pastel colors, the earth tones here are very appealing, and the whiter-than-white kitchens and bathrooms are spotless. The only drawback to this place is that it has no pool.

1711 South Surf Road, Hollywood Beach. 305-922-7500. Moderate. No checks or credit cards.

Where to Eat

CAPONE'S FLICKER LITE
Italian/Hollywood Beach

This is a great place for pizza but it also serves hoagies, subs, and salads, and it has a pretty good raw bar. There are outdoor tables on the Intracoastal and a lounge with a television for sports fans and a jukebox for music lovers.

1014 North Ocean Drive, Hollywood Beach. 305-922-4232. Inexpensive. Lunch and dinner daily.

DOCKSIDE
Seafood/Hollywood Beach

If you were any closer to the Intracoastal Waterway, you would have to ask for a life preserver. The luncheon burgers and fried fish sandwiches with onion and tomato are marvelous and the dinner fillets of grouper, dolphin, and whatever else they proclaim to be fresh are very good, especially if given a light—and we do emphasize "light"—Cajun peppering.

908 North Ocean Drive, Hollywood Beach. 305-922-2265. Inexpensive to moderate. Lunch and dinner daily.

FRANK AND MARIO'S PIZZERIA
Italian/Hollywood Beach
Arguably the best pizza on the beach and popular with most of the locals, including the lifeguards, but the general tackiness of the place is not very inviting—so order take-out.

1104 North Broadwalk, Hollywood Beach. 305-923-3174. Inexpensive. Lunch and dinner daily.

HUNKY DORY'S
Seafood/Hollywood Beach
Would you believe that this was named for a family named Dory? A family that loved this hunk of Hollywood and wanted some good reason to remain forever. *Ergo* the picnic tables alongside the 400 feet of dock space on the Waterway, the inside room where there's lively entertainment, and a kitchen that makes some of the best conch fritters to be found. After inhaling a dozen or so of those deep-fried mini-grenades, ask about the fresh fish of the day, and order it simply broiled. And enjoy as you watch the traffic on the Waterway and wonder just how much it *does* cost to maintain one of those yachts gliding past.

1318 North Ocean Drive, Hollywood Beach. 305-925-1011. Inexpensive to moderate. Lunch and dinner daily.

ICE CREAM DELIGHTS
American/Hollywood Beach
In addition to all the creamy delights, this place serves real lemonade, made from freshly squeezed lemons.

1202 North Broadwalk, Hollywood Beach. 305-921-5424. Inexpensive. Open 10 A.M. to 9 P.M. daily.

JOE SONKEN'S GOLD COAST RESTAURANT
Seafood/Hollywood Beach

A favorite of Chicagoans—Chicago was the late Joe Sonken's native city—not only for its "my kind of town" feeling (it always reminds us of a 1940s upper-crust roadhouse), but because the front facade is plastered with actual Chicago street signs, removed, we presume, with an okay from the Chicago Police Department. The up-front Cutty Sark Lounge is a good gathering place for night owls, and the rambling dining room is a fine observation platform for watching the boat parade just a few feet away from the Sonken docks. During the stone crab season (October 15 to May 15), this is the best place on the beach for indulging in that great natural resource of Florida waters; but the steaks are also worthy of the Chicago connection.

606 North Ocean Drive, Hollywood Beach. 305-923-4000. Expensive. Lunch and dinner daily.

LA CONCHA BEACH CLUB
American/Hollywood Beach

A lively patio with umbrella-shaded tables perfectly positioned for the morning ritual of watching the sun come up. It opens at 7:30 for breakfast, which is served all day—and a powerful, good, old-fashioned American breakfast it is—and the bar isn't shut down until the last customer leaves. During major happenings that bar is filled with sports fans glued to the tube. The menu is light, the service spiffy, and both are bilingual—in English and French.

900 North Broadwalk, Hollywood Beach. 305-921-4190. Inexpensive to moderate. Breakfast, lunch, and dinner daily.

MARTHA'S ON THE INTRACOASTAL
Continental/Hollywood Beach

This stunner on the Waterway is strictly upscale continental with a full panoply of fussily prepared seafood dishes, pepper steaks, and veal in any state but Wiener schnitzel. Our favorite dishes are coconut shrimp with a piña colada batter, dolphin menuiere, and the peanut butter pie. You can dance off the calories to the beat of golden oldies in between courses. The musicians are marvelous and the staff is formal and finely tuned, but if you come casual or right off your boat at their dock, head upstairs for simpler fare and informality, otherwise known as tropical casual.

6024 North Ocean Drive, Hollywood Beach. 305-923-5444. Expensive. Lunch and dinner daily.

McGOWAN'S
American/Hollywood Beach

This review should really be titled "McGowan's/Ocean View," because McGowan's is a bar and Ocean View is a restaurant next door that accepts orders for such essential snack stuff as burgers and hot dogs, chicken wings, and assorted sandwiches. McGowan's is listed here because it's a great bar for beach-viewing out the windows or just sitting around watching television or listening to the jukebox—you can dance if you want. This is the kind of bar where if you come three nights in a row you'll meet most of the real people in town—or at least on the beach.

298 Arizona Street, Hollywood Beach. 305-923-4885. Inexpensive. Open daily.

NICK'S BAR & GRILL
American/Hollywood Beach

Remember the scene in *Body Heat* where Kathleen Turner and William Hurt are flirting in a bar? It was filmed at Nick's, where the locals gather singly and in bunches, to snack on the sandwiches and sip the beers while listening to soft rock, watching the Broadwalk parade out the open windows, or comparing notes with all the other Nickites who have made this oasis of Key West informality their second—or maybe their first—home.

1214 North Broadwalk, Hollywood Beach. 305-920-2800. Inexpensive. Lunch and dinner daily.

OCEANS ELEVEN
American/Hollywood Beach

Another of the popular beach bars, this one with hamburgers that just might be the best on the beach—along with those served at the restaurant's outpost west on Federal Highway, in another simple little old shack that has incredible drink specials during the cocktail hours. This casual little spot also serves breakfast and two-for-one cocktails all day long.

3111 North Ocean Drive, Hollywood Beach. 305-927-5549. Inexpensive. Breakfast, lunch, and dinner daily.

THE PLACE ON THE BEACH
Greek-Israeli/Hollywood Beach

For souvlaki, shawma, falafel, and gyro-filled pita pockets, this is indeed the place on the beach—although it's a little ragged around the edges. It also serves Italian and Polish subs, BLTs with French fries, chicken and tuna salad plates, New York strip steaks, Moroccan couscous (only on Tuesday), kosher hot dogs, Buffalo chicken wings, all kinds of burgers, and 12 flavors of ice cream.

1000 North Broadwalk, Hollywood Beach. 305-923-6168. Inexpensive. Lunch and dinner daily.

RUFFY'S
Seafood/Hollywood Beach

Dine inside, where there's a certain amount of Art Deco elegance, or alfresco for the freshly shucked oysters and clams served ever so simply—on the half shell with a bit of lemon and a cocktail sauce you can make a bit zestier by asking for the Tabasco. The fish is fresh and carefully handled, the burgers bountiful, and the desserts well worth the calories.

2300 Ocean Drive, Hollywood Beach. 305-920-0600. Inexpensive to moderate. Lunch and dinner daily.

SAHARA INTERNATIONAL
Mideastern/Hollywood Beach

When you have a hankering for a spot of tahini and humus this is the place. We go there for the hot dogs—they are super.

1211 North Surf Road, Hollywood Beach. 305-923-8614. Inexpensive. Open daily.

Where to Shop

Hollywood Beach's 27-foot-wide Broadwalk offers 2½ miles of beachwear, souvenir, and gift shops, interrupted by bars, lounges, casual restaurants, and small market delis.

Intersecting the center of the Broadwalk is Johnson Street—hub of the happy crowd that rallies day and night—with numerous shopping opportunities, including **Beach Carousel Department Store; Hollywood Ocean Gifts; Pink Boutique,** with lots of mod beachwear in uplifting colors; **Shore Department Store; La Maison du Cadeau; Seaworld Swimwear;** and **Surf American,** where you can find surf, skate, and boogie boards and outfits for sun and sand. Largest of them all is **Wings Surf and Sports,** with a huge selection of everything you might have forgotten to pack for your trip plus those special little extras you really don't need but can't resist.

At **600 Plaza,** on the northern side of New York Street up to Filmore Street, there are places to snack and sip—**Soft Licks Yogurt, Hat Rack Restaurant and Bar,** and **Subway,** but if you're dieting don't go past the first one; it serves a great variety of nonfat flavors, including the Honey Hill ten-calorie frozen yogurt delight. **Ocean Wave Beachwear** defines its own name.

Beginning at 707 Surf Road is another string of shops including **Swim 'N' Jog,** with a good selection of sportswear. On the next block, from Indiana to Buchanan streets, there are other beachwear shops, plus the **Seaside Deli and Market** and Greek, Italian, and pizza feederies.

A block from Buchanan and Surf streets is the **Sheldon Ocean Beach Club,** with a trio of shops for those seeking beachwear.

More Fun in the Sun

There are some 80 city-sponsored free shows at the **Beach Theater Under the Stars,** a 750-seat band shell amphitheater. These shows are advertised well in advance by the City of Hollywood Recreation and Parks Department, which publishes a monthly "Recreation Program," including events at **Young Circle,** a few minutes away on U.S. 1. Most popular of the concerts are those on Monday night, when there's dancing on the Broadwalk by the band shell. The music is strictly vintage 1930s and 1940s, the dancing the old-fashioned pre-twist variety, and the participants primarily the senior set. They love it and are in place a couple of hours before the first note is played.

For more sedentary entertainment there's the ten-screen **AMC** theater at Ocean Walk, wedged into the Hollywood Beach Hotel, a magnificent expression of Florida Spanish architecture, that opened in 1926, the same year as the Boca Raton Hotel, and was targeted to the same affluent crowd. When boom turned to bust, the onetime pride of Hollywood was converted to other uses, and today it's a condominium with the first two floors serving as a struggling mini-mall and a pitiful imitation of Miami's Bayside.

For waterborne exercise, check into the **Hollywood Beach Sailing Club,** 101 North Ocean Drive (305-925-2863), and check out the 16- or 18-foot catamarans, the Sunfish, Windsurfers, one- or two-person kayaks, water bikes, or sailboats. Dry land simulators are used to teach novitiates how to negotiate once on the water. There are special group rates.

The **Art & Culture Center of Hollywood,** 1301 South Ocean Drive (305-921-3274), has rotating exhibits of the works of contemporary as well as traditional artists, including some locals, and art classes for children. There are also a lecture series, various workshops and seminars, and on Sunday afternoons, classical or jazz concerts.

Jet Skis and waverunners can be rented at **Gulfstream Watersports** (305-457-3533), on the 3500 block of A1A on the Intracoastal just south of Days Hotel Gulfstream Beach Resort. Also, you may want to rent a boat and check out the Intracoastal on a pair of water skis or go deep-sea fishing. **Suncoast Watersports Rentals** is located one mile north of Sheridan Street on the Intracoastal Waterway at 5400 North Ocean Drive (305-920-2574); **Hollywood Jet Ski Rentals,** three blocks north of Sheridan Street at 4501 North Ocean Drive (305-921-8343), is located at Parkside Inn, also on the Intracoastal.

Land lovers can rent bikes at **Sun & Fun Bicycles** (305-925-0735), just behind **Miami Ice** at 1500 North Broadwalk and Hayes Street.

Those interested in deep-sea fishing (half-day or two- and three-day voyages to the Bahamas aboard *Sea Legs IV* and *Island Hopper*) can contact the docks at 3400 North Ocean Drive, a mile north of Sheridan Street on A1A (305-923-2109 or 921-7487).

Where to Write

Greater Hollywood Chamber of Commerce, P.O. Box 2345, Hollywood, Florida 33022. 305-920-0330.

◎　　◎　　◎

FORT LAUDERDALE BEACH

I f they made a sequel today to the 1960 hit film *Where the Boys Are*, it would have to be titled *Where the Boys Aren't*. The thousands of Spring Breakers who used to stream to Fort Lauderdale and pack themselves like sardines onto a few square inches of sand for the annual rites of pinking the skin have been reduced to a trickle. Now, 350,000 of them head for Daytona Beach—with fewer than 20,000 making the trek to Fort Lauderdale, and only half as many wandering a bit farther south, down to the keys. Why the shift of students? They were very clearly given the message that the city fathers no longer wanted the annual madness and excessive drinking, but instead wanted a $35 million general rehab of the beachfront, the three miles of palm-fringed road that ribbons its way along the coast and is a unique union of city and sea that is denied to so many other beachfronts in the state. The high-rises on the far side of the road are not that high and do not shut off the view as they do elsewhere on the Gold Coast. The road—which is officially called Atlantic Boulevard, but is known to the locals only as A1A—makes an almost mystical merging of man with his origins, of the land and sea, of the modern paved road and 21,000 feet of crushed shell and coarse sand.

The parking has been moved and some of the traffic has been diverted from A1A to the side roads. Tropical plantings have been added to median strips and the beach is now protected by handsome walls and elaborate entrances. The roadway, only a few inches from all that water lapping at the shoreline, is a Fort Lauderdale landmark every bit as distinctive as the nearly 400 miles of canals and navigable waterways and the many marinas and boat yards that have earned the town the dual titles of the Venice of America and the Yachting Capital of the World.

Nearly 35,000 boats are registered in the county, and many more are for sale at the numerous brokers found at the major marinas, where charter fleets are also available for fishing trips and cruises to nowhere. In Fort Lauderdale you can take the water routes at minimum expense, traveling from point to point and paying a set fee for all day on and off one of the water taxis. Painted a distinctive yellow and green, these taxis cover any part of the waterways where they can dock. Their busiest times are during the high season (from December 15 to April 15), on the Fourth of July (when there are free concerts and fireworks on the beach along with a super Sandblast and a sculpture contest), and in mid-December (during the annual Sunshine Festival, which is climaxed by a waterborne parade of brightly lighted, gaily decorated boats and yachts of all sizes and shapes). It's Florida's answer to Macy's Thanksgiving Day Parade in the Big Apple, a kind of Big Orange challenge with a hundred boats participating and hundreds of others watching and wishing they had been chosen for the grand review of the waterborne wealth.

Fort Lauderdale is a stop on the Whitbread Round the World Race, when 30 to 40 sailboats blow into port, and during the city's annual Navy Days, usually held in October, the slips and docks are awash with the gray of our fighting ships. Between 150 and 200 military vessels visit Port Everglades each year, and the city is a favorite liberty stop of the officers and men of several nations' navies. Their arrivals and departures can be seen by beachgoers as the gray forms glide in and out of the port like the cruise ships sailing in and out of the harbor—only Miami serves more cruise ships than Fort Lauderdale.

Where It Is

Fort Lauderdale Beach is about halfway between Miami Beach and Palm Beach on State Road A1A, and can be reached by several roads leading from U.S. 1: 17th Street and Las Olas, Oakland Park, and Sunrise boulevards. From the Fort Lauderdale–Hollywood International Airport go north on U.S. 1 at the exit from the airport.

Where to Stay

BAHIA CABANA BEACH RESORT
Hotel/Fort Lauderdale

A low-rise located on the Intracoastal next to the docks of the *Jungle Queen* (see page 83), with charter boats for deep-sea fishing and scuba diving and rentals of all types of water sports equipment. It has 116 rooms, including efficiencies and apartments, three pools, two saunas, and the largest Jacuzzi on the beach. You'll love the waterfront patio and bar overlooking the marina, rated "Number 1 in the World" by *Boating Magazine*. The Cabana Café serves breakfast and what it claims is the "best barbecue on the beach," along with reasonably priced all-American home-cooked dinners. There's a great little souvenir shop, the Cabana Cargo General Store, which also sells beachwear, sundries, magazines, and snacks. This place has a very rustic appearance and reminds us of Ruffy's in Hollywood without the touches of Art Deco.

3001 Harbor Drive, Fort Lauderdale 33316. Toll-free (in Florida): 1-800-922-3008, (outside Florida): 1-800-BEACHES, (in Canada): 1-800-3BEACH4. Moderate.

BAHIA MAR RESORT AND YACHTING CENTER
Resort/Fort Lauderdale

We once visited this resort during the annual International Boat Show (see page 85). It was packed! Buses, taxis, automobiles, and people were everywhere. There is a rooftop pool with bar and grill; a walkway to the beach; the Spyglass Lounge, with a fine view of the ocean; a restaurant serving straightforward steaks and seafood; and Florida's largest marina, with boat rentals, diving excursions, and instructions in sailing and power boating. The marina has a total of 350 slips, including one with a plaque marking it as the spot where mystery writer John MacDonald's Travis McGee kept his *Busted Flush*.

801 Seabreeze Boulevard, Fort Lauderdale 33316. Toll-free: 1-800-327-8154. Expensive.

DAYS INN–LAUDERDALE SURF HOTEL
Hotel/Fort Lauderdale
A block and a half from Bahia Cabana (see page 75), with pool, restaurant, and overall neat appearance. Behind the hotel is the parasailing headquarters, but before making plans to go flying, you might want to check into the inn's patio bar.

440 Seabreeze Boulevard, Fort Lauderdale 33316. 305-462-5555. Moderate.

HOWARD JOHNSON OCEANS EDGE RESORT
Hotel/Fort Lauderdale
All rooms have two double beds, a private balcony, a refrigerator, cable television, and HoJo-coordinated colors. Room rates vary depending on the view. The pool is fresh and clean, with a poolside bar; the restaurant is a HoJo all the way; and the lounge features nightly entertainment.

700 North Atlantic Boulevard, Fort Lauderdale 33304. Toll-free (in Florida): 1-800-343-9213, (outside Florida): 1-800-327-8578, (in Canada): 1-800-654-2000. Inexpensive to moderate.

IRELAND'S INN
Hotel/Fort Lauderdale
A family-owned operation sitting directly on the beach, with two heated freshwater pools bordered by bars and an oceanside patio. Accommodations range from standard hotel rooms to two-bedroom apartments and studio suites. Rooms are spacious; all are equipped with refrigerators. There's an old-timey, Fort-Lauderdale-the-way-it-used-to-be feel about this place, popular among those who have seen many a mango season.

2220 North Atlantic Boulevard, Fort Lauderdale 33305. Toll-free (in Florida): 1-800-423-4359, (outside Florida): 1-800-327-4460, (in Canada): 1-800-451-4777. Moderate to expensive.

LAGO MAR
Hotel/Fort Lauderdale

An old-shoe hideaway with a loyal legion of repeat guests who like the comfort of a bar and dining room reminiscent of a 1940s country club in the burbs of the Midwest. The guest rooms, however, are reminiscent of nothing more than fairly modern motel rooms, but the landscaping allows some sense of privacy far, far from all the action on the Strip. There are tennis courts, a pair of swimming pools, a restaurant and bar, and down-home-friendly staff. The beachfront here is far less crowded than to the north.

1700 South Ocean Lane, Fort Lauderdale 33351. 305-523-6511; toll-free: 1-800-366-5246. Moderate.

MARRIOTT'S HARBOR BEACH RESORT
Resort/Fort Lauderdale

A class act giant among Lauderdale's many beachfront hotels, this 645-room model of modern design and decoration sits on 16 acres of pricey real estate encompassing an 8,000-square-foot free-form pool complete with waterfalls, five tennis courts, whirlpools, saunas, a health club, and out on the shore, 50 cabanas and water sports gear. The lobby is a knockout, and the guest rooms, each with a mini-bar and private balcony, are tropically compatible with all that water and the lush landscaping; the three dozen suites have larger balconies and wet bars made of marble, and if you simply must have a grand piano in your room, reserve the Presidential or Vice-Presidential pads. There are restaurants everywhere; they range from Japanese to garden terrace, coffee shop, seafood specialist, and the signature Sheffield's, a bit too like a British tavern in concept, but formally serving the kind of food found in a grand hotel front-runner.

3030 Holiday Drive, Fort Lauderdale 33301. 305-525-4000; toll-free (in Florida): 1-800-222-6543, (outside Florida): 1-800-228-9290. Expensive.

SHERATON YANKEE CLIPPER BEACH RESORT
Hotel/Fort Lauderdale
Directly on the beach, with 485 rooms, each with two double beds and some with ocean view, some without. There are tennis courts, three pools with accompanying bars, a pair of cocktail lounges, an okay restaurant, and entertainment nightly.

1140 Seabreeze Boulevard, Fort Lauderdale 33316. 305-524-5551; toll-free: 1-800-325-3535. Moderate to expensive.

SHERATON YANKEE TRADER BEACH RESORT
Hotel/Fort Lauderdale
465 rooms furnished in predictable Sheraton style, with restaurants for three meals a day indoors and out, and a pair of pools. Entertainment in the lounge nightly.

321 North Atlantic Boulevard, Fort Lauderdale 33304. 305-467-1111; toll-free: 1-800-325-3535. Moderate to expensive.

SUN TOWER MOTOR HOTEL
Hotel/Fort Lauderdale
A good budget-stretcher with standard rooms, efficiencies, and one-bedroom apartments with full kitchens. The management promises that the balconies are so private you can sunbathe in next to nothing—or nothing at all.

2030 North Atlantic Boulevard, Fort Lauderdale 33305. 305-566-7827; toll-free (outside Florida): 1-800-458-4997. Inexpensive to moderate.

Where to Eat

COCONUTS
American/Fort Lauderdale

Waterfront setting ideal for sunset-watching from the deck, followed by indulging in huge portions of excellent food starting with good soups and fresh salads. Dinners of swordfish, dolphin, filet mignon, New York strip, and chicken teriyaki are served with a humongous baked potato or a healthy dose of excellent rice pilaf. The generous portions continue with the desserts—key lime pie, carrot and chocolate marble cakes—all way above average.

429 Seabreeze Boulevard, Fort Lauderdale. 305-467-6788. Moderate. Dinner daily.

LITTLE ITALY ON THE BEACH
Italian/Fort Lauderdale

This restaurant is great if you are looking for a casual place on the beach with a full menu. This one is loaded with choices of appetizers, entrees, and salads, and there's even a small wine list. Or you can go for the subs and pizzas. Since the place sits right on the main Beachfront Boulevard you can watch the sun come up while you dig into one of the super breakfasts.

401 South Atlantic Boulevard, Fort Lauderdale. 305-763-2186. Moderate. Breakfast, lunch, and dinner daily.

MIKE'S ITALIAN RESTAURANT & PIZZERIA
Italian/Fort Lauderdale

The locals meet here for lunches and light dinners between and after sunnings. With its casual atmosphere and buffet-style service, this is a good place to cool off and enjoy a bite in your beach coverups.

Poinsettia and South Atlantic Boulevard, Fort Lauderdale. 305-462-2058. Inexpensive. Open daily.

OCEAN ROOM
American/Fort Lauderdale

An echo from the not-so-distant past, when restaurants did not get too cute with themeploitation or view dining out as theater. There is a pianist—he's been here forever—and a grand view of the ocean, but the room is basically a throwback to the 1940s and the menu is an abiding joy, reminding us of Sunday dinners and those restaurants where you'd celebrate special family occasions. We can even taste a bit of Mom's home cooking when we dig into the fried chicken with all the trimmings or one of the pies for dessert. The beef and seafood are also handled with respect by the back room.

Ireland's Inn, 2220 North Atlantic Boulevard, Fort Lauderdale. 305-565-6661. Moderate to expensive. Breakfast, lunch, and dinner daily.

R.J.'S LANDING
Seafood/Fort Lauderdale

This Intracoastal beauty affords excellent waterfront views through its walls of windows or from umbrella-shaded tables out on the deck. For lunch we like the seafood salads and lightly fried fish sandwiches, and for dinner, the scallops, salmon, and swordfish simply grilled. When we're in the munching mood we order the gator fritters, Buffalo chicken wings, or R.J.'s "famous baby-back ribs."

515 Seabreeze Boulevard, Fort Lauderdale. 305-763-5502. Moderate to expensive. Lunch and dinner daily.

SALTY SALLY'S
Seafood/Fort Lauderdale

This salty lady is sensational, serving schools of fresh fish, imported Maine lobsters, and those great delicacies of the deep known as stone crab claws, as well as burgers and steaks. Another plus is the attractive setting, and another is the fresh fruit daiquiris. As some locals told us: "This is the only real restaurant on the beach."

3134 Northeast Ninth Street, Fort Lauderdale. 305-566-0366. Moderate. Lunch and dinner daily.

SURFSIDE CAFE
American/Fort Lauderdale
If you enjoy breakfast on the beach while watching the sun come up, this little café is the place to be. Order an omelet or maybe a fried egg to duplicate on your plate what you see on the horizon. For munching later in the day, try the hot dogs with buns so fresh they remind us of the ones dispensed by the little mom-and-pop dairy bars years ago, before fast food demanded prefabs and warming under lights. They also serve subs and roast beef, chicken, and tuna salad sandwiches. Cool off here anytime with a soft-serve ice cream, sundae, milk shake, or frozen yogurt ordered from the walk-up window.

607 North Atlantic Boulevard, Fort Lauderdale. 305-564-5211. Inexpensive. Breakfast, lunch, and dinner daily.

TONY'S BEACH PIZZA SHACK
Italian-Seafood/Fort Lauderdale
The name may fool you. Downstairs there's definitely pizza, but upstairs is a raw bar with an excellent view of the ocean. And it's open for breakfast so here's another vantage point for sunrise-watching.

901 North Atlantic Avenue, Fort Lauderdale. 305-566-2614. Inexpensive. Breakfast, lunch, and dinner daily.

WEDNESDAYS ON THE BEACH
Italian-American/Fort Lauderdale

Wednesdays restaurant and bar claims to be world famous for its subs, pastas, salads, and calzone. This all-day eatery sits right in the middle of the Strip where all the action is. Beachgoers as well as nightlifers like the setting, filled with neon lights and facing the beach. There is a sports bar section as well as a music lovers section with live entertainment and dancing.

101 South Atlantic Boulevard, Fort Lauderdale. 305-763-2226. Inexpensive. Breakfast, lunch, and dinner daily.

Where to Shop

You'll be glad to know that most of the shops on the Fort Lauderdale Beach Strip have signs in their windows that read NO PRESSURE SELLING, PLEASE BROWSE, so you can take your time finding that suit for the tan line that fits your style. On Southeast Fifth Street and South Atlantic Boulevard is the **Hall of Fame Plaza,** with the following temptations:

Clubhouse Bar and Grill, 2933 Southeast Fifth Street (305-463-0325), for snacking while shopping.

Southside Market, 2941 Southeast Fifth Street, to stock up on items for the fridge or cooler.

Daniel's Beachwear, 3007 Southeast Fifth Street (305-761-9084), for inexpensive but good, up-to-date T-shirts, beachwear for all ages, and souvenirs.

Bikinis Galore, 3011 Southeast Fifth Street (305-467-7063), where you can create your own bikini with an on-premise designer, Glenn Hall.

And just around the corner are the shops of South Atlantic Boulevard:

Rysan Surf & Sports, 435 South Atlantic Boulevard (305-761-8972), for mod sportswear and boogie board rentals.

Southbeach Swimwear, 441 South Atlantic Boulevard (305-462-2847), for more mod swimwear and sportswear.

J.J.'S Souvenirs, 445 South Atlantic Boulevard, defines its own name.

Beach Boy's Plaza, at the top of the stairs, located on the same 400 block of South Atlantic Boulevard, is another set of shops for beachwear, souvenirs, and gifts, and snacks at **Little Italy** (see page 79).

Surf Shack, at 917 North Atlantic Boulevard (305-566-9221), is where you'll find everything you need for your visit to the beach: swimwear, tanning products, sunglasses, and surf "toys" for young and old.

On the corner of Atlantic Boulevard and Northeast Ninth Street is a clump of shops: **Tidal Wave** for beachwear and tanning supplies; **Peter's Gifts** for jewelry, beach supplies, and swimwear; **Mama's Market** for foodstuffs; and **Splish Splash** for oodles and oodles of bikinis of every shape and style.

More Fun in the Sun

The *Jungle Queen,* **Bahia Mar Yacht Center,** at A1A, Fort Lauderdale 33316 (305-462-5596), offers a four-hour dinner cruise to a destination called Our Exotic Island on the New River, where you partake of a stuff-yourself-silly feast of barbecue ribs, chicken, and steamed shrimp. There's an on-board bar and entertainment that includes a vaudeville revue and a sing-along. Sightseeing cruises depart twice daily from the Yacht Center on 550- or 180-passenger vessels, and spend three hours chugging up the Intracoastal Waterway and New River to such attractions as a Seminole Indian Village with alligator wrestling and Everglades wildlife. A sight-seeing cruise to Miami and Bayside Market Place departs in the morning and returns approximately six hours later. Reservations are necessary.

The **International Swimming Hall of Fame,** at 501 Seabreeze Boulevard, Fort Lauderdale (305-462-6536), is a swimmer's and coach's dream, with its own superstar walk of fame with foot and hand imprints, a museum with displays of the history of the sport along with tributes to the legends—past and present—an extensive library, and giant outdoor pools that are heated in the winter and cooled in the summer. This is also the setting for important national and international swimming and diving competitions. The complex glistens as a result of a recent $9 million refurbishing. It is open to the public for scheduled lap swimming, water aerobics, and diving. For information on pool hours and regulations call 305-523-0994.

Bonnett House, 900 North Birch Road (305-563-5393), is located between the beach and Intracoastal Waterway just south of Sunrise Boulevard. This is truly a testament to another time, a 35-acre subtropical paradise unnoticeably nestled in the shadow of the condominiums, named for the bonnet lilies, and lived in by Evelyn and Frederic Bartlett, northern artists who created a 30-room plantation-style home built around a courtyard and surrounded by a thick jungle of banyans, mangroves, and chattering monkeys. In the orchid house there are some 1,500 species, and in a shell room are the treasures of conchology. From May 1 to November 30 there are home tours on Tuesday, Thursday, and Sunday, and garden tours on Thursday and Sunday. Tours are by reservation only and there is a charge.

Bill's Sunrise Boat Rental, 301 Seabreeze Boulevard, is the place for parasailing and rentals of boats, waverunners, water skis, Windsurfers, and beach cruiser bicycles. Most of them require a $100 deposit. To reserve call 305-467-1316; if no answer, 305-941-4044. Parasailing is a real thrill, for you can view Fort Lauderdale from on high.

Skyrider (305-462-SAIL), located at the west entrance of the Days Inn, operates aerial recliners designed to seat two passengers comfortably and sail 600 feet into the clouds.

Hugh Taylor Birch State Recreation Area, 3109 East Sunrise Boulevard (305-564-4521), comprises 180 acres of protected wilderness with 400 feet of beach and fishing in the Intracoastal Waterway. A gift from Birch during World War II, the area has picnic tables, pavilions, playgrounds, and canoes and pedal boats for rent. Open from 8:00 A.M. until sunset daily with a nominal fee.

Voyager Sightseeing Train, 600 Seabreeze Boulevard (305-463-0401), takes you on an 18-mile narrated tour of the highlights of Fort Lauderdale. Departures daily at 10:00 A.M. and 12:00, 2:00, and 4:00 P.M.

Water Taxi, Intracoastal Waterway (305-565-5507), will transport you from any safe dock at private homes, hotels, restaurants, or marinas on demand like a land-based taxi. Call the dispatcher for pickup or advance reservation. There are special rates for all-day cruising and weekly frequent floaters. Guided tours of the historic New River are available for groups of 15 or more.

Dragon II, a deep-sea fishing boat located behind the Days Inn, makes daily four-hour group trips morning, noon, and evening. Private charters are available and the boat is equipped with a color electronic fish finder, an experienced crew, and ship-to-shore radio.

Pro Dive (305-761-3413), at the Bahia Mar Resort and Yachting Center, is the area's oldest dive shop and provides all the necessary equipment, instruction, and guidance on where and how to get to the reefs, wrecks, and ridges—17 of them from 10 to 150 feet deep—in Lauderdale waters.

The **Fort Lauderdale International Boat Show** is an annual event that usually takes place the last week in October and is held at the Bahia Mar Resort and Yachting Center. This is the world's largest in-water boat show, with dealers and buyers from around the world and more than 1,200 boats on display including mega yachts over 100 feet long, family cruisers, sport-fishers, high-performance racers, motor yachts, and sailboats.

Where to Write

Greater Fort Lauderdale Chamber of Commerce, P.O. Box 14516, Fort Lauderdale, Florida 33302. 305-462-6000.

◎　　◎　　◎

BOCA RATON AND DELRAY BEACH

Storied Palm Beach still wears with pride all those graceful trees for which the town and county were named. Their sentinel-like presence across the seascape forms a backdrop for some of the finest shoreline in all of Florida, fine enough for an article in *Harper's Bazaar* on America's best beaches to proclaim the 47 miles of Palm Beach County's oceanfront "the biggest dazzler of them all." In north county is the John D. MacArthur State Recreation Area, with more than 225 acres of undeveloped, uninhabited (except by colonies of wildlife) barrier island with hammocks and stands of mangrove. In south county there are beautifully developed beaches in a near-pristine state, safe and secure from the endlessly encroaching condominiums and commercialization. Our two favorites are Boca Raton, with all its waterfront parks, and to the north, Delray Beach, with a beautiful boardwalk and rigid building restrictions. In between are the 2.7 miles of Highland Beach between the ocean and the Intracoastal Waterway, with more long stretches of Gold Coast sand.

Delray has 7,000 feet of public beach, easily accessible and always in view along State Road A1A, which is also known as Ocean Boulevard in these parts. The road is more elevated than Fort Lauderdale's section of A1A and is bordered by thick growths of sea grape, sea oats, and other salt-resistant, dune-preserving plants. Boardwalks lead down to the water at strategic spots, and a paved walk parallels the road the entire length of the beach. Between road and footpath are sidewalks and parking meters. Other meters are found in a couple of nearby locations off A1A: Anchor Park, a vest-pocket affair behind a namesake anchor, with picnic tables, a bunch of benches under shade trees, and rest room facilities; and the equally small Shadowy Park.

The nearest playground for the younger set is located in a fine park along the Intracoastal just over the bridge by Atlantic Plaza. Past the VFW monument to the veterans of three wars, there are all kinds of slides, swings, and climbing equipment plus benches, boat docks, and shuffleboard and lawn bowling courts. Shade trees are giant and numerous, and while the kids burn off that excess energy, you can take it easy and watch all the boats pass by.

Or you can hike or drive approximately one mile south of the Delray public beach to an escape through a sylvan grove of whispering pines—the seven-acre Atlantic Dunes Park, with its own lifeguards, picnic areas, showers, and rest rooms.

Boca Raton is where the parks are, most of them developed with similar facilities. Largest of all is Spanish River Park, whose entrance is within sight of the intersection of A1A and Spanish River Boulevard. The park is named for a shallow freshwater stream that once flowed through the area. It has a half mile of beachfront, reached by a pair of traffic-avoiding tunnels. Much of that glistening golden sand has been reclaimed in recent years in rather ambitious renourishment projects—yes, they're really called renourishment projects. The beach is embraced by 49 acres of forested picnic pavilions with plenty of tables and grills, and there's an observation tower to climb so you can appreciate what the wisdom of city planners has wrought in a prize piece of real estate between the Atlantic and the Intracoastal Waterway.

Heading south on A1A from Spanish River Park you'll find two and a half miles of park fronting the beach. The southernmost point of the park is marked by the South Beach Pavilion at the termination of Palmetto Park Road, the first and still most important route between town and oceanfront. Newly renovated and open from 5:00 A.M. until 11:00 P.M., the pavilion is neatly landscaped and has a turnaround with parking (limit one hour) for 18 cars. Rest rooms are nearby, as is the Boca Marine Safety Headquarters Station.

The entrance to South Beach Park is two-tenths of a mile north of Palmetto and there is ample parking along with playgrounds, jungle gyms, volleyball nets, and picnic tables. A half mile north of Palmetto is the entrance to the town's Red Reef 9-hole, par 32, 1,628-yard, executive golf course with a pro shop. The Red Reef Park entrance to 67 acres of developed beach is four-tenths of a mile north of the course.

South of Palmetto—in fact, south of the Boca Raton Inlet—is another park with 850 feet of developed beach, a departure point for long beach walks all the way to the Hillsboro Inlet and Lighthouse.

There are few communities in the country that can offer tourists such idyllic access to the ocean. Can you imagine teeing off with the majesty of the Atlantic a few yards away? Or grilling the family dinner in a shaded site after a day on the sand or in surf?

Where It Is

Boca Raton and Delray Beach are about halfway between Fort Lauderdale and Palm Beach and are connected to the rest of the state by the Florida Turnpike, Interstate 95, and U.S. 1, as well as State Road A1A. Access roads from the turnpike and the interstate are Atlantic Avenue in Delray Beach and Palmetto Park Road in Boca Raton, both of which go directly to the ocean.

Where to Stay

BERMUDA INN
Motel/Delray Beach

An ultracasual throwback to a 1950s motel with a million-dollar location, right across the street from the Delray public beach. The functionally furnished rooms have two double or queen-size beds, the larger of the 20 rooms have refrigerators, and each of the two efficiencies (#7 and #17), has a kitchen. There's a pool out front and all accommodations have ocean views.

64 South Ocean Boulevard (A1A), Delray Beach 33483. 407-276-5288. Inexpensive.

BOCA RATON RESORT AND CLUB
Resort/Boca Raton

The ultimate big-time, big-buck, full-scale resort loaded with all the attractions for a super family holiday, or for honeymooners, romantics, or even single vacationers. In the main complex, built around the magic of that Aladdin-like architect Addison Mizner, are rooms in the historic (as in the late 1920s) cloister section. Many more of the thousand rooms are in the 27-story tower, where the awesome Presidential and lesser suites are located. There are two swimming pools, 22 tennis courts, and an 18-hole championship golf course, along with bars and restaurants everywhere, including our favorites, the Top of the Tower and the window-wrapped café overlooking the greens. For full-blown banquets there is nothing for miles around to match the Cathedral Room, and no greater sense of place anywhere on the Gold Coast to compare with the old Mizner lobby and other remnants from the Roaring Twenties. Across Lake Boca Raton, reached by shuttle or a boat named *Mizner's Dream,* is the newer Boca Beach Club, with many more rooms, two restaurants, another pair of swimming pools, and half a mile of private oceanfront with 147 cabanas. If you come by boat, watch for Intracoastal Waterway Marker 67 at the hotel's fully equipped marina, which has 23 slips.

501 East Camino Real, Boca Raton 33432. 407-395-3000; toll-free: 1-800-327-0101. Expensive; modified American plan.

THE BRIDGE HOTEL
Hotel/Boca Raton

A mini-high-rise of 123 rooms occupying a strategic piece of real estate along the edge of Lake Boca Raton leading to the inlet across from the Boca Raton Beach Club. Guest rooms are furnished in an upscale modern manner with all the amenities and each has a balcony facing the ocean or the lake, part of the Intracoastal Waterway. The circular pool is enclosed by a sun deck and the Top of the Bridge restaurant offers an ambitious menu, formal service, and sensational panoramas of city and sea, but it's only open during the season. Our favorite public room is the Patio Bar and Cafe, at Waterway level, where you can look up at the namesake bridge.

999 East Camino Real, Boca Raton 33432. 407-368-9500; toll-free: 1-800-327-0130. Moderate to expensive.

CAMINO REAL HOLIDAY INN
Hotel/Delray Beach

A masterful mix of Mediterranean, Mexican, and a bit of the magic of Addison Mizner characterizes this five-story castle located at the busiest corner of Delray Beach—Atlantic Avenue and Ocean Boulevard. The pool, Jacuzzi, and sun deck are beautifully positioned to provide panoramic views of the Atlantic, as is the top-floor Seacrest dining room (see page 96). There's more food and fun at the tiki bar and the ice cream shop, and there's live entertainment in the lounge. The guest rooms, provided with complimentary . morning papers, are handsomely outfitted in coordinated tropical tones, and there's plenty of parking.

1229 East Atlantic Avenue, Delray Beach 33483. 407-278-0882; toll-free: 1-800-HOLIDAY. Moderate to expensive.

DOVER HOUSE
Inn/Delray Beach

A three-building spread of 48 generous-size rooms complete with kitchen units and well-maintained modern furnishings, the kind we expect to find in such handsome structures built around courtyards and pools. There are special savings on weekly and monthly rentals, but this is an interval ownership operation, so be absolutely certain about your reservation in good time.

110 Ocean Drive (A1A), Delray Beach 33483. 407-276-0309. Expensive.

HARBOR HOUSE
Motel/Delray Beach

For yachtsmen and would-be boaters or for tourists who just want to be near marinas to watch the nonstop waterborne parade, this is the ideal place, overlooking the Intracoastal Waterway and the yacht club. Only 3 of the 21 rooms, the studio efficiencies, and a single one-bedroom suite with kitchenette do not have a view of the Waterway. But they are all furnished in a

manner marvelously compatible with the perfect Florida setting right outdoors. With a swimming pool of course.

124 Marine Way, Delray Beach 33483. 407-276-4211. Moderate.

HOLIDAY INN
Motel/Highland Beach
The ocean-to-waterway community separating Boca Raton and Delray Beach
has one commercial property and this is it, a far-better-than-average link in
the Holiday chain and blessed with a superb oceanfront location. The guest
rooms are functional modern motel in design and furnishings but the center
courtyard, complete with pool, chickee bar, and outdoor grill, the boardwalk
to the beach, and the dining room, with walls of windows overlooking the
ocean, raise the level of comfort considerably. The staff is friendly, and a great
group of ladies runs the restaurant, a reliable place for noontime salads,
sandwiches, and excellent burgers. Maine lobster, Cajun-style or crabmeat-
stuffed dolphin, Delmonico steak, catfish, and a surf-and-turf combo with
snow crab claws are among dinner specialties.

*2809 South Ocean Boulevard (A1A), Highland Beach 33487. 407-278-
6241; toll-free: 1-800-HOLIDAY. Moderate to expensive.*

OCEAN LODGE
Motel/Boca Raton
A money-saver across the street from the lushly planted strip of greenery
separating beach from roadway, with a small swimming pool and kitchens in
some of the rooms.

*531 North Ocean Boulevard (A1A), Boca Raton 33432. 407-395-7772.
Inexpensive.*

THE SEAGATE HOTEL AND BEACH CLUB
Hotel/Delray Beach

Tucked into the trees surrounding the classic Delray hostelry are 70 comfortably furnished rooms and efficiencies facing gardens and pools. Across the road is the hotel's own beach club, with a wonderful little bar and a wall of windows for watching all the action with the security of a roof overhead and a drink in hand.

500 Ocean Boulevard (A1A), Delray Beach 33483. 407-276-2421. Expensive.

SHORE EDGE
Motel/Boca Raton

Directly across the street from South Beach Park and the oceanfront, this immaculate little treasure hangs in there happily as if it's still 1964, long before the Boca boom transformed most of the town into an enclave of affluence. Arlene and George Hoffmeyer are in charge of this retreat of 15-units, some of which have kitchenettes. There's a small pool in center court. And everything is clean, clean, clean. As George is fond of saying about Arlene, "If she were marooned on a desert island, all she would want to have is a broom, a mop, and a pail."

425 North Ocean Boulevard (A1A), Boca Raton 33432. 407-395-4491. Inexpensive.

WRIGHT-BY-THE-SEA
Motel/Delray Beach

Located south of the beachfront in Delray, but with its own fine spread of sand in full view of the 28 rooms, studios, and one-bedroom apartments, all of them spacious and facing the carefully manicured gardens and lawns surrounding the center court swimming pool. In all aspects of design and decor, this is a very comfortable, reassuring home away from home—a very right-by-the sea.

1901 South Route A1A, Delray Beach 33483. 407-278-3355. Expensive.

Where to Eat

BOSTONS
American/Delray Beach

A wonderfully informal beachfront oasis for porchfront people-watching. The inside room is jam-packed most every evening because of the live entertainment—reggae on Mondays is particularly popular. We like to come during the day and linger over lunch, munching on good burgers and terrific toasted cheese sandwiches, or grilled dolphin, tuna, or fillets of other edible creatures from the deep. Come night the menu gets a bit more ambitious but there's nothing outrageous. Even on the hottest days of summer, there's a cooling breeze from the ocean, balmy enough to make guests here realize how special life in southern Florida really is.

40 South Ocean Boulevard (A1A), Delray Beach. 407-278-3364. Moderate. Lunch and dinner daily.

CHEZ MARCEL
French/Boca Raton

This is the gloriously Gallic little empire of Marcel Wortman, maître d' of great care and concern, who arrived on the local scene in the 1970s after distinguished careers in the class operations of Miami Beach and the Caribbean. This is his third successive restaurant in Boca, and his best. The back room is French or French-inspired, the fare more classical than nouvelle, but far less complicated than that of an Escoffier. We like most the Dover sole, fillets of salmon with morel-freckled light cream sauce, calves liver, dolphin Grenobloise, and for climax, the excellent homemade sherbets and rice pudding.

1 South Ocean Boulevard (A1A), Boca Raton. 407-362-9911. Expensive. Dinner daily. Reservations suggested.

CIAO
American/Delray Beach

A sidewalk café that Susan Raymond Bogle has been running with great success and enthusiasm since 1978. The made-to-order specialities range from fresh fruit salads, pizzas on Syrian bread, and fruitberry smoothies to Mexican tostadas, an authentic combo of refried beans, grated cheese, lettuce, and tomato on a soft tortilla dolloped with hot salsa. Our favorites are the pita pocket sandwiches filled with egg or tuna salad, hummus and lots of fresh garlic, the pecan coffee cake, and lemon squares.

1206 East Atlantic Avenue, Delray Beach. 407-278-4520. Inexpensive. Breakfast and lunch Monday through Saturday. Closed July 1 through October 1.

ERNY'S
American/Delray Beach

An honored name in the local restuarant whirl and a reliable provider of solid food prepared without fuss or flourish and delivered by a veteran staff of waitresses. The bar is a rallying point for the locals all through the day and night and there's live entertainment—jazz on Tuesday and a jazz festival during the summer doldrums.

1010 East Atlantic Avenue, Delray Beach. 407-276-9191. Moderate. Lunch and dinner Monday to Saturday.

INCREDIBLE EDIBLES
American/Delray Beach

This cheerful, bright little patio around the corner from Atlantic Avenue is open all day for money-saving, simple meals delivered by a smiling crew. We like the three-egg omelets in the morning and at midday the sandwiches layered with turkey breast or roast beef, preceded by the soup of the day and followed by some mousse or rice pudding. Dinners can be as simple as a burger or jumbo hot dog or as complicated as beef and seafood brochettes—or the house special, Charbonnade (guests grill their own meats and are served home-brewed sauces and baked potatoes).

8 Gleason Street, Delray Beach. 407-278-0645. Inexpensive to moderate. Breakfast, lunch, and dinner daily, and take-out catering.

LA VIELLE MAISON
French/Boca Raton

Typical of very much upscale Boca Raton, there are two superluxe and expensive restaurants close to the beach: Chez Marcel and this encapsulation of all things affluent—a magical setting, one of the best wine lists in Florida, formal service, flowers everywhere, and a French menu executed with great flair and finesse. Even the parking lot is handsomely landscaped and it allows access to a window for observing the chefs assembling such specialties as sautéed trout, quail with raisin sauce, and crepes stuffed with lemon souffle. Fixed-price and à la carte menu, and show-stopping cheese and sherbert carts.

770 East Palmetto Park Road, Boca Raton. 407-391-6701. Expensive. Dinner daily.

RATTLESNAKE JAKE'S
Tex-Mex/Deerfield Beach

This storefront with its uncluttered windows is a super site from which to watch the parade to and from the beach a block away. Straight off a side street in Tijuana, it's the ultimate in simplicity, with mounted fish to accompany the parrots and neon beer signs. The chips are the crispiest, the salsa the sauciest, and the fajitas really do sizzle. We like the steak burritos, the saffron rice, refried beans, and ice cold Mexican beer.

2060 Northeast Second Street, Deerfield Beach. 305-421-4481. Inexpensive. Lunch and dinner daily.

SANDWICHES BY THE SEA
American/Delray Beach
A block from the beach, assembling what it proclaims to be "The Best Sandwiches in Town," this simple snackery also serves yogurt and salads and will do your catering.

1214 East Atlantic Avenue, Delray Beach. 407-272-2212. Inexpensive. Breakfast and lunch and take-out daily.

SEACREST
Continental/Delray Beach
Yes, it's in a Holiday Inn, but this is not your everyday, ordinary Holiday Inn, as should be apparent from the write-up on page 91. And this is no ordinary restaurant. First of all, there's a great view from the top floor of the inn; second, there's the Sunday brunch, one of the best in the area; third, there's the regular menu, with simply broiled fresh catch of the day, fettuccine Bolognese, shrimp marinara, tortelline Alfredo, poached salmon, and chicken or veal piccata.

Holiday Inn, 1229 East Atlantic Avenue, Delray Beach. 407-278-0882, ext. 135. Moderate to expensive. Lunch and dinner daily; Sunday brunch.

WHALE'S RIB
American/Deerfield Beach
A terrific raw bar with a wonderful jam-packed, sheer fun feeling—ceilings and walls are hung with nautical nonsense, hats, the world's currency, and mounted fish that did not get away. Sit at the raw bar or in one of the booths and work through Buffalo chicken—no, Whale—wings, a half dozen escargot drowned in garlic butter, conch fritters, fried shrimp, or clams or oysters served with Whale fries (terrific!). Or stretch your mouth with the sandwiches, all of them on whole wheat Whale buns.

2031 Northeast Second Street, Deerfield Beach. 305-421-8880. Inexpensive. Lunch and dinner daily. No credit cards.

WHALE RIB'S ATLANTIC WHALER
American/Delray Beach

Opened in 1992, this spacious, poolside spinoff from the popular Whale's Rib a few miles south brings the same kind of quality control and freshness to the beachfront. Dive into the raw bar menu for starters, then have a whale burger, cappicola, or fried fish sandwich, baked scallops, stuffed shrimp, or Maine lobster, accompanied of course by their wonderful whale fries. Follow with key lime pie.

1111 East Atlantic Avenue, Delray Beach. 407-274-9320. Inexpensive to moderate. Lunch and dinner daily.

Where to Shop

IN BOCA RATON

The Boca Beach Market & Deli (407-395-0154), with ready-made salads and sandwiches and all kinds of soft drinks, is across A1A from the South Beach Pavilion. Around the corner is a small string of shops on the north side of Palmetto Park Road, a block from the pavilion. There's an ice cream and yogurt outlet at 897 Palmetto with a beach market convenience store next door and **Papa John's Pizza** (407-368-9229) a few steps away at number 887.

For beachwear there's the **Second Skin Swimwear** shop (407-393-4600), at number 893, and the **Force—E at Dive, Surf & Ski** shop (407-368-0555) at number 881.

A more extensive selection of fun stuff for the sun can be found a few minutes south of the Boca beaches in the neighboring community of Deerfield Beach, where there's a strip of 16 shops on Northeast Second Street just off the beach. **Sea Girl** (305-428-2693) specializes in ladies' apparel, **Sea-Things** (305-428-3545) in gifts and souvenirs, and **Beach Comber** (305-421-7870) in both gifts and beach garb. The biggest store is **Wings** (305-570-8017), a beach five-and-ten with a huge collection of T-shirts, ready-made or plastered with your own design. **Island Bike and Beach Rental** (305-427-4647) defines its name, close to the Post Office. For snacking in between shops there's **Bob's Pizza** (305-426-1030), which also has subs and sandwiches, and **Rattle Snake Jake's** (305-421-4481) for Tex-Mex pizza, burritos, and chimichangas. Next door is a small food market and deli that sells subs and will also provide four-hour film developing.

IN DELRAY BEACH

Stroll, window-shop, and buy all along Atlantic Avenue as far as your legs and wallet allow:

Del Hurd, 1165 East Atlantic (407-276-6093), is a very upscale men's clothing store specializing in the Delray Beach look.

Key West Design, 1122 East Atlantic (407-265-3958), features their famous hand-painted fabrics for women.

Coconut Collection, 1118 East Atlantic (407-276-3418), has their own hand-painted fashions for women.

Kemp's Shoe Salon, 1104 East Atlantic (407-278-0377), sells shoes, handbags, and accessories.

Snappy Turtle, 1034 East Atlantic (407-276-8088), has the same kind of ladies' resortwear they sell in their shop at Kennebunkport, Maine.

Petite Connection, 1020 East Atlantic (407-276-8088), takes care of ladies in sizes 2 to 14.

Delray Drugs, 900 East Atlantic (407-276-7416), is the nearest pharmacy to the beach.

Quilters Marketplace, 524 East Atlantic (407-243-3820), defines its own name with gifts and supplies.

Robert's Gift Center, 518 East Atlantic (407-276-5447), specializes in Hummels, Lucite, and glassware.

Delray News & Tobacco 429 East Atlantic (407-278-3399), is the place for out-of-town papers and magazines in Delray Beach.

More Fun in the Sun

Windsurfers are available for rent a few feet from the southern boundary of the Delray public beach. The only fishing pier in the area is a few hundred yards south of the Boca beach in Deerfield Beach. There's plenty of metered parking and a 3,000-foot undeveloped beach to the south of the pier. Surfers might find some solace in the beaches of Delray and Boca, but the best waves in Palm Beach County, sometimes high enough to compete with those splashing in Saint Augustine, Daytona Beach, and Sebastian Inlet, can be found where the Florida peninsula reaches its easternmost point, at Reef Road north of Delray Beach, just south of the Lake Worth Inlet, where waves peak from November to April. For current conditions call 407-976-WAVE, and be sure to pick up a copy of the Florida Surf Map at the surf shop.

For ecologists and environmentalists who want to learn more about life along the shore—study indigenous trees, plants, and marine life—there's the **Gumbo Limbo Nature Center** on A1A one mile north of Palmetto Park Road, 1801 North Ocean Boulevard (407-338-1473), in the heart of one of the largest tropical hammocks between Miami and West Palm Beach. It's the headquarters of the Boca Turtle Patrol, and at certain times of the year you can watch the young hatchlings enrolled in Boca's own Head Start program. In 1992 a $2.8 million expansion added another classroom and biology laboratory, and four outdoor saltwater aquariums that are 20 feet across and 4 feet deep, fed continually by a pipe 200 feet out in the Atlantic. One is a touch tank where various sea creatures can be felt and picked up; another has constantly swirling water for those turtles in need of such; a third is for sea turtles; and a fourth is for special exhibits. A state-of-the-art testing lab for the local university's Ocean Engineering Department, experimenting with the action and effects of salt water on various building materials, is open to the public only through observation windows.

The most important community happenings in the area are the annual **Delray Affair,** held the first weekend after Easter when more than 400 exhibitors display their wares along Atlantic Avenue, and the incredible **St. Patrick's Day parade** along the same route—one of the greatest, and most famous, salutes to Paddy anywhere in the country.

Where to Write

Boca Raton Chamber of Commerce, 1800 North Dixie Highway, Boca Raton, Florida 33432. 407-395-4433.

Delray Beach Chamber of Commerce, 64 Southwest Fifth Avenue, Delray Beach, Florida 33447. 407-278-0424.

◎　◎　◎

VERO BEACH

In the WPA Guide to Florida (part of the Federal Writers' Project during the Great Depression), Vero Beach is singled out for its broad streets, "bordered with coconut, royal and date palms, and a profusion of tropical shrubs." Thanks to a strictly enforced ordinance against the cutting of trees and the obvious-everywhere determination of the residents to make their corner of Florida a city of flowers, you see brightly blooming plants wherever you drive or walk. Oleanders are especially plentiful, but they compete with a rich assortment of hibiscus, the bold yellows of alamanda, and the reds of bougainvillea.

The broad boulevards lead to shaded streets and Ocean Drive (A1A) to winding lanes flanked by lushly landscaped homes and estates. To the south on A1A, past the well-tended greens and fairways of a private country club, are many well-insulated developments sporting such names as Castaway, Smugglers Cove, Porpoise Point, Bonita Beach, Surfside, Atlantis, and The Moorings. The No Trespassing signs indicate the insularity, but there are other avenues of affluence and comfort that are open to the public interested in gaining some insight into the general level of living in these parts.

Drive south a dozen miles past all the well-manicured, faultlessly maintained enclaves of economic achievement to the Pepper State Park and Visitor's Center, just north of the Fort Pierce Inlet. You'll find a couple of thousand feet of developed beach—more firm underfoot than the beaches farther south—with showers, rest rooms, lifeguards, and a small local history museum, close to the equally modest UDT-Seal Museum honoring the navy's frogmen. A thousand feet north is the mainland entrance to the Jack Island State Preserve, a 950-acre mangrove island and official bird sanctuary with more than a hundred species in residence at various times of the year. A wooden walkway and footbridge take you onto the island, past thick clumps of sea grape alongside a coastal hammock, to the four-mile nature trail on perimeter dikes. There's also an observation tower where you can mount sentries and log your sightings of our feathered Floridians.

Two miles north of Vero Beach, also reached by a leisurely drive along A1A past other impressive estates and guarded developments, is the Government Tracking Station, with its nine and a half acres of developed beach reached by access roads—Pebble Reef and Surf lanes. Five hundred feet north is another beach, equally as isolated, at the Indian River Shores Walkway on Beachcomber's Lane.

There are many more parks in this special stretch of Florida waterfront. Indian River County (Vero Beach is the county seat) has more beachfront parks per mile of ocean and more oceanfront park acreage per capita than any other county in the state.

Using Sexton Plaza, the intersection of A1A and State Road 60, as your base point in this special settlement of 20,000 souls, go about one and a half miles north to the Jaycee Park, with its 2,000 feet of developed beach. A half mile south is the undeveloped Conn Beach, accessible via Conn Way, Lilac Road, and Avenida Palm. South is the actual Vero Beach, undeveloped and easily reached by a dozen roads with such delightful names as Coquina and Gay Feather, Ladybug and Flamevine, Jasmine and Turtle Cove. Sexton Plaza has its own 150 feet of developed beachfront.

The park a few hundred yards north of Sexton Plaza has playground equipment for the kids, barbecue grills for Dad, and picnic tables and pavilions for the whole family. A boardwalk leads across the dunes to the beach and there are freshwater showers. Another boardwalk behind a row of shops is three-tenths of a mile long. The diagonal parking alongside the park is free.

South of Sexton Plaza is Humiston Beach Park, with its own set of gym equipment, showers, picnic tables, rest rooms, and 500 feet of developed beach. Three-quarters of a mile off shore are the rusting remains of the S.S. *Breckenshire,* which foundered on the reef in April 1884. Today it's home to large schools of fish and a popular site for scuba divers.

But "popular" does not mean masses of people or fleets of commercial dive boats roaring across the waves. "Popular" is a relative term in these parts where the crowds do not really congregate. There's no spring break in Vero Beach; and no summer, fall, or winter break. But there are tourists: families and couples looking for a laid-back lifestyle, and residents of southeast and central Florida who think of Vero Beach as their own kind of Cape Cod or Long Island, as important an oceanfront getaway as those northern summer outposts are to Downeasters and New Yorkers. For them, for sun-seekers looking for relief from the glitz and glitter of the Gold Coast, or for those who want to settle the kids down after all the rigors of central Florida's theme parks, Vero Beach is the perfect change of pace.

Where It Is

Vero Beach is thirty-two miles east of the Florida Turnpike and nine miles east of Interstate 95. From both, take the State Road 60 exit and follow State Road 60 which ends in Vero Beach at Sexton Plaza on A1A.

Where to Stay

DAYS HOTEL
Hotel/Vero Beach

A five-story modern hotel on the beach with 109 rooms that are comfortably but not imaginatively furnished. Each has two double or king-size beds and such conveniences as a telephone and a television with in-room movies. For views of the water, poolside and oceanside rooms are available for an additional cost of 10% and 20% respectively. For 30% more there are efficiency units with kitchenettes. The so-called corporate rooms have a desk and comfy chairs that recline for those who want to take some shaded, maybe even air-conditioned, rest from all those golden rays and all that sand just out the door. Another respite can be found in the hotel's signature restaurant, Duke Snider's, good enough to have its own write-up (see page 106).

3244 Ocean Drive, Vero Beach 32963. 407-231-2800; toll-free: 1-800-325-2525. Moderate to expensive.

DRIFTWOOD RESORT
Resort/Vero Beach

Another outpouring of the Waldo Sexton bag of tricks (see page 108), en-larged and stripped of many of its unique furnishings and artifacts over the years, but still with enough bells, railings, tiles, and carved wood to make this—originally Sexton's home—an interesting escape. Make sure you have a confirmed reservation, as this is a time-share facility and they may not always be able to guarantee rooms booked too far in advance. The rooms are strictly mod, whether you're tucked into a regular hotel accommodation or one of the suites with kitchenette and whirlpool. The developer who converted a lil' ole' inn into something with as ambitious a title as "resort" tried to retain the pecky cypress-weathered wood on the facades of the additions. When they expanded the restaurant named after Vero's legendary pioneer they kept much of the spirit of the massive Sexton, whose size was equaled only by his energy and entrepreneurial achievements.

3150 Ocean Drive, Vero Beach 32963. 407-231-0550. Moderate to expensive.

GUEST QUARTERS
Hotel/Vero Beach

An all-suite oceanfront hotel with 55 one- and two-bedroom accommodations, each with a balcony overlooking the Atlantic, ideal for a leisurely breakfast watching the sun rise out of the wear, or for later lounging and sipping while planning a dinner destination. Breakfast is served in the rooms or in the coffee shop, and there's a poolside bar for light fare during the day. The level of maintenance is high and the standards of service are very high.

3500 Ocean Drive, Vero Beach 32963. 407-231-5666; toll-free: 1-800-424-2900. Expensive.

HOLIDAY INN OCEANSIDE
Motel/Vero Beach

The name is no idle boast. If this Holiday Inn were any closer to the water, it would be floating, and if the dining room/lounge had windows open to the ocean breezes it would more than live up to its name—Windswept. The rooms and suites, with some efficiencies, are standard motel modern and have all the conveniences, but those facing pool or ocean have fine views of the water. There's a beauty shop on the premises and live entertainment in the lounge, plus groaning board Sunday brunches. For those who want more of Vero Beach on a permanent basis, there's a real estate office on the premises.

Sexton Plaza, 3384 Ocean Drive, Vero Beach 32960. 407-231-2300; toll-free: 1-800-HOLIDAY. Moderate to expensive.

THE ISLANDER MOTEL
Motel/Vero Beach

Superbly situated 300 feet from park and shoreline (lifeguards are on duty) and in the heart of the many shops and snackshops that radiate from the streets flanking Sexton Plaza. There's a quaintness, a Cape Cod cottage look to the building, which boasts a courtyard, pools, patios, and second-floor porches. But the guest rooms are strictly Florida tropical, with pecky cypress-paneled walls and cathedral ceilings. Each room has two double beds, a snack-size refrigerator, and the usual modern amenities including ceiling fan, temperature control, color cable television, and telephone; but also complimentary morning coffee. A final plus—the level of upkeep is faultless.

3101 Ocean Drive, Vero Beach 32963. 407-231-4431. Moderate.

Where to Eat

THE BLACK PEARL
Continental/Vero Beach

An intimate, intense, and formally served gem as special as its name declares. There's no bar, but the wine list is very good, as it should be, considering the output of the kitchen, from the chilled leek-watercress soup to the butterscotch cheesecake and key lime pie. In between are feta-spinach-walnut fritters with cheese-dijonaise sauce; fettuccine primavera; grilled dolphin, swordfish, snapper, and shrimp; roast duckling with apples and cashews; and sea trout with caviar as black as the restaurant's namesake pearl. The tables are close, the noise level high, but don't let that deter you from making a reservation—which is necessary at least two days in advance during the season.

1409 A1A, Vero Beach. 407-234-4426. Moderate to expensive. Dinner nightly.

BOBBY'S
American/Vero Beach
There are two Bobbies here, Bob Kost and Bob McCarthy, and together they run this informal oceanfront 200-seater, the perfect place to drop in for a break from the beach. Hunker into the bar, where there's television coverage of all sporting events, or sit out on the covered patio to spoon into brewed-out-back soups or enjoy one of the mouth-stretching, freshly assembled subs or sandwiches. The chili-cheese nachos are a specialty here but make sure you save room for the cheesecake.

3450 Ocean Drive, Vero Beach. 407-231-6996. Inexpensive to moderate. Lunch and dinner daily.

CHEZ YANNICK
French/Vero Beach
The second-best French restaurant on the Treasure Coast, started by the same Yannick Martin who went inland a bit to open Cafe du Soir (21 Royal Palm Boulevard), the best. His assistant stayed on the ocean and we're all greatful for that—and for the refurbishing that added a crystal chandelier and a pair of marble fireplaces as accent pieces. The skill of the designer is matched by that of the kitchen, evident at the outset in the cold or hot soups, the Beluga,

or soft-shell crabs in a heavenly sauce zapped with precisely the right amount of garlic. From that auspicious launching, you can sail into a shrimp-swordfish mode or something featuring sweetbreads, a tender breast of chicken, or tournedos with a terrific sauce freckled with truffle. For finishers there's profiterole, its rich and thick chocolate sauce suggesting a splash or two of brandy; but if that doesn't tempt, then consider one or another of the home-made sorbets, or the white or dark chocolate mousse. Whatever you choose will leave you determined to return—soon.

Riveria Inn, 1605 South Ocean Drive, Vero Beach. 407-234-4115. Expensive. Dinner Monday to Saturday.

DUKE SNIDER'S RESTAURANT AND BAR
American/Vero Beach

Why Duke Snider of Dodger fame? Because Vero Beach has its own Dodgertown a couple of miles from the beach, complete with streets named for Jackie Robinson and Sandy Koufax, oversize baseball streetlights, and complete sports facilities, including a 6,000-seat stadium where the Dodgers do their spring training and their Class A farm club plays 70 games a year. Twice a year a hundred enthusiasts, ages 25 to 71, fulfill their fantasies for a week, rubbing shoulders with the likes of the Duke in the Adult Baseball Camp. You can also see the Duke in this memorabilia-filled restaurant, with its life-size portraits of the slugger and action photos framed in fields of burgundy, green, and mahogany, masculine to the core. Whenever the Hall of Famer is in town, he joins the munchers, lunchers, and diners enjoying the great views of the ocean while homing in on the overstuffed sandwiches, or the crabmeat Bearnaise, liver and onions, chicken marsala, teriyaki steak, and prime Florida beef. You won't strike out here.

Days Hotel, 3244 Ocean Drive, Vero Beach. 407-231-2800. Moderate. Breakfast, lunch, and dinner, with live entertainment, Wednesday to Saturday; Sunday brunch.

THE MENU
American/Vero Beach

A no-nonsense setting that is as straightforward as the food, and that means no elaborate French sauces, overuse of oregano and rosemary, or gobs of garlic. Flavoring standards are typified—and introduced—by the conch chowder, which is chock-full of conch and chunks of vegetables, but has no excess of pepper, Tabasco, and spices. The same solid, easy-on-the-tastebuds approach characterizes the roast lamb, the roast pork chops, the lightly battered broiled fillets of fresh fish, and the Yorkshire pudding with the prime rib, which has a very good creamy horseradish sauce as platemate. So for those who like their food refreshingly free of nouvelle, this is the place, and it's all served family style. And for vegetable lovers, The Menu is heaven. A wonderful harvest of lightly steamed vegetables accompanies each entree. This is precisely the kind of place that should have good Black Forest, German chocolate, and cheese cakes—and it does.

1517 South Ocean Drive, Vero Beach. 407-231-4614. Moderate to expensive. Dinner daily.

OCEAN GRILL
American / Vero Beach

The most distinctive restaurant in and well beyond Vero Beach, the Ocean Grill is a vibrant monument to the irrepressible Waldo Sexton, indefatigable promoter of the area, developer, and builder with a scratch-in-the-sand approach to architecture and an insatiable urge to collect. This is only one of his lantern, wrought-iron, stained-glass, and statuary-filled buildings in town, but it's the best place to start the Sexton pilgrimage by elbowing into the tiny bar that dangles over the water and munching on such midday marvels as crab burgers (anything with crab is good at the Ocean Grill), a chicken or Cobb salad, or a sandwich thickly layered with thinly sliced roast beef. For dinner in the dining room, we like to start with the velvety cream of chicken soup accompanied by a cornmeal muffin and follow that with the broiled catch of the day served with wild rice. The steaks are also a reliable choice and, if we have room, we don't like to pass up the cole slaw, sweetened with bits of apple. Sexton is long gone (he died at age 82 in 1968), but—gratefully—his memory lingers on.

1050 Sexton Plaza, Vero Beach. 407-231-5409. Moderate to expensive. Lunch Monday to Friday; dinner daily.

VILLAGE SOUTH
Continental/Vero Beach
This is an unheralded hideaway with a fine inventory of excellent specials from scallops Rockefeller and mushrooms imperial to veal treated the Italian way and beer-battered shrimp. The fish is fresh and handled with intelligence by the kitchen crew, which also puts out a cabaret menu late at night—for the lounge crowd listening to the piano or guitar in the kind of informal setting that encourages the patrons to do their own solo gigs.

2900 Ocean Drive, Vero Beach. 407-231-6727. Moderate to expensive. Lunch Monday to Saturday; dinner daily.

WALDO'S
American/Vero Beach
Originally the grew-like-Topsy bar, lounge, and restaurant that started its beachfront existence as Waldo Sexton's kitchen. That was during the Great Depression, when Sexton made the rounds of the Palm Beach auctions buying up anything and everything, paying cash on the barrel head, and then using

the geegaws and doodads and the heavier, more elaborate furnishings to supplement the decor of the weathered wood buildings he was putting up on the shore and in town. Waldo's may be only a slight shadow of those halcyon days, but it's a grand place to pay homage to the unique Sexton, whether idling away a lazy few hours on the open-air deck watching the waves splash in and out, or digging into an early morning omelet, a noontime burger, or a dinner fillet of broiled dolphin and the best Cobb salad for miles and miles around.

3150 Ocean Drive, Vero Beach. 407-231-7091. Moderate. Breakfast, lunch, and dinner daily.

Where to Shop

Across from the park north of **Sexton Plaza** there's a string of shops selling a variety of resort ready-to-wear. Immediately south of Sexton Plaza is another series of shops that includes a newsstand and swimsuit sellers (bikinis are definitely not the most popular mode of dress in these parts). **Crickets Too** has upscale beach and resort wear, and **The Hawaiian Shop** sells fashions from those distant islands, including the well-known floral-patterned shirts. For those who like to snack and shop, or for long-suffering husbands who want to take a break, across from all that shopping by Humiston Park is **Christy's Raw Bar,** for sandwiches, pizza, and of course, raw bar offerings. Next door are the **Candy Shoppe,** for fudge, roast nuts, and saltwater taffy; and **Mrs. Max's Kitchen,** with wonderful breakfast specials.

More Fun in the Sun

Deep Six Dive and Watersports (407-562-2883) is a few blocks from the ocean on State Road 60 near Fifth Avenue, next door to **Houlihan's,** which is the place for everything related to water sports—boogie boards and surfboards, scuba tanks, water skis, snorkeling gear, wet and dry suits, and sunglasses.

Where to Write

Dodgertown, P.O. Box 2887, Vero Beach, Florida 32961-2287. 407-569-4900.

Vero Beach Chamber of Commerce, P.O. Box 2947, Vero Beach, Florida 32961. 407-567-3491.

CENTRAL FLORIDA AND THE SPACE COAST

C O C O A B E A C H

Cocoa Beach is smack in the center of the greatest stretch of sandy shore (75 miles of it) of any county in the state, and it is arguably the most user-friendly, family sort of beach as well. Kind to vacation budgets, and easy to reach from the major population centers of central and south Florida, it is at once a place of almost endless fun-in-the-sun activities and a quiet, easygoing spot with a 25-mile stretch of National Seashore, splendidly isolated from the teeming tourist trade. You can stroll or cycle the hard-packed sand, and ride the waves when you hear the cry "Surf's up!" checking first with a surf shop to find out where the pros are going in this surfing capital of Florida. You can watch the wildlife on a driving or walking tour of the Merritt Island National Wildlife Refuge or leap to the modern age and beyond by visiting the Space Center, which has an excellent complex dispensing information on the many sights to be seen at the center, at the refuge, and elsewhere.

You can easily reach it all from your base camp in Cocoa Beach, which, more than any other area in central or southeast Florida, makes a pretty good stab at being Florida as it used to be sometime back in the 1940s and 1950s. And the beaches along State Road A1A beckon from one end of town to the other, easily accessible from accommodations on or off the beach. Parking can be found without a hassle, there are playgrounds and picnic areas, and when the tides are right there are all kinds of shells for collectors of all ages. Forty-five of the town's streets provide access to the ocean, and there are nine acres of developed beach with facilities and a promenade at Sheppard Park at the ocean end of State Road 520 leading from the mainland. Sidney Fischer and Lori Wilson parks are close by, the former with 300 feet of beach and parking for 200 cars, the latter with pavilions, dune crossovers, and parking for 46 cars.

Where It Is

Cocoa Beach is on State Road A1A, three miles south of Cape Canaveral and five miles from the town of Cocoa and U.S. 1 via State Road 520, which includes a bridge and a causeway.

Where to Stay

COCOA BEACH HILTON & TOWER
Hotel/Cocoa Beach

This relatively new hotel with 300 rooms and 11 suites sits on some of the state's most uncrowded beachfront. It's a class act in these parts, sporting a pool and a spacious sun deck, a pair of lounges, a stylish restaurant, and Coco's, a nightclub with live entertainment.

1550 North Atlantic Avenue, Cocoa Beach 32931. 407-799-0003; toll-free: 1-800-526-2609. Expensive.

DAYS INN OCEANFRONT
Hotel/Cocoa Beach

This 120-room hotel occupies 300 feet of oceanfront and has a large pool and badminton, volleyball, and shuffleboard courts. Some of the accommodations are efficiencies with microwaves to help save the dining-out dollars.

5600 North Atlantic Avenue, Cocoa Beach 32931. 407-783-7621. Moderate.

HOLIDAY INN COCOA BEACH RESORT
Hotel/Cocoa Beach

This local link of the chain stands out from the rest, having 500 guest rooms including extra large units with king-size beds, three-room ocean villas, and two-level ocean lofts, all occupying over 25 acres of prime Atlantic-front property. With tennis courts, an oversize swimming pool, and a whirlpool spa, this lushly landscaped vacationland is a great place to unwind. The children's activity center keeps the little ones busy with a variety of projects. Baby-sitting service is also available, so parents can take advantage of the nightlife at Plum's, a lounge where there's live entertainment and dancing.

1300 North Atlantic Avenue, Cocoa Beach 32931. 407-783-2271; toll-free: 1-800-HOLIDAY. Moderate to expensive.

HOWARD JOHNSON PLAZA-HOTEL
Hotel/Cocoa Beach

In this new beachfront hotel all 210 rooms are done in tropical pastels and each has an ocean view and a balcony. Amenities include two large pools with 62 cabanas, a wading pool, an exercise room, water sports facilities, and a sunbathing deck. Carlyle's is the restaurant of choice, and Herbie K's, a 1950s vintage diner.

2080 North Atlantic Avenue, Cocoa Beach 32931. 407-783-9222; toll-free (in Florida): 1-800-FLORIDA, (nationwide): 1-800-356-7432. Moderate.

THE INN AT COCOA BEACH
Inn/Cocoa Beach

This charming inn sits on 750 feet of beachfront and has 50 rooms decorated in tones of mauve and teal. French country furniture fills the breakfast room, where complimentary continental breakfast is served at dawn and wine and cheese is offered at sunset. The innkeepers work hard to create an at-home feeling and they have a variety of rooms, most of them with private balcony or patio.

4300 Ocean Beach Boulevard, Cocoa Beach 32931. 407-799-3460; toll-free 1-800-343-5307. Expensive.

MARLIN APARTMENTS
Apartments/Cocoa Beach

Efficiencies and one-bedroom apartments, some with oceanfront views, are comfortably but simply furnished and have fully equipped kitchens. They are available by the week or month and are ideal for families concerned about vacation budgets. There is no pool.

22 Tulip Avenue, Cocoa Beach 32931. 407-783-8712. Moderate.

OCEAN SUITE HOTEL
Hotel/Cocoa Beach

An all-suite hotel with balcony, refrigerator, and wet bar in each room, all of which overlook the pool and beach. A restaurant and a lounge with live entertainment add to the extras.

5500 Ocean Beach Boulevard, Cocoa Beach 32931. 407-784-4343; toll-free (in Florida): 1-800-843-9680, (nationwide): 1-800-367-1223. Moderate.

RAMADA OCEANFRONT RESORT
Hotel/Satellite Beach
This hotel is truly a dazzler, with its grand lobby entrance and such facilities as a lighted beachfront tennis court, a fitness center complete with sauna and steam room, a video game room, and a gift shop. There's oceanfront dining in the Off Broadway restaurant and nightlife in the Stage Lounge. We like to sip and snack at the surfside boardwalk or poolside bar.

1035 State Road A1A, Satellite Beach 32937. 407-777-7200; toll-free: 1-800-272-6232. Moderate.

SEA AIRE MOTEL
Motel/Cocoa Beach
Fifteen oceanfront efficiencies in an ole-timey, pre-space-race setting. The patio has a barbecue grill, picnic tables, and benches with umbrellas, and there's a small playground for the kids.

181 North Atlantic Avenue, Cocoa Beach 32931. 407-483-2461. Inexpensive to moderate.

WAKULLA MOTEL
Motel/Cocoa Beach
With 814 square feet of living space in each of the 116 two-bedroom apartments, this is the best value in the area for a family vacation. Walk-in closets, a living room, a full kitchen and dining room, a large bathroom, and cable TV with free HBO are standard for each apartment, and there is a heated pool plus a kiddie pool in the tropically landscaped courtyard. This is apartment living with the extras of a hotel, and the standards of maintenance are very high.

3550 North Atlantic Avenue, Cocoa Beach 32931. 407-783-2230. Moderate.

Where to Eat

ALMA'S ITALIAN RESTAURANT
Italian/Cocoa Beach

Chef-owner Tim Morgan has passed the quarter century mark in this pre-fifties building. His specialties include seafood Alfredo; fresh catch of the day broiled, blackened, grilled, or fried; and a six-ounce filet mignon. Standard Italian dishes such as pizza, pastas, veal, and eggplant Parmesan are also available. There's a full bar and a wine list.

306 North Orlando Avenue, Cocoa Beach. 407-783-1981. Inexpensive to moderate. Dinner daily.

BERNARD'S SURF
Seafood/Cocoa Beach

One of the great restaurants of Florida and a favorite of ours for years. With its own fishing fleet guaranteeing freshness and quality, it confidently features fillets of snapper and grouper, rock and regular shrimp, and those special scallops caught off the coast, plus excellent land-locked fare and a terrific bread basket.

2 South Atlantic Avenue, Cocoa Beach. 407-783-2401. Expensive. Lunch and dinner daily.

BLUEBERRY MUFFIN
American/Indialantic

A bright little blockhouse that specializes in blueberry muffins—of course—but also old-fashioned breakfasts, solid luncheon sandwiches, and freshly made salads.

1130 North A1A, Indialantic. 407-725-7117. Inexpensive. Breakfast and lunch daily.

GATSBY'S DOCKSIDE EATERY
American/Cocoa Beach
Eat along the water or make reservations for a dinner, sunset, or sight-seeing cruise. Sunday brunch, cocktail hour snacking, and outdoor waterfront dining with live entertainment and a solid menu of seafood and steaks characterize the land-based operation, which has absolutely nothing in common with the Great Gatsby.

500 West Cocoa Beach Causeway, Cocoa Beach. 407-782-2389. Moderate. Lunch and dinner daily.

HEIDELBERG RESTAURANT
German/Cocoa Beach
The place on the Space Coast for all the best of the wurst, plus smoked pork loin, red cabbage, kraut, lots of beer—and *gemütlichkeit.*

7 North Atlantic Avenue, Cocoa Beach. 407-783-1981. Expensive. Lunch and dinner Monday to Saturday.

THE ITALIAN COURTYARD
Italian/Cocoa Beach
The Bianco bunch—Mom, Pop, Dominick, and Francisca—put it all together from *a* to *v*—antipasto to veal Parmesan. Remember to save space for the Italian rum cake and cappuccino torte.

Merritt Island Causeway (State Road 520), one block west of A1A, Cocoa Beach. 407-783-0413. Moderate to expensive. Dinner daily.

JACK BAKER'S LOBSTER SHANTY
Seafood/Cocoa Beach

This fantastic waterfront setting is the perfect place to consume schools of fish fillets and the lobsterlike rock shrimp. And there are burgers to please the younger set.

2200 South Orlando Avenue, Cocoa Beach. 407-783-1350. Moderate. Lunch and dinner daily.

JUNGLE JIM'S
American/Merritt Island

Jim works hard to live up to his boast of having the greatest burgers on Earth. They do have the zaniest names—Rhino, Hippo, Safari, Blue Max, and Tarzan. Also featured are "World Famous Monte Cristo Sandwiches," a real blast from the past. A fun spot for munching, lunching, sipping, and supping.

777 East Merritt Island Causeway, Merritt Island. 407-459-2332. Moderate. Lunch and dinner daily.

THE MANGO TREE
Continental/Cocoa Beach

This is a great place for a romantic evening or a celebration—or just because you deserve it! The setting is elaborate, with beautiful fresh-cut flowers flown in from Hawaii, impressive butterfly collections on the walls, and a continuous art show with a net worth of about a quarter of a million dollars. Large fish ponds are located indoors and out and small bowls of Siamese fighting fish are on tables in the restaurant. The menu, although not as elaborate as the setting, has such headliners as Calico scallops St. Jacques, Dover sole, rack of lamb, and various dishes featuring grouper, veal, beef, and pasta. Appetizers include Scottish salmon and Beluga caviar.

118 North Atlantic Boulevard, Cocoa Beach. 407-799-0513 or 783-5533. Expensive. Dinner Tuesday to Sunday.

OLD FISHERMAN'S WHARF
Seafood/Cocoa Beach

After you watch the catfish feeding frenzy a few feet from your waterfront table, start your meal with a slab of smoked mullet or the superlative smoked fish spread before proceeding to peel-'em-yourself gulf or rock shrimp served with tasty slaw and hush puppies. Then get serious with broiled dolphin, flounder, or red snapper.

Crescent Beach Drive, Cocoa Beach. 407-783-2731. Moderate to expensive. Lunch and dinner daily.

THE PIER HOUSE RESTAURANT
Seafood/Cocoa Beach

Our favorite time to eat at this spectacular setting, jutting 800 feet over the ocean, is during a full moon, but whenever, we start our evenings here with coconut shrimp or smoked amberjack, continue with scallops, lobster, or flounder, then finish off with cheesecake. Beef and poultry are available for the land-lovers, and the Sunday seafood brunch is sensational.

401 Meade Avenue, Cocoa Beach. 407-783-7549. Moderate to expensive. Dinner daily; Sunday brunch.

RUSTY'S RAW BAR
Seafood/Cocoa Beach

Located inside Bernard's Surf, this great little bar is the casual side of a great restaurant, serving the freshest of raw bar snacks, thickly stacked sandwiches, and good burgers.

2 South Atlantic Avenue, Cocoa Beach. 407-783-2401. Moderate. Lunch and dinner daily.

SPINNAKER'S
American/Cocoa Beach
Located on Cocoa Beach Pier, and ultracasual, this oceanview delight has live entertainment on the weekends, so after you have sunned your bod or cast for a catch of the day at the end of the pier, relax with a burger, a piled-high sandwich, or a dinner of ribs, chicken, or steak. Then indulge in one of the exotic drinks and enjoy the show.

401 Meade Avenue, Cocoa Beach. 407-783-7549. Inexpensive to moderate. Lunch and dinner daily.

Where to Shop
Oceanotions, on Cocoa Beach Pier (407-783-7549), is a tropical gift shop for souvenirs and gifts for friends and family back home.

Ron Jon Surf Shop, 4151 North Atlantic Avenue (407-799-8820), is one of a kind—the world's largest surf shop, where you can purchase all of your beach supplies and toys for the sun fun.

Seaside Mall, located on South Atlantic Avenue across from Bernard's Surf, has souvenir and gift shops such as **Mysteries of the Sea,** the **Rags to Riches Beachwear Shop,** and several snackshops—**Seaside Pizza,** where New York–style pizza is served until late hours daily; **Betties Buns and Dogs,** where you can buy snowballs in 20 flavors to cool you from your beaching; and **Key West Taco,** for a quick Tex-Mex fix.

Tropical Threads (407-783-2002), a boutique located on Cocoa Beach Pier at the 400 block of Meade Street, has the latest styles for the beach set.

More Fun in the Sun
Cocoa Village Playhouse, 300 Brevard Avenue, in Cocoa Village across the river (407-636-5050), is a handsomely restored theater from the Roaring Twenties and home for local drama, dance, and musical performances.

The Water Works, 1891 Merritt Island Causeway, State Road 520 (407-452-2007), is open seven days a week for rentals of sailboats, waverunners and sailboards, powerboats, and water-skiing equipment. Call ahead.

Coconuts on the Beach, 2 Minuteman Causeway (407-784-1422), located in the area directly behind the Seaside Mall, is the county's best beach party, an oceanfront happening that delivers with great gusto on its promises of "music, fun, and sun" and of "edibles and elixir"—in other words, munchies, a full menu, a deejay spinning your favorite tunes, and bartenders mixing your favorite drinks. The place jumps on Sunday afternoons. Sit at the beachfront patio bar or go find some shade; either way, you'll have a "hot" day at Coconuts.

The **Merritt Island National Wildlife Refuge** comprises 131,143 acres of forest and wetlands filled with furry creatures as well as gators, turtles, and manatees, and such birds as gulls, terns, egrets, herons, cormorants, pelicans, and rarest of all, the southern bald eagle. Some 350 different bird species have been sighted along this Atlantic flyway, a major migration route. Make your own count while driving the seven-mile **Black Point Wildlife Drive**, or walking either the path through a half mile of subtropical forest and a couple of miles of hardwoods and on the boardwalk over the wet areas, or the five-mile Cruickshank track, which circles a marsh and has a photo blind as well as an observation tower.

Spaceport USA is the most exciting contrast to all those natural sur-roundings. Start with the visitor center, then sign up for the IMAX films, tour the art gallery and the satellite center, where you can study just what it is we're learning up there, and then take one of the guided tours—they are excellent.

At each of the city's oceanfront parks is a branch of **Beach Rentals of Cocoa Beach** (407-783-1682) for cabanas, beach umbrellas, and lounges.

The **Cocoa Beach Recreation Complex**, on Banana River and Minute-man Causeway, has tennis and racquetball courts, an Olympic-size swimming pool, and an 18-hole championship golf course.

Mountasia Fantasy Golf, 6355 North Atlantic Avenue, Cape Canaveral (407-799-4861), has two miniature 18-hole courses in jungle settings with mini-waterfalls, rivers, caves, and mountains.

If you're a vacationer with fishing on your mind, check with **Bait and Tackle**; they arrange all-day fishing excursions, furnishing all the equipment you need to catch the big one. They're located at the end of Cocoa Beach Pier, a half mile north of State Road 520. **Port's End Park** is another site for the fishing enthusiast—you can fish from the seawall or from a boat you rent at a nearby dock. This is a four-acre water park that has been called a fisherman's dream because you can fish directly in the channel at the deep-water turning basin of the port.

Club Nautico, located at Gatsby's Dockside (407-784-0000), has power-boat rentals of various sizes, and skiing equipment is available.

Where to Write

Brevard County Tourist Development Council, P.O. Box 1969, Cocoa, Florida 32923. 407-453-0823; toll-free: 1-800-USA-1969.

Canaveral National Seashore, P.O. Box 2583, Titusville, Florida 32780. Ranger headquarters: 407-267-1110; tape information: 407-867-2805.

Cocoa Beach Area Chamber of Commerce, P.O. Box 1988, Merritt Island, Florida 32954-1988. 407-452-4390.

Merritt Island National Wildlife Refuge, P.O. Box 6504, Titusville, Florida 32782. 407-867-0667.

Spaceport USA, TWRS, Kennedy Space Center, Florida 32899. 407-452-2121. For information on launch schedules, call toll-free (in Florida only): 1-800-432-2153.

Titusville Area Chamber of Commerce, 2000 South Washington Street, Titusville, Florida 32780. 407-267-3036.

DAYTONA BEACH

Daytona Beach was the first of Florida's many, many beautiful beaches to become world famous. This strip of hard-packed white quartz sand is where the Babe Ruth of racing, Barney Oldfield, and the moguls of Motown, Henry Ford, Louis Chevrolet, and Ransom Olds, rallied every winter to race their engines, test new cars, and set new speed records. Cheering crowds and screeching gulls watched the cars roar along the 23 miles of the Daytona Raceway—from the first years of the automobile age (pre–World War I) until 1961, when the racers moved inland to the Daytona International Speedway. Daytona Beach is still the World Center of Racing, but it's no longer the Millionaire's Colony, as it was known at the turn of the century, when the Astors, Vanderbilts, and Rockefellers wintered in the salubrious sunshine. The home of John D. Rockefeller, called The Casements because of its many diamond-shaped windows, survives and serves today not only as a reminder of the last stages of the Gilded Age but as a cultural center and gallery, fronting handsomely laid-out gardens, restored to their original design with fountain and pond. But the home is located in Ormond and not Daytona Beach, a few thousand conch shells south. Why Ormond Beach? Because Rockefeller, who built his own private accommodations when he discovered that the hotel where he usually stayed charged him more than the other guests, asked his doctors to find the most healthful climate in the country, one in which he could live to be 100. But not even J. D. Rockefeller could realize all his goals—he died at the age of 97.

You too can enjoy the climate in Ormond, or Daytona Beach, or anywhere else along the 23 miles of the world-famous raceway. Actually, only 5.2 miles of it are in Daytona Beach proper; another 5.2 are in Daytona Beach Shores, 1.2 are in the adjacent Wilbur-by-the Sea, 3.9 are in Ormond Beach, and 8.2 are in Ormond-by-the-Sea.

From one hour before sunrise until one hour after sunset you can take your car on those many miles of shoreline, which is an incredible 500 feet wide at low tide, but only along clearly designated rutted trails in the sand, and never to race—in fact, you can never go more than 10 miles per hour, and that rule is strictly enforced.

There is no lack of access roads, although in the high season for beachgoers, from the end of January to the second week in April and from the end of May to Labor Day, a toll is charged for the privilege of rolling on the sand and parking your four-wheel headquarters—perpendicular to the water and in single rows only.

Six main lifeguard stations cover the 40 miles of county beaches, with a couple of hundred guards on duty during the high season perched on close to a hundred towers. Interspersed are rest rooms and portable toilets, a couple of dozen showers, and nearly 150 concessions with food and beverages and all kinds of rental gear.

In Lighthouse Point Park, located on the north side of the inlet, there are two main picnic pavilions with grills; other oak-shaded picnic facilities along with an observation deck—strategic sites for watching the birds and the boat parade while you lunch—are reached by wooden walkways. There are also nature trails, a playground, and rest room facilities with showers.

The crowds do not congregate at this southern extremity of Daytona's beaches, and we have never had trouble finding isolated pockets of privacy. Interrupt your beachgoing with walks around this sleepy little settlement, with its fishing camp sense of place, its easy-to-recommend restaurant called Down the Hatch (see page 131), and its 175-foot lighthouse that first flashed in 1887, about the time the millionaires were establishing a Florida mission of exclusivity. Climb the 203 steel stairs to the balcony, which provides a 360-degree panoramic view of land and sea and the Ponce de Leon Inlet, known as Mosquito Inlet in the days prior to the promotion of tourism. The lighthouse is open daily to the public and there's a gift store and a pair of mini-museums, one filled with the original lens and artifacts from the old lighthouse era, the other with various beachcomber findings and renderings of other lighthouses in the country.

During Spring Break you might want to flee to where the keeper who tended the 200,000-candlepower lamp used to live, unless you don't mind braving the onslaught of some 350,000 collegians who have earned Daytona Beach another world title—Spring Break Capital of America. Fort Lauderdale used to have that distinction, but its 20,000 breakers constitute a drop in the chugalug bucket compared to Daytona Beach. So check in advance for the dates of the spring break crowd and make your plans accordingly.

Where It Is

Daytona Beach is on the east coast of central Florida, reached by clearly marked exits off Interstates 4 and 95 as well as U.S. 1 and State Road A1A, which becomes Atlantic Avenue along the beachfront.

Where to Stay

The Daytona Beach resort area has more than 16,000 guest rooms in hotels, motels, inns, and rental condominiums. The high-rise hotels stand shoulder-to-shoulder along much of the beachfront, and it's sometimes mind-boggling trying to pick out the best among all those gaudily painted towers with cute names and figures of pirates and Vikings and the like propped out front as come-ons. Here's our selection of current favorites.

ACAPULCO INN
Hotel/Daytona Beach Shores

At the southern edge of the strip, this eight-floor Mexican resort lookalike has 133 rooms, each with a private oceanview balcony, a refrigerator, cable TV with Home Box Office, two double beds or one king-size bed, a safe, a clock-radio, and a telephone. Efficiencies have fully equipped kitchens. Out back are separate pools for adults and children and a pair of whirlpools, along with an oceanview lounge and a restaurant called Fiesta that is more or less Mexican. Across the street is a miniature golf layout. No student groups or unchaperoned students are permitted from March through June.

2505 South Atlantic Avenue, Daytona Beach Shores 32118. 904-761-2210; toll-free: 1-800-874-7420. Moderate.

AKU TIKI INN
Hotel/Daytona Beach Shores
Another smaller (a relative term on this beach) choice on the quieter, less-congested southern stretch of sand, this five-story, 132-room hotel has one of the largest pools, complete with a one-meter board at the deeper end. There's also a lounge with live entertainment and a dining room serving three meals a day. The pool bar is open during the high season, February to April.

2225 South Atlantic Avenue, Daytona Beach Shores 32118. 904-252-9631; toll free: 1-800-AKU TIKI. Inexpensive to moderate.

BEACH HUT
Motel/Daytona Beach Shores
A simply outfitted money-saver on the ocean with all the conveniences. Available are single rooms; ground-floor studio efficiencies with mini-kitchens; regular efficiencies with fully equipped kitchens, two beds or a queen-size bed and a sofa bed; and two-bedroom apartments with two double beds and a queen-size bed. There are the usual pool, sun deck, shuffleboard court, and game room, but also barbecue grills and complimentary morning coffee.

3247 South Atlantic Avenue, Daytona Beach Shores 32118. 904-761-8450. Inexpensive to moderate.

DAYTONA BEACH HILTON
Hotel/Daytona Beach
A class act of the area, an understated expression of taste with all the dash and professionalism of a Hilton. The lobby is a delight, with its lounge—open for breakfast, lunch, and late-night entertainment—offering beach views on one flank and the lobby people parade on the other. There's also a coffee shop and the top-floor Roof Restaurant, with far more ambitious fare, including some tableside flash and flame and a school of good seafood dishes featuring red snapper and shrimp. The 215 guest rooms are quietly outfitted in subdued

tropical tones, and of course there's a pool and the usual accompaniments one should expect in a class act.

2637 South Atlantic Avenue, Daytona Beach 32118. 904-767-7350; toll-free: 1-800-445-8667. Moderate.

DAYTONA BEACH MARRIOTT
Hotel/Daytona Beach

The newest of the oceanfront giants, opened in 1989 at the north end of the strip at a cost of $47 million, this 17-story 402-room wonder, located directly across the street from the Peabody Auditorium, has its own kind of performing arts complex. On one side of the hotel sits the coral stone amphitheater built by the WPA during the Great Depression (saved by the Marriott), as does its companion clocktower. The face of the clock bears letters spelling "Daytona Beach" in place of the usual numbers. Brass and real and faux marble have been generously utilized to provide a touch of modern hotel class and strategically planted foliage is everywhere. Each of the handsomely furnished guest rooms affords a fine panoramic view of the ocean and the raceway beach. A lounge, poolside bar, coffee shop, and signature dining room called Coquinas provide for sipping and supping.

100 North Atlantic Avenue, Daytona Beach 32118. 904-254-8200; toll-free: 1-800-228-9290. Expensive.

HOWARD JOHNSON'S OCEANFRONT
Hotel/Daytona Beach

One of the best-looking links of this chain to be found in Florida, all eggshell white with light, light pink trim and hot pink neon lighting, attractively furnished guest rooms including singles, doubles, efficiencies, and suites with balconies and the usual extras. Oceanfront pools with chickee bars, lounges and restaurants, and plenty of deck for sunning and swimsuit-watching.

2500 North Atlantic Avenue, Daytona Beach 32118. 904-672-0990; toll-free: 1-800-874-6996. Moderate.

SHERATON INN

Hotel/Daytona Beach Shores

The Sheraton representative on high-rise hostelry row, with 144 rooms with private balconies, motel modern furnishings, and the usual amenities. Efficiency units have fully equipped kitchens. Among the extras that make this destination stand out from the crowd are the large pool with adjacent kiddie pond, an upper deck for sunning or relaxing in the whirlpool (alongside which is the Sea Shanty bar and grill), and the Seagarden Restaurant, loyal to its name with lush tropical plantings and grand panoramas of the ocean through the wall of windows. Students, alone or in groups, are welcome.

3161 South Atlantic Avenue, Daytona Beach Shores 32118. 904-761-2335; toll-free: 1-800-874-7420. Moderate.

SUN VIKING LODGE

Motel/Daytona Beach

No, the Vikings never came this far south—if they had, they might have abandoned the frigid fjords forever. But the external decor is strictly Leif Eriksson—helmeted Hagars, paintings of the famous ships. Don't expect "lefse" and "lutefisk," however, or even a dining room. But do expect a lot of family-oriented facilities: indoor and outdoor pools; a 60-foot water slide; exercise and game rooms; shuffleboard, basketball, and volleyball courts; a spa and sauna (now that's Viking!); and comfortable, modern guest rooms—91 of them—including efficiencies with fully furnished kitchens and sofa beds, each with an oceanfront or oceanview balcony. The lodge also rents one-, two-, and three-bedroom private homes across the street—perfect for the extended family.

2411 South Atlantic Avenue, Daytona Beach 32118. 904-252-6252; toll-free: 1-800-874-4469. Inexpensive to moderate.

Where to Eat

A-AAAH AT'SA PIZZA

Italian-American/Daytona Beach

The origins of pizza go back to the time of the Etruscans, a little bit farther back than the family running this classic pizzeria a block from the beach can trace their roots. But they do have four generations of lil ole pizza-makers in the family album and they are doing it just right. They also churn out credible hot dogs and hamburgers and deliver within an area large enough to cover many of the hotels and motels.

614 Broadway, Daytona Beach. 904-258-3249. Inexpensive. Lunch and dinner daily.

AUNT CATFISH'S
American/Port Orange

This wonderfully rustic waterfront shack, located at the western edge of the Port Orange Causeway, serves some of the best-value-for-the-money food in Florida. Come for the Sunday brunch and eat enough for a week while watching the omelet-pancake teams go through their paces, showering the flapjacks with such zingers as chopped pecans and chocolate chips. There's food aplenty, all of it good old down-home stuff, including chicken and crab fritters, beautifully breaded catfish fingerlings you eat like corn on the cob, cheese grits, baked beans, hush puppies and fries, and all kinds of salads.

Corner of Dunlawton and Halifax Drive, Daytona Beach. 904-767-4768. Inexpensive. Lunch Monday to Saturday, dinner daily; Sunday brunch.

DOWN THE HATCH
Seafood/Ponce Inlet

When you make the excursion to the Ponce de Leon Lighthouse and get away from the crowds, this is the place to do your lunching, munching, and dining. It's fish-camp simple with straightforward service and seafood fresh from its own fleet, which docks a few feet from the restaurant. Watch the boat parade while you work through the platters of shrimp and scallops, fresh fillets of grouper, superior soft-shell crabs, good chowders, and the kind of bar you'd expect to find on the water.

Timmons Fishing Camp, Ponce Inlet. 407-761-4831. Inexpensive to moderate. Lunch and dinner daily.

HOG HEAVEN
Barbecue/Daytona Beach
Conveniently located across from the Marriott Hotel, this classically back-country rustic cabin serves the best barbecue on the beach. Our favorite pig-out? The perfectly barbecue-browned pork ribs slathered with gobs of finger-lickin' sauce.

37 North Atlantic Avenue, Daytona Beach. 904-257-1212. Inexpensive. Lunch and dinner daily.

J.C.'S OYSTER DECK
American/Port Orange
An inviting and informal riverfront spread of rusticity with a raw bar and palm-shaded picnic tables under the massive girders of steel and concrete spanning the Halifax River. Commercial fishermen unload their harvests a few feet away and there's a never-ending parade of boats, great to watch while you're digging into combo platters of fried shrimp, deviled crabs, clam strips, and freshly shucked oysters. But don't overlook the humongous hamburgers—they're terrific!

East Dunlawton underneath the bridge, Port Orange. 904-767-1881. Inexpensive. Lunch and dinner daily. No credit cards.

PARK'S
Seafood/Daytona Beach
This veteran (since 1976) stop on the budget trail has a fine waterfront—on the Halifax River—location. Schools of fish stream out of the kitchen, everything from Maine lobsters to Maryland crabs, Carolina scallops and locally caught grouper, flounder, snapper, and shrimp, all served in a no-nonsense setting with high-volume speedy delivery. Their seafood market is next door.

951 North Beach Street, Daytona Beach. 904-258-7272. Inexpensive. Dinner daily. Closed December.

RED SNAPPER
Seafood/Daytona Beach Shores

Jimmy Stavracos must be doing something right. He's been in business at this comfortably casual location across from the beach since 1960, specializing in serving Florida's most famous fish—red snapper—in a variety of ways. Our favorite way to go is the Greek, broiled or pan-fried with lemon, butter, and just enough oregano to take us back in time and taste to a taverna on Mykonos. Shrimp and other seafood are also treated with respect by the Stavracos clan, which also knows what to do with duckling and quality beef.

2058 South Atlantic Avenue, Daytona Beach Shores. 904-252-0212. Moderate. Lunch and dinner daily. Closed for three weeks in December.

ST. REGIS HOTEL
French/Daytona Beach

The memories of Al and Etta Mae Bruchez are kept alive in this little landmark hotel a couple of blocks from the ocean. The chef from their charming and intensely personal Chez Bruchez bistro across the street— shuttered for several years—is in residence, and he has all the old Bruchez recipes and magic touch. French onion or black bean soup are on the lunch menu, along with chicken piccata and a petit filet mignon smothered with port-soaked mushrooms. Dinners start with house-made pâtés, carpaccio, or crabmeat Caribbean in a spicy sauce, while the main action revolves around veal marsala or Française, a variation of scampi-style shrimp called Carlucci, and a special St. Regis Quartet consisting of frog legs with crabmeat, scallops, and shrimp in a splendid lemon-butter sauce.

509 Seabreeze Boulevard, Daytona Beach. 904-252-8743. Moderate to expensive. Lunch Monday to Friday, dinner Tuesday to Saturday; Sunday brunch.

SAPPORO JAPANESE STEAK HOUSE
Japanese/Daytona Beach Shores

A steak house on a smaller, considerably more modest Benihana scale, with one of those Samurai warriors standing before you flashing swords and slicing beef and shrimp while some stranger at the community table tells you about his Toyota. There's a sushi bar off to the side, and that's where we usually spend our time here.

3340 South Atlantic Avenue, Daytona Beach Shores. 904-756-0480. Moderate to expensive. Dinner daily.

SINBADS
American/Port Orange

A king-size waterfront (on the Intracoastal) high-volume feeder run by the Van Hollebeke family, who have been on these shores since 1986. But they did not arrive as newcomers in the business—their restaurant up north, on the Detroit River, opened in 1949. The experience shows—in the supersize, thickly layered sandwiches; the shrimp salads and sardine plates; the orange roughy; lobster; and pickerel imports. From the extensive menu we find comfort in the oysters Freddie (with a cheese-garlic cream sauce), the broiled Canadian sea scallops, the half pound of red snapper, or the pork chop served with applesauce.

78 Dunlawton Avenue, Port Orange. 904-756-2921. Moderate. Breakfast, lunch, and dinner daily.

T.C.'S TOP DOG
American/Daytona Beach

Located one block south of Seabreeze, this is *the* place on the strip for hot dogs. T.C. himself says, "If you haven't been here yet, you haven't lived—nobody builds better weenies than T.C.!" The self-proclaimed hot dog king is open until 4:00 A.M., and he hands out special awards to anyone who buys and survives a T.C. Super Top Dog.

425 North Atlantic Avenue, Daytona Beach. 904-257-7766. Inexpensive. Lunch and dinner daily. Eat in or take out.

TOPAZ CAFE
Nouvelle American/Flagler Beach

A dozen miles north of Ormond Beach but certainly well worth the trip, because the sisters Hampton, Catherine and Lisa, are doing wondrous things with all kinds of fresh ingredients. Start with some truly old-fashioned chicken soup or a brew made with baked onions and barley braced with provolone and Romano or fresh fruits tossed with chopped nuts in a creamy coconut dressing. Then move onto some steak or grouper Oscar, shrimp sautéed in extra virgin olive oil with herbs and cilantro-butter, or fresh breast of chicken with mushroom and scallion dotted ginger-and-garlic sauce. This is clearly one of the best restaurants in the area, and it also does catering.

1224 South Ocean Shore Boulevard, Flagler Beach. 904-439-3275. Expensive. Lunch Friday, dinner Tuesday to Saturday.

TOP OF DAYTONA
American/Daytona Beach Shores

The view is the thing from the summit of the 29 floors that soar skyward like a space shuttle. Everything else seems secondary, but there are dancing and entertainment nightly, early-bird savings, good prime rib, and a slew of specials created by owner Sophie Kay, who is good enough to have her own television cooking show.

2625 South Atlantic Avenue, Daytona Beach Shores. 904-767-5791. Moderate to expensive. Dinner daily.

Where to Shop

Most of oceanfront Atlantic Avenue across from the hotels is dotted with strips of stores interspersed with various snack shops and convenience stores filled with the kinds of provisions needed by visitors who have accommodations with kitchens. Beach supplies and clothing are available everywhere but the one outlet that is outrageously larger than all the rest is the **Big Kahuna Surf Shop** with two locations, 2540 and 2739 South Atlantic Avenue (904-760-5265 and 904-672-1757). They are stocked with the latest in swimwear, tanning products, beach equipment, sporty casuals—1700 square feet of shopping.

Note: Tune in to beach radio 77 AM for weather conditions, beach rules and regulations, and area happenings.

More Fun in the Sun

For a special Sunday brunch on the water, or noontime buffet, or evening dinner-dance, board the *Dixie Queen* at the southwest side of Seacrest Bridge, 841 Ballough Road (904-255-1997). You'll be entertained by a Dixieland show band. If you want to bounce over the waves at speeds up to 40 miles per hour, or take a scenic inlet cruise, check into the **Critter Fleet** (904-767-7676), located at the docks across from the Ponce Inlet Lighthouse, for a 90-minute ride (great for the whole family) on a 100-passenger speedboat.

The 2,560-seat **Peabody Auditorium** (904-255-1314 and 252-0821), 600 Auditorium Boulevard, across from the Marriott Hotel, 100 North Atlantic Avenue, is the home of both the Daytona Beach Civic Ballet and Symphony Society and the Concern Showcase. Broadway musicals are also performed here. The **Ocean Center** (904-254-4545), a convention, trade show, and sports complex, presents such family shows as Sesame Street Live, the Ringling Brothers and Barnum & Bailey Circus, and Walt Disney's Magic Kingdom on Ice. It's across the street from the auditorium.

The main street pier on the boardwalk, adjacent to the **Oceanfront Bandshell and Park**, where there are free concerts during spring break and in summer, offers a gondola ride that affords great views of the beachfront. South of the pier and at many other strategic locations all along the shoreline, you'll find rental boogie boards, three-wheeler fun cycles, ATV four-wheelers, and for the sand potatoes, lounge chairs, umbrellas, and floats. **Holiday Golf**, at

2500 South Atlantic Avenue in Daytona Beach Shores, is a great little miniature course providing all kinds of strange challenges and laughs.

Unlike the good old days here when there were only low-rises and simple little cottages on the beach, and little to do at night except wait for the moonlight, there's lots of after-dark action, including: The **Coliseum** (904-257-9982) at 176 N. Beach Street, is regarded by the locals as the ultimate dance club. **The O.P.** (904-672-2461), which stands for the Other Place, is another favorite of the locals and is located in Ormond Beach at 642 South Atlantic Avenue. **701 South** (904-255-8431) is at that address on South Atlantic Avenue and features progressive music. **Finky's Tonight** (904-255-5059), 640 North Grandview Avenue at the intersection of Seabreeze Boulevard and A1A, has rock music, light dining, and Finky's Pig Out between 6 P.M. and 9 P.M. when you can eat and drink for one low price and receive a free T-shirt and mug.

Where to Write
Daytona Beach Convention and Visitor's Bureau, 126 East Orange Avenue, Daytona Beach, Florida 32114. 904-255-0415; toll-free: 1-800-854-1234.

NORTHERN FLORIDA: PENSACOLA TO JACKSONVILLE TO ST. AUGUSTINE

PENSACOLA

There's a splendid isolation about the beaches of Pensacola, even during the annual Memorial Day and Labor Day weekend invasions, when the Panhandle earns its title of Baja Georgia. Off-season, we've walked for miles and never encountered any other surfer, swimmer, stroller, or body-bronzer. The beaches are easily accessible from the city, where there are countless historic attractions and parking is free almost everywhere. Closest to town, across the three-mile Bay Bridge, is Gulf Breeze and the northernmost section of the Gulf Islands National Seashore, part of a 150-mile chain of barrier islands stretching along the Gulf of Mexico from Florida's Santa Rosa Island in the east to West Ship Island, Mississippi.

U.S. 98 dissects Gulf Breeze and the National Seashore, giving easy access to one of the longest fishing piers in the world, to boat ramps for those who bring their own, and to the Naval Live Oaks Area, the nation's first timber preserve, set aside in 1828 when 30,000 acres of live oak were declared off-limits to all but naval shipbuilders. The area has picnic shelters, showers, rest rooms, and a visitor center with information and exhibits on the National Seashore and the art of shipbuilding.

South of 98 and Bob Sikes Bridge leads to some of Florida's newest and most inviting beaches, beckoning sun-seekers to the National Seashore on Santa Rosa. Nine miles west of the bridge is the entrance to the beach. The Fort Pickens Area was named for the largest of the area's forts, a pentagon covering seven acres that was constructed by 400 slaves in the 1830s. Apache warrior Geronimo and 50 of his followers—men, women, and children—were incarcerated here in the late 1880s. Now open to the public and protected by the National Park Service, the fort lies at the tip of the island, past a 200-site campground and picnic area, indoor showers and bathhouses, a marina with charter boats, and a small museum with an auditorium where daily programs are given.

Santa Rosa Island has 17 miles of natural beach with lifeguards on duty during the summer at Fort Pickens and at Langdon Beach, but not at the beach called Unnamed. It's halfway between Fort Pickens and Pensacola Beach, which comprises 2,500-foot Quietwater Beach on Santa Rosa Sound, with boat ramps and picnic sites, and Casino Beach by the fishing pier, with beach bars and Tiki Island amusement park. Public access to the beaches is alongside the pier and on Avenida 10 through Avenida 23 off Ariola Drive, which runs parallel to the main road, Pensacola Beach Boulevard. On the other side of the boulevard there's a fine paved jogging-bicycle path.

East of the developed area, just beyond Avenida 23, the Santa Rosa Island section of the Gulf Islands National Seashore stretches for ten miles with 106 acres of beach on both the Gulf and Santa Rosa Sound. The stretch leads to the small development of Navarre Beach, with access to the Gulf via nine streets named after states—Indiana, California, Missouri, Michigan . . . There's a fishing pier and the small, community-maintained Shoreline Park, with picnic and playground facilities.

The western section of the state's National Seashore is on Perdido Key, 14 miles of natural sand with dramatic dunes. At Johnson Beach there are showers, rest rooms, concessions selling snacks, a nature trail, and a picnic area. Lifeguards are on duty during the summer. Perdido Key State Preserve has 250 acres of more of the same—wonderfully white sand and dunes dotted with rosemary and sea oats. The road to the key goes through the Naval Air Station, which has a fascinating museum presenting the history of naval aviation from its beginnings in 1941. Close by is Fort Barrancas, built at the same time as Fort Pickens to guard the entrance to Pensacola Bay.

Where It Is

Gulf Breeze is crossed by U.S. 98, the coastline road running from Panama City Beach to Pensacola. Pensacola Beach is reached by the Bob Sikes Bridge, which leads south from 98 as it turns north and crosses the Pensacola Bay Bridge. State Road 399, called Fort Pickens Road west of its beginning at the end of Sikes Bridge, and Via de Luna east of that intersection, runs from one end of the barrier island to the other. Perdido Key is reached by taking State Road 292, Barrancas Avenue, from Main Street in downtown Pensacola. As it crosses State Road 295, Navy Boulevard, 292 is called Gulf Beach Highway and it leads directly to the bridge connecting Perdido Key and the mainland.

Where to Stay

There are many beachfront homes, cottages, and condominium units for weekly and monthly rentals on Santa Rosa Island covering a wide range of cost, comfort, and taste. Advanced reservations and deposits are required. All accommodations have fully furnished kitchens and most have telephones and TVs. Pets and groups are not permitted. Most of the real estate companies offer such properties. Pensacola Beach Realty (1-800-874-9243) has a fine inventory and a 16-page booklet complete with photographs and all the details. Rates range from moderate to expensive.

BARBARY COAST MOTEL
Motel/Pensacola Beach

Two dozen one- and two-bedroom suites, king-size and standard rooms spread in a half dozen units on the Gulf with pool and picnic area in between. All but two of the accommodations have kitchens, and that means saving money at breakfast and snack time.

24 Via de Luna Drive, Pensacola Beach 32561. 904-932-2233. Inexpensive.

COMFORT INN
Motel/Navarre

Located two minutes from the beach directly across from Bob Sikes Bridge and close to the fishing pier, this motel is next door to the Navarre Square Shopping Plaza and six minutes from the zoo. A complimentary continental breakfast, a playground, a picnic area, and a swimming pool are among the attractions.

8494 Navarre Parkway, Navarre 32566. 904-939-1761; toll-free: 1-800-868-1761. Inexpensive.

COMFORT INN
Motel/Pensacola

Close to but not directly on the beach and featuring a swimming pool, hot tub, and free continental breakfast, this is a convenient location for those who want to go to the dogs at pari-mutuel Greyhound Park or visit the National Museum of Naval Aviation.

13585 Perdido Key Drive, Pensacola 32507. 904-492-2755. Inexpensive.

THE DUNES
Hotel/Pensacola Beach

The class act of the beach, this eight-story, 140-room (including penthouse suites) hotel has a prime location on the pristine white sand and sports a pair of swimming pools (one that is part indoor, part outdoor), great sunning decks and lawns, a 'round-the-clock café, and an okay dining room–lounge overlooking the shore where there are weekend cookouts. Friday night splash parties feature such movies as *Jaws* with free popcorn and Kool-Aid for the kids, who have their own Beach Bunch program of activities, organized with the nearby Holiday Inn. There are also volleyball nets and croquet courts and special rates for golf at a sister property, the Tiger Point Country Club, over on Gulf Breeze. The two 18-hole courses here were designed by Jerry Pate, a principal owner.

333 Fort Pickens Road, Pensacola Beach 32561. 904-932-3536; toll-free: 1-800-83-DUNES. Moderate.

FIVE FLAGS MOTEL
Motel/Pensacola Beach

Advertised as offering the lowest rates in town, the motel faces the beach and has a fine pool and patio. The 49 functionally furnished rooms have such amenities as color TV and air-conditioning, and guests are provided complimentary morning coffee. Pets are permitted.

299 Fort Pickens Road, Pensacola Beach 32561. 904-932-3586. Inexpensive.

HOLIDAY INN
Motel/Pensacola Beach
Superbly situated close to the turnoff onto Fort Pickens Road from the Bob
Sikes Bridge, this nine-story, 150-room box on the beach has a wonderful
penthouse lounge and Gulf-view dining room called Casino (but without
gambling), its own tennis courts, and a Beach Bunch children's (ages 4 to 12)
program Friday and Saturday from Easter to Memorial Day and then Wednesday through Saturday from the beginning of summer through Labor Day.
This is not merely a baby-sitting service but an active program of water-
oriented activities and contests, games, puppet shows, and storytelling, plus
movies and more games from 6:00 P.M. to 10:00 P.M., allowing the parents to
do some serious restaurant reconnaissance.

*165 Fort Pickens Road, Pensacola Beach 32561. 904-932-5361; toll-free:
1-800-HOLIDAY. Moderate.*

PERDIDO SUN
Condominium/Pensacola
At a perfect beachfront location, 12 stories of one-, two-, and three-bedroom
apartments fully furnished in modern tropical tones. Each has a kitchen and
a Gulf-view balcony. There are indoor and outdoor pools, a whirlpool hot tub,
a fitness room with an adjacent sauna, and a convenient boardwalk over the
dune line.

*13753 Perdido Key Drive, Pensacola 32507. 904-492-2390; toll-free:
1-800-227-2390. Moderate to expensive.*

TRISTAN TOWERS
Condominium/Pensacola Beach

The closest accommodation to the Fort Pickens National Seashore, this is a carefully maintained, handsomely landscaped 16-floor high-rise offering daily and weekly rentals of two- and three-bedroom fully furnished apartments. Each unit has corner windows providing maximum panoramas of the Gulf and its beach a few hundred feet away. Other amenities include a pair of lighted tennis courts, a large pool and sun deck, a boardwalk to the beach, a gazebo, and a security gate.

For reservations, contact Pensacola Beach Properties, at 1200 Fort Pickens Road, Pensacola Beach 32561. 904-932-9341; toll-free: 1-800-932-9341.

Where to Eat

BOY ON A DOLPHIN
Greek/Pensacola Beach

In 1986, when the chef at the in-town Angus Steak House split off from his partner, he came to the beach and opened a better-than-average restaurant. Named after the legendary statue, it features Greek-style, open-hearth charcoal-broiled scampi, snapper, and grouper, along with excellent steaks and such Macedonian standbys as moussaka, garlic chicken, and fela, a mixture of ground meat and rice wrapped in cabbage leaves rather than the customary grape leaves, and served with a lemon-egg sauce. Greek wines are available but no belly dancers or bouzouki.

400 Pensacola Beach Boulevard, Pensacola Beach. 904-932-7954. Moderate to expensive. Lunch and dinner daily.

FLOUNDER'S CHOWDER & ALE HOUSE
Seafood/Pensacola Beach

Here's the best—and most popular—restaurant on the beaches, a fun-loving spinoff from the in-town McGuire's Irish Pub & Brewery, and filled with the same high spirits, served with the same gusto by a hearty crew of lads and lasses, and featuring live entertainment nightly out on the sand. There are rum and reggae every Sunday along with bikini contests, and it's the site of the annual Save the Beach concerts in May. The menu is a real joy—to read *and* to order from. Steaks are hickory grilled and of the same top quality as those served at McGuire's; Gulf shrimp, whether scampi-style, barbecued, battered, or steamed in beer, are super; oysters are freshly shucked; and the spider po'boy—deep-fried soft-shell crab—is sensational. Among the drink delights are those labeled fogcutter, bilgewater margarita, blue marlin, cappuccino l'amour, and diesel fuel—you can fuel some of the people some of the time. . . .

800 Quietwater Beach Road, Pensacola Beach. 904-932-2003. Moderate to expensive. Lunch and dinner daily.

GOLDEN CHINA
Chinese/Gulf Breeze

Best Chinese cuisine on the beaches, whether you order one of the specialty combination dinners or straight off the menu as we do, starting with the dim sum dumplings and teriyaki steak bits, moving on to hot and sour soup, General Tso's chicken, orange beef, or anything with garlic sauce, before finishing with the fried bananas.

830 Gulf Breeze Parkway, Gulf Breeze. 904-932-2511. Moderate. Lunch and dinner daily.

JUBILEE RESTAURANT & OYSTER BAR
American/Pensacola Beach

A well-dressed second-floor spread of surprising sophistication for this section of the state, with walls of windows for wonderful views of Santa Rosa Sound. It's a place where butter really is better, the addition of honey and coconut making it a great spread for the sourdough and whole wheat rolls. For the main action we like the mesquite-grilled swordfish or the tournedos given a variation of the Rossini treatment—artichoke hearts and lump crabmeat sautéed with white wine. A freshly assembled salad of seafood mingled with greens is a good starter, and bread pudding is the perfect finisher. On the ground level, the Oyster Bar has a much more informal atmosphere, with outside tables, a couple of bars, good snack food, and live, loud entertainment.

400 Quietwater Beach Boardwalk, Pensacola Beach. 904-934-3108. Jubilee Restaurant: moderate to expensive; dinner daily. Oyster Bar: inexpensive to moderate; lunch and dinner daily.

THE MOORINGS
Seafood/Pensacola Beach

A third-floor restaurant and lounge up a deck from The Ship's Store and loaded with all the necessities for a nautical look. There's a fine view of the marina and Little Sabine Bay, so start your evening with a sip in the lounge or the outside deck where you can watch the sunset. Then settle into one of the restaurant's steaks or chicken specialties, or something with pasta. Or sign up for the nightly seafood buffet. Fish sandwiches and seafood salads headline the lunch menu.

655 Pensacola Beach Boulevard, Pensacola Beach. 904-934-3606. Moderate. Lunch and dinner daily.

NERO'S
American/Pensacola Beach

Good pizza and heavily stacked steamed sandwiches are what you find at Nero's, along with dartboards, pool tables, and video games. For the ultimate monster meal, order a forklift pizza.

49 Via de Luna, Pensacola Beach. 904-932-4590. Inexpensive. Breakfast, lunch, and dinner daily.

PEG LEG PETE'S
Seafood/Pensacola Beach

Rugged second-deck raw bar where oysters—baked, steamed, raw, Cajunized, or given the casino-Rockefeller treatment—are the specialty of the shack, which is completely casual. Live entertainment Friday and Saturday.

1010 Fort Pickens Road, Pensacola Beach. 904-932-4139. Inexpensive. Lunch and dinner daily.

SANDSHAKER SANDWICH SHOP AND LOUNGE
American/Pensacola Beach

Late-night oasis for the cool set and lunch-dinner budget stretcher with home-brewed soups, overstuffed sandwiches, and such daily specials as chicken and dumplings and taco salads.

731 Pensacola Beach Boulevard, Pensacola Beach. 904-932-0023. Inexpensive. Lunch and dinner daily.

SUN RAY TACO SHOP
Mexican/Pensacola Beach

"Mexican food comes from Mexico . . . please be patient!"—this is their clever way to advise that the food is made to order, including our favorites—chili

Sanchez, made with turkey; nacho salad, crowned with marinated chicken or taco beef; and tampico chicken or steak, served on Spanish rice topped with sautéed veggies and accompanied by refried beans. There is the usual Tex-Mex menu, and another one for the 12-and-under set, with sloppy joes, burgers, and taquitos the best-sellers.

20 Via de Luna, Pensacola Beach. 904-932-0118. Inexpensive. Lunch and dinner daily.

THE SUNDECK
American/Pensacola Beach
Here's a great place for starting your outdoor beach day at sunrise—it opens at 6:00 A.M.—with some fresh OJ, eggs and bacon, strong coffee. Later in the day there's pizza, burgers, pinball and darts, and savings on drinks before dinner. There's outdoor cooking on the weekends and parachute drops any time—this is the headquarters of the Panhandle Parachute Association.

12 Via de Luna, Pensacola Beach. 904-932-0835. Inexpensive. Breakfast, lunch, and dinner daily.

Where to Shop
Alvin's Island, 400 Quietwater Beach Road (904-934-3711), is on the Boardwalk and offers most major brands of sportswear, the latest in swimwear, and all kinds of beach supplies. The **Treasure Chest** (904-932-6883), in the same complex of Boardwalk shops and snackeries, is the domain of Jim and Martha King, who stock a wide variety of gift items and souvenirs. Around the corner, at 786 Quietwater Beach Road, next door to **Flounder's,** is the **Oasis Shirt Shop** (904-932-6638), with a fine assortment of T-shirts and other coverups stocked by owners Bill and Janice Sutherland. At 20 Via de Luna, the **Sun Ray Casual Shop** (904-932-9550), next door to the **Sun Ray Taco Shop** has a wide range of casual beachwear, and claims to have the best bargains in T-shirts.

More Fun in the Sun

Fishing enthusiasts who want to spend time out in Gulf waters angling for the big ones—flounder, grouper, amberjack, snapper, and barracuda—or venture out to the much heralded De Soto Canyon, where the sail and swordfish and the blue-and-white Marlin hide, have to go back over the bridges to the mainland and the in-town marinas. Check with **Captain G. Kay Lough,** at 935 Fairway Drive (904-455-4892), docked at Pitt Slip, located downtown next to the Port of Pensacola. That's also the home port of the **AAA Charter Service** (904-438-3242). **The Scuba Shack,** on the water at 719 South Palafox Street (904-433-4319), has a new 50-foot party fishing boat called *Wet Dream;* and at 801 South Palafox (904-434-6977) trips are made aboard the *Chulamar.*

Jet Skis, waverunners, powerboats, and sailboats are available on Pensacola Beach at **Key Sailing,** 500 Quietwater Beach Road (904-932-5520); **Port Side Sailing,** 430 Pensacola Beach Boulevard (904-932-2000); and **Bonifay Water Sports,** 460 Pensacola Beach Boulevard (904-932-0633)—the last two on the sound across from the bridge toll station.

The perfect place to learn boardsailing and windsurfing is **Surf & Sail,** 11 Via de Luna (904-932-SURF), with new stock boardsails—Mistral, Bic F2, and O'Brien. It's also the place for the latest in beachwear, reef sandals, sunglasses, and rollerblade equipment.

Waverunners, paddle boats, canoes, fishing and pontoon boats are available for rent at **Pier 1** (904-934-3500), at the southern end of the three-mile Bay Bridge on Gulf Breeze. Parasailing—600 feet up, up, and away—can be arranged at the same location (904-934-8106).

Southwind Divers (904-934-2224), offers daily wreck trips, instruction, and certification sessions from basic to advanced leadership levels. All necessary scuba gear is available for rent, and the divemasters know the sites in Gulf waters where artificial reefs complete with fighter planes, sunken battleships, freighters, barges, tugboats, and oil rigs—all of them active fish havens—have been created through the combined efforts of the U.S. Navy, the Department of Commerce, and the Escambia County Marine Recreation Committee.

For entertainment of a far different sort, check into **Tiki Island,** an amusement park that was completely refurbished in 1991. Your aspiring major leaguers will love the batting cage, and the whole family will enjoy the miniature golf course, site of the Pensacola Beach Celebrity Golf Tournament.

You can also rent bikes—one- or ten-speed, for 1, 2 or 24 hours—for riding along the beach bike paths, which stretch both east and west.

To the east, in Gulf Breeze, at 5801 Gulf Breeze Parkway (904-932-2229), is the **zoo,** with 500 animals, including the world's largest gorilla, and a petting enclosure. Other features are outdoor puppet and animal shows and elephant rides. To the west, at the southern tip of the mainland, on the grounds of the Pensacola Naval Air Station, is the **National Museum of Naval Aviation** (904-453-NAVY; toll-free: 1-800-327-5002), filled with aviation memorabilia from the early years of the century to the present, do-it-yourself flight simulators, scale models, and a hundred authentic aircraft from the type of TBM Avenger flown by President Bush during World War II to modern-day jets.

There always seems to be some special event on the beach. In February it's **Mardi Gras,** organized by the lighthearted Krewe of Wrecks; in March and April, **Easter egg hunts and tosses,** and an **international windsurfing Pro/Am.** The second week of June means the area-wide main event of the Pensacola year, the **Fiesta of Five Flags,** with reenactments of the landing of Spanish conquistador Tristan de Luna; a yacht parade; sand sculpture contests; arts, crafts, and music on the boardwalk; volleyball and tug-of-war competitions; and a beach treasure hunt for the under-nine set.

In July there are fireworks and an air show by the world-famous **Blue Angels,** stationed at the Naval Air Station; in November, a seafood festival, and at Christmas, a procession of decorated boats to end the year.

Only one Pensacola Beach event can be found in the *Guinness Book of World Records.* That's the world's longest beach party, an annual first-week-in-April **mullet-tossing competition** that stretches across Perdido Key all the way to Alabama Point. That's right, a contest to see how far you can throw a mullet. Participants jam along the key across the Florida-Alabama state line all the way to Alabama Point. They also toss beer kegs, Frisbees, and horseshoes, or engage in such sports as spearfishing, skydiving, and volleyball. There are cross-state competitions in softball, billfishing, and black belt karate; a 5K race; and car and swimsuit shows, with many of the activities taking place at the one-of-a-kind **Flora-Bama Lounge,** smack on the state line.

Where to Write
Gulf Breeze Chamber of Commerce, P.O. Box 337, Gulf Breeze, Florida 32562. 904-932-7888.

Gulf Islands National Seashore, P.O. Box 100, Gulf Breeze, Florida 32562. 904-934-2600.

National Museum of Naval Aviation, Naval Air Station, Pensacola, Florida 32508. 904-452-3604.

Pensacola Visitor Information Center, 1401 East Gregory Street, Pensacola, Florida 32501. 904-434-1234; toll-free (in Florida): 1-800-343-4321, (outside Florida): 1-800-874-1234.

Pensacola Beach Chamber of Commerce, P.O. Box 1174, Pensacola Beach, Florida 32561. 904-932-1500; toll-free: 1-800-635-4803.

Perdido Key Chamber of Commerce, Coquina Shops Information Center, 14110 Perdido Key Drive, Perdido Key, Florida 32507. 904-492-3714.

Santa Rosa Island Authority, P.O. Drawer 1208, Pensacola Beach, Florida 32562. 904-932-2257.

Superintendent, Gulf Islands National Seashore, 1801 Gulf Breeze Parkway, Gulf Breeze, Florida 32561. 904-934-2600.

◎　　◎　　◎

OKALOOSA AND
WALTON COUNTIES

W̶e discovered this area in the mid-fifties, returning again and again in
subsequent years to enjoy the isolation of the sugar-white beaches, the
clumps of undisturbed sea oats, the gently rolling dunes with tidal lakes, and
the ponds brimming with starter fish waiting their turn to head for deeper
waters. We were glad when an important segment of all that sand—a 356-
acre oasis of white beaches and freshwater lakes surrounded by pine flat-
woods—was designated the Grayton Beach State Recreation Area. And when
we learned that those sands were named the best beach in the continental
United States, in a survey that included 31 other Florida beaches as among the
best 50 in the country, we were not at all surprised.

The emerald-green waters splashing those beaches are crystal clear, as we
learned when flying over the area several times in the process of preparing this
book. No concessionaires were to be seen, no swimming pools or high-rise
condominiums or low-rise developments wedged tightly together as though
frightened of wide-open spaces.

There are other isolated patches of solitude along the coastline, which
stretches from Santa Rosa Island east of Pensacola Beach to the western border
of Panama City Beach. Starting with the small Phillips Inlet area of undeveloped beach and continuing with Seagrove Beach, a one-and-a-half-mile
Gulf frontage leading to Grayton Beach. Then come Dune Allen Beach, Beach
Highlands, Four Mile Village Beach, and Miramar Beach, a couple of miles

east of the Okaloosa County border. All of these beaches are among the finest in the country, characterized by sands that look like vast fields of snow, so pure are the quartz crystals, ground to the consistency of fine-texture sugar.

The entire strip of Santa Rosa east of Eglin Air Force Base has the highest dunes in the state, and is accessible via the First through the Seventh Beach freeways, the 55-acre Ross Marler Park, the 40-acre Newman Bracklin Wayside Park (where there are recreation facilities), and the 22-acre John C. Beasley Park. Across East Pass leading from the Gulf of Mexico to Choctawhatchee Bay there are the Silver Beach Wayside Park and the 208-acre Burney Henderson Beach State Recreation Area.

In addition, there's access for swimming and various water sports at strategic sites along the bay, which is one of the Hobie Cat and windsurfing centers of the world.

Such athletic activities are a long way from the splendid isolation of the best of the Gulf beaches in these two counties, but that's part of the appeal of the area. You can get away from it all without making a major expedition. You can have the best of both possible worlds: the mod-mod conveniences of up-to-date accommodations and the satisfaction of good restaurants, maybe a charter fishing trip out into the Gulf or a shot at sailing or windsurfing.

Where It Is
The beaches of Okaloosa and Walton counties are located 25 miles south of Interstate 10 on U.S. 98 midway between Pensacola and Panama City Beach.

Where to Stay

ALOHA VILLAGE
Hotel/Fort Walton Beach
A beachfront money-saving link in the Best Western chain, with standard motel-type rooms and functional modern furnishings. Each room has twin or queen-size beds, and some have kitchenettes. There's a small pool. "Student-age guests" are required to leave a $250 damage deposit on check-in.

866 Santa Rosa Boulevard, Fort Walton Beach 32548. 904-243-3114; toll-free: 1-800-458-8552. Inexpensive.

BLUE HORIZON

Hotel/Fort Walton Beach

On the Okaloosa Island gulf with an indoor pool, hot tub and sauna, a pair of restaurants, water sports gear, and volleyball courts. Kitchenette units are available, and many of the rooms have large private balconies. Within easy walking distance are the Okaloosa Fishing Pier and the Gulfarium.

1120 Santa Rosa Boulevard, Fort Walton Beach 32548. 904-244-5186; toll-free: 1-800-336-3630. Inexpensive to moderate.

CAROUSEL BEACH RESORT

Hotel/Fort Walton Beach

This hotel boasts 105 rooms—singles, efficiencies, and one- and two-bedroom units—with private balconies. Beautiful beachfront location, two swimming pools, sun-sheltering gazebos, a gift shop, and a lounge.

571 Santa Rosa Boulevard, Fort Walton Beach 32548. 904-243-7658; toll-free (outside Florida): 1-800-523-0208. Inexpensive to moderate.

CONDOMINIUM RENTALS

Okaloosa and Walton counties are dotted with a great variety of condominiums, on or very close to the Gulf shore. They offer homes away from home in high-rise accommodations—one-, two-, and three-bedroom units—with fully furnished kitchens and all the facilities. Most of them have swimming pools and some have tennis courts. Numerous realty firms in the area specialize in such rentals. One of the largest, with an impressive portfolio, is Abbott Realty Services, Inc., 35000 Emerald Coast Parkway, P.O. Box 30, Destin, Florida 32541. 904-837-GULF; toll-free: 1-800-874-8914.

HOLIDAY INN

Hotel/Fort Walton Beach

All 385 rooms, including those on the Emerald Floor (with special concierge services), have a view of the hotel's 800 feet of sparkling white-sand beach. A couple of lighted tennis courts, three pools, and a weight room are on the grounds, along with the necessary equipment for snorkeling, sailing, and deep-sea fishing. J.P.'s Restaurant serves light lunches and full-scale steak and seafood dinners. On the ground floor of the seven-story atrium are shops specializing in gifts and women's clothing. Nightly dancing in the lounge.

Highway 98 and Santa Rosa Boulevard, Fort Walton Beach 32548. 904-243-9181; toll-free: 1-800-465-4329. Moderate to expensive.

JAMAICA JOE'S ISLANDER
Hotel/Fort Walton Beach

Includes 106 one- and two-bedroom units, efficiencies with kitchenettes, and some deluxe penthouse-style accommodations, all with balconies. The swimming pool with beach bar is only a few feet from the gentle surf of the Gulf.

790 Santa Rosa Boulevard, Fort Walton Beach 32548. 904-244-4137; toll-free: 1-800-523-0209. Inexpensive to moderate.

RAMADA BEACH RESORT
Resort/Fort Walton Beach

Largest of the chain complexes in the Okaloosa-Walton area, with 454 units, a dramatic lagoon pool with grotto bar, a patio snack bar on the beach, and a place for guests to barbecue by the pool. Among the restaurants, the Lobster House features seafood, the garden Cafe presents Southern-style cuisine in a setting of lush tropical greenery, and the Pelican's Roost offers raw bar selections. There's live entertainment in the lounges, and for those eager to burn off calories there are two tennis courts, whirlpools, saunas and exercise rooms, and an indoor pool, plus the lagoon for swimming.

U.S. Highway 98 East, Fort Walton Beach 32548. 904-243-9161; toll-free: 1-800-2-RAMADA, (in southeast states): 1-800-874-8962. Moderate.

SANDESTIN BEACH HILTON
Resort/Destin

A real stunner on the beach, this ultramodern 15-story tower houses 400 suites, each with private balcony, oversize dressing area, separate bunks for the kids, and the usual Hilton amenities. There are indoor and outdoor swimming pools with spacious sunning decks and beachfront cabanas, and the tennis and golf facilities of the 2,600-acre Sandestin Resort are available—the Hilton is on its land, its sand. The Sandcastles Lounge is graced by a tinkling piano, the poolside Beach Club Grill offers a snack-sandwich menu, and the Sandcastles Restaurant features a menu with stuffed shrimp scampi and broiled amberjack in a pecan-freckled lemon sauce. The restaurant's Sunday brunch, with glazed Cornish game hens, beef Burgundy, roast beef, Belgian waffles, eggs Benedict, and made-to-order omelets, is the best in the two-county area.

5540 Highway 98 East, Destin 32541. 904-267-9500; toll-free: 1-800-367-1271. Expensive.

SANDESTIN BEACH RESORT
Resort Community/Destin

A world-class resort, all 2,600 acres of it, with a total of 575 rooms located in a hotel, in beachfront condominium units, and in villas fronting the golf course or marina, and with more than seven miles of waterfront along the Gulf of Mexico and Choctawhatchee Bay. There are two par-72 championship golf courses and 16 tennis courts, including 3 on grass—and not many resorts can boast that kind of greenery. But then this is one of the top getaway destinations in the nation, carefully manicured and well maintained, and with a fine variety of escapes for snacking and sipping—Babe's Seafood House, with wonderful Friday night seafood buffets; Harry T's, with sandwiches and Sunday brunch; and The Elephant's Walk, with such winners as sautéed jumbo Gulf shrimp spiked with dill and garlic and mingled with angel hair, and pan-fried fresh Gulf snapper with a sauce of peppers and mangoes.

Emerald Coast Parkway, Destin 32541. 904-267-8000; toll-free (outside Florida): 1-800-874-3950. Expensive.

SEASIDE RESORT
Resort/Santa Rosa Beach

If you're ready for a real surprise, the kind that soothes the spirit and stimulates the intellect, make reservations at this 80-acre nugget of nostalgia crisscrossed by white picket fences, fronted by gazebos leading to the incomparable shoreline, and graced by a New England–type commons where classical concerts are given. The village, whose vernacular architecture is unspoiled by high-rises or anything blatantly out of keeping, fans out from a center-stage post office and understated shops. The guest houses, all fully furnished, boast front porches that recall the innocence of a more youthful time, inviting you to rock a spell and relax. When you move in to one of these homes, you'll find a welcoming bottle of wine in the fridge, as well as all the necessities for a continental breakfast. You can prepare your other meals if you wish, but then you'd be missing Bud & Alley's, one of the best restaurants in the Panhandle.

Seaside Community Development Corporation, Box 4730, County Road 30-A, Seaside Branch, Santa Rosa Beach 32459. 904-231-4224. Expensive.

SHERATON CORONADO BEACH RESORT
Hotel/Fort Walton Beach

A beachfront spread of low-rise units with Sheraton standard advantages and amenities, a pool with Jacuzzi and chickee hut shelter, water sports gear, a restaurant, and a lounge. Room furnishings are tropical modern.

1325 Miracle Strip Parkway East, Fort Walton Beach 32548. 904-243-8116; toll-free: 1-800-874-8104. Moderate.

TOPS'L BEACH AND RACQUET CLUB
Resort/Destin

A full-blown resort community large enough to require a tram to take guests from the two- and three-bedroom suites to such diversions as the 12 tennis courts and three racquetball courts; the lighted jogging, walking, and exercise path; the aerobics and Nautilus centers; the sauna, steam room, and health spa (with whirlpools); the indoor and outdoor pools; and all the beach activities—including sailing lessons. The Blue Heron spa features a weeklong fitness program of nutritionally balanced cuisine, supervised exercise, and various beauty-body treatments right down to hair and makeup styling, aromatherapy (herbal treatment to the body), clay baths, and skin-care consultation.

5550 Highway 98 East, Destin 32541. 904-267-9222. Expensive.

Where to Eat

THE BACK PORCH
Seafood/Destin

Directly on the Gulf, which means sparkling days and superb sunsets while you're sipping and snacking on cold smoked shrimp and tuna dip, steamed oysters, and beer-battered onion rings. Although fresh seafood such as char-grilled amberjack is the specialty, you can get a good hamburger, cheeseburger, or char-grilled chicken breast sandwich.

Old Highway 98, a quarter-mile from the junction with new Highway 98 on the Gulf, Destin. 904-837-2022; 904-837-2023. Inexpensive to moderate. Lunch and dinner daily.

BAY CAFE
French/Fort Walton Beach

The French brothers Lamont—Julian in the kitchen, and Pierre out front as manager-maître d'—are at the helm of this simple little bit of waterfront rusticity on Choctawhatchee Bay. We like to sit out on the deck, especially during romantic moon-filled nights, charmed by the Cinzano umbrellas, seduced by the duckling in a brandy-spiked cherry sauce, the seafood pasta primavera, the grouper Wellington flattered with lobster and a splash of champagne—clearly the best French food in the area.

233 Alconese Avenue, Fort Walton Beach. 904-244-3550. Moderate to expensive. Lunch daily, dinner Monday to Saturday.

BAYOU BILL'S
Cajun-American/Santa Rosa Beach
A crab house of the first rank—informal, with nautical decor, a garden room with a skylight that filters in the moon and stars, and reasonable prices for such specialties as buckets of oysters, shrimp, and garlic-laden crabs. The fresh fillets of fish are fried or char-grilled, and the gator tail, favorite of the locals, is sautéed.

Highway 98 East (4 miles east of Sandestin Resort), Santa Rosa Beach. 904-267-3849. Moderate. Dinner Tuesday to Sunday.

THE BEACHSIDE CAFE AND BAR
Continental/Destin
This handsomely decorated retreat is about 700 yards from the beach and sports a fine bar with live music, great for drinking and dancing after a dinner of sautéed snapper, blackened grouper, grilled amberjack, or a sizzling steak. Good wine list.

950 Gulfshore Drive, Holiday Isle, Destin. 904-837-1272. Expensive. Dinner daily.

BUD & ALLEY'S
American/Seaside

This is a beachfront winner, with the ambience of something on a New England shore, a superior wine list, and some of the most imaginative chefs on the Panhandle. From pasta to steaks, soups to snapper, the cuisine is championship caliber. Our favorite meals here start with fresh ceviche, crostini with grilled tomato, or chicken livers coated with onion marmalade, then proceed to the New York strip steak, with roast garlic and fresh horseradish, accompanied by grilled polenta and sautéed greens; or the grilled lamb loin soaked in port with laurel, fresh herbs, and juniper berries.

State Road 30A, Seaside. 904-231-5900. Expensive. Lunch and dinner Wednesday to Monday.

CRIOLLA'S
Creole-Caribbean/Santa Rosa Beach

One of the best restaurants in Florida, owned and operated by chef Johnny Earles, a back-bayou boy with the touch of genius and the desire to expand horizons, here and abroad. We recommend anything and everything on Johnny's menu, but count yourself lucky if the fare of the day includes starters of crawfish beignets, conch escabeche, and criolla colado—grilled tenderloin chili layered with masa, steamed in banana leaves, and served with ancho tomato salsa—and such terrific entrees as curried shrimp with coconut spring roll, creole-curried oysters, wood-grilled lamb chops, or tuna mignon, wrapped with zucchini and smoked bacon, finished with key lime beurre blanc.

Highway 30A, 1 mile west of Surfside, Santa Rosa Beach. 904-267-1267. Moderate. Dinner daily.

FLAMINGO CAFE
American-Creole/Destin

A superior restaurant in a superlative location, ideal for watching the sunset. We start our meals here with either the crab-laced asparagus soup, the blackened shrimp on angel hair smoothed by pecan butter, or the oysters Bienville, then move on to the hot crayfish salad before tackling the soft-shells, or the grouper Pontchartrain, or the veal Oscar, all while indulging in an excellent selection of wines by the glass and enjoying the trendy black-white decor.

414 Highway 98, Destin. 904-837-0961. Expensive. Dinner daily.

GRAYTON CORNER CAFE
American/Grayton Beach

This converted beach cottage, informally furnished with wickerware, serves as the setting for a solid selection of deli sandwiches, raw bar treats, salads, burgers, and terrific char-grilled fish sandwhiches.

1 Defuniak Street, Route 2, Box 831, Grayton Beach. 904-231-1211. Inexpensive. Lunch and dinner daily.

HARBOR DOCKS
Seafood/Destin

Overlooking Destin Harbor with its own seafood market alongside and an outside deck for dining on the water, this eatery specializes in the fresh Florida catch of the day broiled, fried, char-grilled, or Cajunized—all in the traditional manner. For something completely different try some of the Thai dishes.

Highway 98, Destin. 904-837-2506. Moderate. Lunch and dinner daily.

THE LAKE PLACE
Continental/Santa Rosa Beach

You can be sure everything served here is fresh. Owners Susan and Peter Mulcahey dispense with menus because they're a by-the-market restaurant. Our favorite meals here commence with the crab bisque and then proceed to pasta followed by some of their wonderful seafood.

Route 30A, Santa Rosa Beach. 904-267-2871. Moderate. Dinner Tuesday to Saturday. No credit cards.

LeBLEU'S CAJUN KITCHEN
Cajun/Santa Rosa Beach

We love the catfish, served either broiled or fried; the barbecue pork sandwiches, with potato salad and baked beans; the Cajun steak and shrimp specialties; and of course, the red beans and rice. The cole slaw is fresh and crisp and the crawfish pie delicious. Breakfasts are homemade-wonderful, with biscuits and gravy, omelets—including a Cajun-style one—grits, home fries, and pancakes. This is a favorite of the locals and of ours—our caps are among the hundreds, maybe thousands, adorning the walls and ceiling.

Highway 98 East (between Highways 393 and 331), Santa Rosa Beach. 904-267-3724. Inexpensive. Breakfast, lunch, and dinner daily.

MARINA CAFE
Continental/Destin

A sensational setting, complete with an outdoor deck overlooking the harbor from the second floor of the Destin Yacht Club. The prime steaks and filets mignon are outstanding, but so are the Louisiana-inspired dishes—the crawfish, oysters, and crabcakes—and those farinaceous high-flyers, including our favorite, the penne mingled with chunks of baby eggplant, buffalo mozzarella, plum tomatoes, and pine nuts, and dressed with extra virgin olive oil zapped with fresh basil and garlic. The seafood medley is marvelous, with its combination of soft-shell crab, shrimp, scallops, and fresh fillets of snapper, amberjack, or swordfish.

Destin Yacht Club (2nd floor), 320 Highway 98E, Destin. 904-837-7960. Moderate to expensive. Dinner daily.

NENA'S
American/Santa Rosa Beach

Transplanted Texan Nena Prejean is the main force in this happy, family-pleasing 100-seater with money-saving early-bird and off-season dinners and a regular menu built around her homemade everything, including excellent baked-out-back breads and such desserts as Louisiana bread pudding spiked with brandy. We especially like the shrimp Marie, a mingling of shrimp, artichokes, tomatoes, and snow peas on angel hair pasta crowned with crabmeat and showered with pine nuts. Another favorite is the Fish Czanzary, grilled fresh fillets layered with creole-seasoned vegetables and shrimp.

Highway 98 East, Santa Rosa Beach. 904-267-3663. Moderate to expensive. Dinner daily.

NICK'S
Seafood/Freeport and Santa Rosa Beach
From the outside each of these restaurants looks like just another roadhouse, but inside you'll find some of the best fried fish in Florida. We are not great fans of fried oysters—except at Nick's, where they approach the level of heavenly perfection. The steamed crabs are also terrific. Frank and Bonnie Nick should win an award for such performances.

Route 1, Basin Bayou Highway 20, Freeport; 904-835-2222. Highway 30-A, Santa Rosa Beach; 904-267-2117. Inexpensive to moderate. Lunch and dinner daily at the Freeport location; dinner daily at Santa Rosa Beach.

THE SOUND
Continental/Fort Walton Beach
A family pleaser with a good selection of dishes featuring snapper and shrimp, grouper, crabs, oysters, and scallops. But not to be overlooked are the prime rib and the steaks, although it's usually hard for us to pass up the char-grilled or blackened amberjack. Its location on Santa Rosa Sound and the Intracoastal Waterway is another reason to find this spot.

108 Miracle Strip (West Highway 98), Fort Walton Beach. 904-243-2722; 904-243-2772. Moderate to expensive. Lunch and dinner daily.

Where to Shop

Alvin's Island Department Stores, 1204 Highway 98 East, Fort Walton Beach (904-244-3913); and 1073 Highway 98, Destin (904-837-5178), have everything from clothing to beach toys, tanning products, and picnic supplies.

Angelika's Gift Shop, Highway 30A, Route 1, Box 334-A, Santa Rosa Beach (904-267-3053), has an assortment of souvenirs and quality gifts.

The **Market at Sandestin,** Highway 98 East, Destin, has over 20 shops, including the **Islander** (904-654-4144), with contemporary beach and casual wear for the young and young at heart; **Jamaica Joe's** (904-837-1149), for ladies' resort, casual, and beachwear with a small selection for men and children; **Sandestin Signature** (904-267-5550), featuring casual cotton clothing for the beach, T-shirts, sweats, and souvenirs of all sorts for the family; and **Tarzana's** (904-654-1762), with the latest in swimwear for ladies and children.

Santa Rosa Mall, at Mary Esther Cutoff, three blocks from the beach, has 120 more vendors, including restaurants, a video arcade, a pharmacy, and just about any type of shop imaginable.

The intimate little spread of **Shops at Seaside** harmonizes beautifully with the spirit of the place and offers upscale resortwear for men and women, unique gifts, books, snacks, and an all-purpose food market with gourmet deli items.

Shores Shopping Center, across from Holiday Isle in Destin, is home to the **Mole Hole** (904-837-8070), for original handcrafted items, unusual gifts, art, and toys; **Sporty Lady of Destin** (904-837-6763), for beach, sports, casual, and evening wear; **Today's** (904-837-3150), for the latest in jewelry, clothing, prints, and gifts; and the **Rainbow Connection** (904-837-2055), the place for ladies' and children's clothing of all sorts.

More Fun in the Sun

The **Billy Bowlegs Festival,** held annually the second week of June in Fort Walton Beach, began in 1955 and gets bigger and better each year, with a new Captain Billy Bowlegs named to head his crew of pirates landing to take over the city. One hundred booths are filled with food and arts and crafts, and there's nonstop entertainment. The Torchlight Parade, the coronation of Captain Billy Bowlegs, performances by the Northwest Florida Ballet Association, concerts, sailing regattas, volleyball tournaments, beauty contests, and a fireworks display are all crowd-pleasers.

The **Fort Walton Beach Seafood Festival** is held the second week of April at the Okaloosa County Fairgrounds. Started in 1981 by the Fort Walton Beach Art Museum Association, the annual festival features art shows, fairs, boat cruises, fish fries, a flea market, antique and model car shows, a train ride, and 'round-the-clock entertainment including puppet shows, clowns, and country and rock music.

Cash's Faux Pas, 106 Santa Rosa Boulevard, Okaloosa Island (904-244-2274), with live entertainment in season, is one of the favorites of nightclubbers in North Florida.

Charter boat fleets in the Destin area, otherwise known as "The World's Luckiest Fishing Village," number over 100 and are among the best equipped in the United States. A list would take the next several pages, so strike out on your own and inquire at your home-away-from-home or at the marinas that dot this coast. The **Destin Fishing Rodeo** (P.O. Box 296, Destin 32541) is an annual October tournament that began in 1948 and awards cash prizes to men, women, and juniors.

Okaloosa Island Pier, Highway 98 East, four and a half miles west of Destin and three-quarters of a mile east of Fort Walton Beach (904-244-1023), stretches 1,261 feet out into the Gulf for a good day's fishing. You can rent poles, bait buckets, and tackle at the **Pier Bait Shop,** and when it's time for lunch, take a break at the **Pier Snack Bar.**

Fantasea Scuba Headquarters, 1 Highway 98 East (toll-free [in Florida]: 1-800-326-2732), sells and rents equipment for underwater ventures with dive charters available. **Paradise Beach Service** (904-664-7872), on Choctaw Bay near the Ramada Inn, is the headquarters for Jet Skis, waverunners, pontoon boats, catamarans, and parasailing and windsurfing equipment. **Baytown Marina at Sandestin** (904-267-7777) is another outlet on the bayside where you can rent water sports equipment. These vendors close December through February.

Gulfarium, Okaloosa Island (904-244-5169), on the beach next to the pier, features otters, penguins, tropical birds, alligators, and harbor seals, along with performing porpoises and sea lions. At the Living Sea exhibit you can see moray eels, sharks, stingrays, giant sea turtles, and various types of exotic marine life in their natural habitats. A large gift shop with a great selection of souvenirs and gifts is on the premises.

Indian Temple Mound Museum, U.S. Highway 98 (904-243-6521), exhibits relics of the first 10,000 years of habitation in this north Florida area. The Temple Mound was designated a National Historic Landmark and has been restored to its original condition.

Museum of the Sea and Indian, 4801 Beach Road (Old Highway 98) (904-837-6625), has been in operation for 30 years. Located on the beach eight miles east of Destin, this museum features exhibits from Indian tribes throughout North, Central, and South America and hundreds of marine exhibits, mostly from the Gulf but also from the waters around the world. There are live alligators, monkeys, and exotic birds. At the **Shell Shop Trading Post** you can purchase souvenirs such as Indian jewelry, clothing, and artifacts, and choose from the best selection of seashells in the area.

Santa Rosa Golf & Beach Club, Highway 98, Route 1 Box 3950 (904-267-2229), a member-owned 18-hole course open to the public, is located on the beach, which means you can take your rays with the balmy breezes while improving your handicap. Tennis courts, a restaurant, and a lounge are also on the premises.

Where to Write

Destin Chamber of Commerce, P.O. Box 8, Destin, Florida 32541. 904-837-6241.

Emerald Coast Tourist Development Council, P.O. Box 609, Fort Walton Beach, Florida 32549. 904-681-9200; toll-free: 1-800-322-3319.

Fort Walton Beach Chamber of Commerce, P.O. Drawer 640, Fort Walton Beach, Florida 32549. 904-244-8191.

Grayton Beach State Recreation Area, Route 2, Box 6600, Santa Rosa Beach, Florida 32459. 904-231-4210.

Greater Fort Walton Beach Chamber of Commerce, P.O. Box 640, Fort Walton Beach, Florida 32548. 904-244-8191.

Northwest Florida Emerald Coast Tourist Development, P.O. Box 609, Fort Walton, Florida 32549-0609. 904-651-7131.

South Walton Chamber of Commerce, P.O. Box 29, Defuniak Springs, Florida 32433. 904-267-3511.

South Walton Tourist Development Council, 1248 Santa Rosa Beach, Florida 32459. Toll-free: 1-800-822-6877, (in Canada): 1-800-248-8344.

Walton County Chamber of Commerce, P.O. Box 29, Defuniak Springs, Florida 32433. 904-892-3191.

◎ ◎ ◎

PANAMA CITY BEACH

The narrow strip of Gulf shore between Panama City and Pensacola is the popular weekend and summer vacation ground for many Alabamans who travel less than 100 miles to achieve a salt-water tan." Those words from the 1939 WPA Guide to Florida are just as true today, but we can also add other states of the Deep South whose sun-seekers and body-bronzers have claimed this portion of Florida as their own beachfront "Riviera."

From Memorial Day to Labor Day the vacationers stream like lemmings to the beaches, as soft and seductively white as new-fallen snow, washed ever so gently by the emerald-turquoise waters of the Gulf of Mexico. During those months the Miracle Strip, as this section of the coast is known, comes alive. The cruising lanes are filled with modern-day Confederates, and the motels, hotels, and resorts overflow with work-weary wanderers who make a summer holiday in Panama City Beach an annual family tradition.

Amusements and attractions abound, and there are restaurants and snack shops to suit any and all tastes and pocketbooks. By the middle of September, however, the crowds recede like the tides, and in the winter months, when central and south Florida are invaded, the Panhandle and Panama City Beach shutter many of their doors, and a different kind of Southerner starts arriving—in trickles. There are those from South Florida who want to flee the snowbirds flying in from the Northeast and Midwest, and those who yearn for the isolation and more bracing temperatures—without going to any frozen extremes. This area is "the other Florida," which we first learned to love in the early 1950s, not during its crowded summer season but at other times of the year, when we luxuriated in splendid isolation on some of the most beautiful beaches in the world.

The St. Andrews State Recreation Area, reached by Thomas Drive off U.S. 98, has superior swimming from its sandy shores and in a pool by the shallow, protected jetty; there's superb fishing from that jetty—or from a pair of piers—for bluefish and bonito, dolphin, flounder, and redfish. There are nature trails into the wilderness and modern conveniences—snack stands, showers, rest rooms, a boat ramp and rentals, group camping accommodations, changing rooms, and picnic sites—spread over 1,063 acres of piney woods, marshland, and rolling dunes covered with the vital, protective dune grasses, sea oats, marsh hay, and panic grass.

Also at St. Andrews is a carefully reconstructed "teppentine" still, the kind once found all over the area when turpentine production was a vital part of the economy. Just as interesting an insight into the past is the reconstructed saltworks, the kind that proliferated in the Panhandle during the War Between the States until they were systematically destroyed by the Yankees in 1862.

The eastern section of the recreation area, Shell Island, is reached by boat (ferry and charter information is available at St. Andrews Recreation Area or at Panama City Beach marinas) and is well worth the trip—but only if you want to experience one of the greatest beaches in the world, seven miles spread along a barrier island covered by undulating dunes cloaked with grasses, wild myrtle, dwarf magnolia, and endless clumps of rosemary, said to have been introduced by the English when Florida was part of their colonial empire. Carefully preserved in a primitive state, the island is free of facilities and modern encroachments of any kind. So if you're planning to spend more than a few hours, remember to take your own refreshments and sun shades—and remember to remove all of your refuse when you catch the boat back to civilization.

When you get back you'll find easy access to many other beaches, including Biltmore Beach, adjacent to the western end of St. Andrews; the Panama City Beach, with some 1,500 feet of developed shoreline and nine miles still undeveloped; and the Bay County Pier and Park on the Miracle Strip Parkway. Access points from a string of streets leading to the beach are too numerous to mention, but they're easy to find; and of course, there are numerous accommodations fronting the Gulf's bluer-than-blue waters.

Where It Is

Panama City Beach is in the middle of the Florida Panhandle, 107 miles east of Pensacola and 97 miles west of Tallahassee, reached by Thomas Drive off U.S. 98 to east Panama City Beach, or directly by 98, which runs along the coast of West Panama City Beach.

Where to Stay

CHATEAU
Motel/Panama City Beach

With 152 rooms and kitchen-furnished suites, private balconies, and coffee and gift shops, this misnamed motel is across the road from the Miracle Strip Amusement Park—an ideal destination for those who want a non-Disney retro-trip to a remake of the movie *Grease*.

12525 Highway Alternate 98, Panama City Beach 32407. 904-234-2174; toll-free: 1-800-874-8826. Moderate.

EDGEWATER BEACH RESORT
Resort/Panama City Beach

High-rise and low-rise accommodations are gathered around a sensational free-form lagoon swimming pool caressed by thousands of tropical plants. There are also heated whirlpools here and there. Elsewhere in the complex are a dozen each of shuffleboard and tennis courts, a 9-hole par-3 golf course, and a few thousand feet of beachfront. Plus, there's a pretty good restaurant on the premises; for lunch, we like the fried grouper sandwiches and the steak-and-cheese Phillys; for dinner, the lobster in champagne sauce and the crab-filled shrimp.

11212 Alternate Highway 98, P.O. Box 9850, Panama City Beach 32407. 904-235-4044; toll-free (outside Florida): 1-800-874-8686. Expensive.

FLAMINGO
Motel/Panama City Beach

All the rooms and apartments have a fridge or fully furnished kitchen, and all but one have a view of the Gulf or the unique dome-covered tropical garden, lushly landscaped with ferns and palms, surrounding the swimming pool that overlooks the beach.

15525 West Highway 98, Panama City Beach 32407. 904-234-2232; toll-free: 1-800-828-0400. Inexpensive to moderate.

GULFCREST
Motel/Panama City Beach

A standard two-story motel functionally furnished and featuring a variety of accommodations ranging from rooms with two double beds to efficiencies and two-bedroom apartments with kitchenettes. There's a swimming pool and acres of powdered sugar sand out front.

8715 Surf Drive, Panama City Beach 32407. 904-234-3328. Inexpensive to moderate.

GULFVIEW INN
Inn/Sunnyside

This country inn owned by a family from Tennessee, the Nances, offers out-of-the-ordinary accommodations across the street from the beach. The owners boast that their homemade jams are reason enough to stay and, coupled with their Southern hospitality, they might be right. All five rooms have a private bath and entrance, and most of them have a beautiful view of the Gulf. The inn is located across from the dunes—you can't beat this for "Old Florida" sunset-watching.

21722 West 98A, Sunnyside 32461. 904-234-6051. Moderate.

MARRIOTT BAY POINT RESORT
Resort/Bay Point–Panama City Beach
If there's anything this 1,100-acre fun-creational resort lacks we haven't found it. There are two and a half miles of waterfront, 30 stocked ponds, three miles of canals, 300 acres of forest, 36 holes of championship golf, a dozen Har-Tru tennis courts, half a dozen swimming pools, seven restaurants, three lounges, sailing, windsurfing, golf and tennis lessons, free use of cycles and Windsurfers, *plus* harbor rides on a modern Mississippi paddle-wheeler, *plus* an active program—including aquarobics—for the young ones. Transportation to the pristine wilderness of Shell Island is available. With the largest private yacht marina on the Gulf Coast, 355 guest rooms and suites, rental condominium villas, and a full flood of meeting and conference facilities, this is the premier resort of the Panama City Beach area and one of the finest to be found anywhere in Florida.

100 Delwood Beach Road, Bay Point 32407. 904-234-3307; toll-free: 1-800-974-7105. Expensive.

MIRACLE MILE RESORT
Hotels/Panama City Beach
Not one but four hotels, anchored by the Sheraton Miracle Mile Inn, with the Barefoot Beach Inn, Gulfside Miracle Mile Inn, and Sands Inn alongside, comprising a total of 640 rooms, suites, and kitchenette units with modern tropical furnishings. There are restaurants, snack shops, and lounges, along with swimming pools and the usual amenities. It's the ideal location for those who want the advantages of a large-scale resort and a location away from all the hustle and bustle of the amusement and commercial sections of the Miracle Strip. In the Gulfside Inn, a ballroom has been converted to a 300-seat theater to serve as summer home for the ten-week season for the Florida State University Summer Music Theater.

9450 South Thomas Drive, Panama City Beach 32407. 904-234-3484; toll-free: 1-800-874-6613. Inexpensive to moderate.

PORTERS COURT
Hotel/Panama City Beach

For more than three decades, this multiunit money-saver has been catering to families in its beachfront units, some with two double beds and a fridge, others with a suite-size living room and sofa bed, fully furnished kitchen, and private balcony. Our favorite accommodations are the cottages, with two bedrooms, living room with sofa bed, kitchen, and front porch facing the Gulf a few feet from the swimming pool.

17013 West Highway 98A, Panama City Beach 32407. 904-234-2752; toll-free: 1-800-421-9950. Inexpensive to moderate.

THE REEF
Hotel/Panama City Beach

Here's a real budget-pleaser—and it's directly across the street from the Miracle Strip Amusement Park and not far from the Bay County fishing pier, longest in the Gulf of Mexico. The comfortably outfitted rooms have private balconies, and some have fully furnished kitchenettes with large refrigerators. There's also a small swimming pool directly on the beach.

12011 Front Beach Road, Panama City Beach 32407. 904-234-3396. Inexpensive.

SEA LODGE
Motel/Panama City Beach

A modern and immaculately maintained beachfront hugger with single and double rooms, some with fully furnished kitchenettes. A few feet from the aquamarine waters of the Gulf is a fine little swimming pool with chickees and sunning decks.

14825 Front Beach Road, Panama City Beach 32413. 904-234-3394; toll-free: 1-800-874-2882. Inexpensive to moderate.

SHALIMAR PLAZA
Motel/Panama City Beach

One of the more attractive motels on the strip, with a private tennis court and a swimming pool flanked by fine sunning decks. Accommodations range from simple single rooms to one- and two-room units with kitchenettes. There's no restaurant or coffee shop on the premises, but across the street are a popular diner and a convenience store, and not far distant are many other places to please palates and pocketbooks.

17545 Front Beach Road, Panama City Beach 32407. 904-234-2133; toll-free: 1-800-232-2435. Inexpensive to moderate.

SUGAR SANDS MOTEL
Motel/Panama City Beach

The perfect name for a motel on the 27 miles of Panama City Beach area, and another budget-happy destination. Nothing fancy and with truly functionally furnished rooms, many with a kitchenette and a private balcony, some consisting of two bedrooms and a living room. And there is a pool, plus volleyball nets and shuffleboard courts and outdoor grills for barbecuing your catch— from the Gulf or the grocery.

20723 Front Beach Road, Panama City Beach 32407. 904-234-8802; toll-free: 1-800-367-9221. Inexpensive to moderate.

Where to Eat

ANGELO'S STEAK PIT
American/Panama City Beach

Steak prepared on an open pit is the specialty at this down-home-western family feedery with the huge bull out front. The chicken, barbecue ribs, and seafood are as reliable as the steaks.

9527 West Highway 98, Panama City Beach. 904-234-2531. Moderate. Dinner daily. Closed October 1 through March 1.

BILLY'S OYSTER BAR I & II
Seafood/Panama City Beach

These are classic raw bars in the best Florida sense of the word, with the beauteous bivalves of the state's hard-shell harvest transported from Apalachicola or Mobile bays. The rugged honesty of the setting is matched by the quality and freshness of the seafood served. We come here for the baked oysters, steamed Florida blue crab, and the combination platters.

I: 3000 Thomas Drive, Panama City Beach; 904-235-2319. II: one mile west of Phillip's Inlet, Panama City Beach; 904-231-5487. Inexpensive to moderate. Lunch and dinner daily.

BISHOP'S GULF FAMILY BUFFET
American/Panama City Beach

Here's hog heaven for the stuff-yourself-silly set: morning, noon, and night buffets at budget prices. Start your day with a half dozen waffles, at noon devour a few dozen popcorn shrimp and a burger or two, and at dinner make a round-trip to the table for the fried and broiled seafood, the chicken, and the roast beef. And of course, indulge in a few desserts here and there.

12628 West Highway 98, Panama City Beach. 904-234-6457. Inexpensive. Breakfast, lunch, and dinner daily.

BOAR'S HEAD
American/Panama City Beach

Tourists flock here for the seafood, consuming by the thousands the fried blue crab fingers, oysters in mustard sauce, and charbroiled shrimp, before digging into the sautéed swordfish layered with onions and peppers, or the broiled or fried flounder, grouper, and snapper. But the locals love the products from the plains: the thick, perfectly grilled steaks and the prime rib. And of course the barbecue ribs and the best baby-back bones in the Panhandle—from domestically raised porkers, not wild boars, despite the imposing boar's head at the entrance.

17290 Front Beach Road, Panama City Beach. 904-234-6628. Moderate to expensive. Dinner daily, May 15 to September 15; dinner Tuesday to Sunday, September 16 to May 14. Closed the month of December.

CAPTAIN ANDERSON'S
Seafood/Panama City Beach

The brothers Patronis, Johnny and Jimmy, have been at the helm of this dockside delight since 1969. Named for the captain who sent his fleet out from these docks a century ago, this spacious and closely supervised super-success is a perennial winner of *Florida Trend* magazine's Golden Spoon Award as one of the best restaurants in the state. You'll give your own awards after you've tasted the grilled shrimp or churrasco steak, the Greek salad tossed with shrimp and crabmeat, or the crab-stuffed Gulf flounder, or what the brothers promise is "The World's Finest Seafood Platter."

5551 North Lagoon Drive, Panama City Beach. 904-234-2225. Moderate. Dinner Monday to Saturday. Closed November 1 through February 1.

CAPTAIN DAVIS DOCKSIDE RESTAURANT
American/Panama City Beach

The name is an accurate one. This captain is very definitely dockside, with a wall of high, wide, and handsome windows overlooking all the action of the marina and the boat parades on the Grand Lagoon. It should come as no surprise that seafood is the specialty, but do not overlook the steaks or the prime rib.

5550 North Lagoon Drive, Panama City Beach. 904-234-3608. Moderate. Dinner Thursday to Tuesday.

FIDDLER'S GREEN
American/Panama City Beach

Start your evening here with a trip to the nearby water-surrounded, tin-roofed Teddy Tucker's for phase one of the nightly sunset ritual. Phase two takes place on the Fiddler's deck or in the dining room, where you watch the Gulf take its final gulp of the sun while you work through the superior crabcakes in a mustard-spiked beurre blanc, followed by a fillet of the Gulf's famous snapper, or the swordfish, plainly grilled or lightly layered with Parmesan and served with fettuccine, and a jiggling plate of flan to finish. The setting is comfortably upscale, with dramatic decorative touches and top-quality table appointments. The luncheon salads and sandwiches are kind to diets, and the bountiful breakfast buffets are real eye-poppers.

100 Delwood Beach Road, Panama City Beach. 904-234-3307. Moderate to expensive. Breakfast, lunch, and dinner daily.

THE MELTING POT
Swiss/Panama City Beach

If you too do fondue, this is the place, part of a small chain of melted-cheese-and-chocolate servers for the do-it-yourself dipping set. Chicken, beef, seafood, bread, veggies, and fruits—they offer it all.

11053 Middle Beach Road, Panama City Beach. 904-233-6633. Moderate. Dinner daily.

MIKATO JAPANESE STEAKHOUSE
Japanese/Panama City Beach

If you're looking for a sushi fix or want to watch ambidextrous Samurai chefs prepare your filet mignon, chicken, jumbo shrimp, mushrooms, onions, and zucchini before your very eyes, check into this Americanized version of a Japanese restaurant and watch the smiling chefs working the teppan grill.

7724 West Highway 98 Alternate, Panama City Beach. 904-235-1338. Moderate to expensive. Dinner daily.

MONTEGO BAY SEAFOOD HOUSE & OYSTER BAR
Seafood/Various Panama City Beach Locations

Here's a budget-pleaser with a wide variety of noontime seafood salads, burgers, and sandwiches, as well as such hearty fare as liver and onions, veal Parmesan, and pork chops. Come dinner, you'll want to consider (while the wee ones are working over the children's menu) such Cajun creations as blackened fillets of fish, back bayou gumbo, and red beans and rice. But don't overlook the farinaceous features or the excellent grilled amberjack.

9949 Thomas Drive; 904-235-3585. 4920 Thomas Drive East; 904-234-8686. The Shoppes at Edgewater, 472 Beckrich Road; 904-233-6033. 17118 Front Beach Road; 904-233-2900. Inexpensive. Lunch and dinner daily.

THEO'S
Continental/Panama City Beach

The chef here prepares American food with a French-Mediterranean flair. The sauces are light, the steaks are beautiful, the seafood and poultry noteworthy. Lobster thermador, broiled grouper, and the house specialty, shrimp Theo— shrimp lightly coated in flour and sautéed in white sherry—are among the fresh seafood choices.

4423 West Highway 98, Panama City Beach. 904-785-2998. Moderate to expensive. Dinner daily.

Where to Shop

Alvin's Island Tropical Department Stores, with 13 outlets on the beach or directly across from it, is one of America's top ten retail chains, with a large selection of swimwear, resortwear, beach supplies and accessories, and an assortment of souvenirs. Located at 12010 West Highway 98 (904-234-3048); 14520 West Highway 98 (904-234-2411); and at Alvin's Magic Mountain Mall, 12010 Highway 98 (904-234-6760).

Fields' World, 12700 West Highway 98 (904-234-6500); **Fields' Family Sportswear,** 5912 Thomas Drive (904-233-1623); **Fields' Sun & Sea,** Front Beach Road and Middle Beach Road intersection (904-235-3677), are good-value family department stores with everything imaginable for the vacationer from beach supplies and tanning lotion and water toys of all sizes to swimwear and casual clothing, picnic essentials, souvenirs, and gifts.

Maharaja of India, Bahama Plaza, 13514 West Scenic Highway 98 (904-234-6488), has wonderful designer jewelry and individually crafted beach and casual wear for ladies.

Shops at Edgewater, 555 Beckrich Road, has a drugstore, grocery, snack shops, and the latest-fashion casual and beach clothing at **Beach Scene** (904-233-1662) and **New Spirit Clothing** (904-233-8560). **Quick Snap Photo** (904-234-7160) is the place for developing those great vacation pictures or for finding film and other camera supplies. Also, if you want to escape sun and shore and watch the latest flicks, **Cinema 6** (904-234-9232) has daily showings from noon 'til night.

World of 25,000 T-Shirts, 12700 West Highway 98 (904-234-2929), lets you wear your own message (custom airbrushed) or something silly from its huge inventory.

More Fun in the Sun

The **Annual Indian Summer Seafood Festival,** usually held during the second week of October, is a three-day event, Friday through Sunday, featuring country music, magicians, jugglers, acrobats, a Saturday parade, and more than 100 food and craft booths.

Captain Anderson's Marina (904-234-3435; toll-free [in the Southern states]: 1-800-874-2415) offers full-day and half-day deep-sea fishing trips, charters, daily sight-seeing trips, and—from Memorial Day through Labor Day—dinner-dance cruises (call 904-234-5940 for dinner cruises).

City Pier, 16101 West Highway 98A (904-233-5080), the longest in the Gulf (1,642 feet), is great for fishing. You can rent all tackle and purchase bait at **Pier Tackle**, owned by **Half-Hitch Tackle** (904-235-2576).

Coconut Creek Mini-Golf, 9807 West Highway 98 (904-234-2625), has two elaborately designed courses filled with rocky mountains and waterfalls, lagoons and bridges, animal figures and tiki huts. **Pirate's Island Adventure Golf**, 9518 Front Beach Road (904-235-1171), is open daily for family fun on two 18-hole courses filled with pirate scenery and located in the midst of tall pine trees, waterfalls, island peaks, and caves complete with dripping stalactites.

The Panama Beach area ranks with Key Largo in affording what is considered some of the best diving in the country. The area has hundreds of natural and artificial reefs as well as wrecks that include a 465-foot British tanker torpedoed in 1942 by a German U-boat, an 1800s shuttle that sank in 1937, and the cargo vessel used by Admiral Byrd in his 1920s Antarctic exploration. Dive shops scheduling excursions to the sites include: **Hydrospace Dive Shop**, 3605-A Thomas Drive (904-234-9463) and 6422 West Highway 98 (904-234-3063), the Gulf's largest; **Diver's Den**, 3804 Thomas Drive (904-234-8717; toll-free: 1-800-832-3483); **Holiday Scuba Center, Inc.**, 481 Beckrich Road (904-769-7842); **Hydrospace Dive Shop**, Bridge Tender Marina, 6400 West Highway 98 (904-234-3063); **Hydrospace Dive Shop West**, 3605-A Thomas Drive (904-234-9463; toll-free: 1-800-874-3483); and **Panama City Dive Center**, 4823-A Thomas Drive (904-235-3390).

Golfers from pro to beginner can do their swinging on these excellent courses: **Holiday Golf and Tennis Driving Range**, 100 Fairway Boulevard (904-234-1800); **The Hombre**, 120 Coyote Pass Highway 98 (904-234-FORE); **Lagoon Legend**, 100 Delwood Beach Road (904-234-3307), with a green surrounded by water, for the precision hitter; **Signal Hill Golf Course**, 9615 North Thomas Drive (904-234-3307), best suited for the average player.

Gulf World, 15412 Front Beach Road (904-234-5271), with a new dolphin petting pool, has a variety of shows starring the bottlenose dolphin, sea lions, and magnificently colored tropical parrots.

Miracle Strip Amusement Park, 12000 West Highway 98 (904-234-5810), has nine fun-filled acres with over 60 rides, 13 arcades of games, live entertainment, and a mass of fast snack food offerings. It's a real blast from the pre-Disney and Six Flags past. We stay dry riding the roller coaster, the oversize pirate ship *Sea Dragon*, the Crazy Daze, the Octopus, or the Scrambler, and when the sun is high we get wet at the adjacent **Shipwreck Island Waterpark** (904-234-0368; closed from the end of September through March 1) on the Pirates' Plunge water slide, in the Ocean Motion wave pool, or roaring down the rapids of the White Water Tube Ride. The strong of heart can shoot 35 miles an hour down the rushing waters of the Speed Slide into the safety of the lagoon. This wet-and-wild theme park covers six acres of beautifully landscaped grounds. After energy levels drop you can relax and cruise on the Lazy River Ride.

Ocean Opry Country Music Jubilee, 8400 Front Beach Road 98A (904-234-5464), features the Rader family as well as such nationally renowned country music performers as Stella Parton, Jeanie Pruitt, and Jim Ed Brown on Celebrity Saturdays. Off-season shows are scheduled Tuesday, Friday, and Saturday. Call ahead for times.

Southern Elegance Cruise Lines, Sun Harbor Marina at the east end of Hathaway Bridge (904-785-3006; toll-free: 1-800-346-SHIP), offers a six-hour cruise filled with the excitement of a real casino with roulette, crap tables, slot machines, and blackjack.

Spinnaker, 8795 South Thomas Drive (904-234-7892), is *the* party place of Panama City Beach. Located directly on the beachfront, this nightclub-beachclub has 20 bars, three stages, and a large free-form pool. The springbreakers know this is the place to be. Tour buses bring the college escapees in daily during the riot days of the season for the vacation of their lives. Call the live entertainment hot line (904-234-7882) to find out who's playing. The fun starts in the morning and goes nonstop until the wee hours of the next morning.

Where to Write

Panama City Beach Chamber of Commerce, 12015 Front Beach Road, Panama City Beach, Florida 32407. 904-234-3193.

Panama City Beach Visitor and Convention Bureau, P.O. Box 9473, Panama City Beach, Florida 32407. 1-800-PCBEACH.

St. Andrews State Recreation Area, 4415 Thomas Drive, Panama City, Florida 32407. 904-234-2522.

◎　　◎　　◎

SANDY SHANGRI-LAS: DOG ISLAND AND ST. JOSEPH PENINSULA STATE PARK

When you're weary of the bustle and hustle of the mod-mad world, when you really want to, have to get away from it all, head for the Panhandle and its strips of island sand standing as silent sentinels between land and sea. Head for our two favorite lonely island escapes, Dog Island, one of the three barrier islands in Apalachicola Bay, or the St. Joseph State Park, the tip of a peninsula pointing the way to the mainland and, for better or worse, civilization.

Dog Island

Dog Island, nearly seven miles long and less than a mile across at its widest point, made its first map appearance in 1690 when French explorers named it Isles aux Chiens, probably because there were wild dogs on the island, possibly because the outline of the land resembled a crouching dog.

The easternmost of the Apalachicola barrier islands, it is reached only by air (you land in a grassy field at the eastern extremity), or via private boat or the 45-minute ferry ride on the *Ruby B*. The ferry is docked at the crossroads called Carabelle, five miles across the bay on U.S. 98, which licks most of the Panhandle shoreline from south of Tallahassee to Pensacola. Carabelle is about halfway between the fishing village of Panacea and the oyster capital of Apalachicola.

What to do when you get there? Nothing, if that's your need. Just sit and ponder the gentle surf, or admire the magnificent dunes, some of the highest untrammeled mounds of sand in the state. Or you can stroll the beaches that fringe the shorelines and protect the shallow sound from the deeper demands of the waves from the Gulf of Mexico.

Study the natural growths of the dunes, the goldenrod and sea lavender; marvel at all the marsh grasses and the black mangrove, whose spidery legs are rooted deep in the water to form over time, lots of time, more padding on the edges of the spit of sand standing so boldly as waterbound protector.

In the elevated stretches of land, there are sand and slash pines, and clumps of rosemary said to have been introduced into these Panhandle parts by the British during their occupation of Florida at the time of the American Revolution.

The island's 1,842 acres were once a federal reservation with a lighthouse and a quarantine station to process the many ships that sailed from world ports to Carabelle to pick up loads of lumber. Today much of the island is once again a reservation. In 1980, the Nature Conservancy, that resource-rescuing organization that has been such a savior of Florida's natural wonders, bought and set aside 1,300 acres.

The remainder of the land is privately owned, including some 80 houses, only a few of which are occupied year-round—there can't be more than a dozen full-time nontourists here. The other buildings are holiday shacks and cottages, some of them looking as though their owners have forgotten where the island is. And then there's the Pelican Inn.

Built in 1963, the two-story cypress inn boasts double-decker, wraparound gallery porches and has eight functionally furnished but spacious efficiencies, each with a private bath, a balcony, and a gloriously unobstructed view of the beach just a couple of hundred conch shells away. There are no TVs or telephones or other such distractions, but there are hibachis on the porches for do-it-yourself grilling of whatever it is you hooked from dock, beach, or boat that day—bluefish, flounder, pompano, or Spanish mackerel.

But you'll have to bring your own charcoal. And your own potatoes, milk, breakfast cereals and bread, and anything else you think you're going to need during your stay.

The helpful, accommodating managers of the inn, Alison and Peter Debnam, will be glad to advise you at the time you're making reservations about provisions to bring. They will also make charter flight arrangements for you, if you wish.

If you're a bird-watcher, you will want to bring binoculars as well as a telephoto lens for your camera to capture the great blue herons and double-crested cormorants, peregrine falcons, black skimmers and snowy plovers, sanderlings and willets, egrets and ruddy turnstones, and of course those dive-bombing pelicans. Some 200 species of birds reside or pass through the island on their migratory patterns.

There are more birds to watch on Dog Island's neighboring barrier islands to the west: St. George, Little St. George, and St. Vincent. Unfortunately, St. George has been bustling with condominium construction of late, ever since it was connected to the mainland by a 4.2-mile causeway and bridge, but Little St. George is a protected reserve—however, both the Georges do have close to 40 miles of undeveloped, near-primitive beach.

St. Vincent is a National Wildlife Refuge, a four-by-nine-mile triangular-shaped barrier that can be reached only by boat, and then only for daytime visits. There is no public transport there, but you can wander along a few of the 80 miles of inland trails or the 14 miles of beachfront in search of endangered species (look but do not touch). For information on access, contact the St. Vincent National Wildlife Refuge, Box 447, Apalachicola, Florida 32320; 904-653-8808.

Much as we like to experience such protected wilderness, we prefer Dog Island, which is as respectful of the need for protection and housing of the human spirit as it is for the flora and fauna.

To rejoice in that kind of blissful environment in today's world, contact the Pelican Inn, P.O. Box 301, Carabelle, Florida 32322; toll-free: 1-800-451-5294.

St. Joseph Peninsula State Park

A long narrow finger pointing the way to the Panhandle interior and protecting St. Joseph Bay from the splashier waters of the Gulf, the St. Joseph Peninsula boasts a 2,516-acre state park, a 1,650-acre wilderness refuge bordered by 20 miles of white sand beach, salt marshes, and freshwater ponds, all framed by some of the most interesting and unusual dune formations in the state.

The splendor of its isolation gives no clues to the peninsula's long history, which dates back to the prehistoric Indians who harvested the oysters, scallops, and fish found in abundance in the bay. In 1838–1839, territorial delegates gathered to write Florida's first constitution in St. Joseph, surely the most famous of all the state's lost towns, destroyed by a hurricane a few years after the constitution was signed.

You can see a static reenactment of the constitutional convention along with displays detailing the short-lived and tragic history of the town at a state museum en route to your escape in the park. You'll pass the Cape San Blas lighthouse, originally built in 1847 and today a loran station.

The park provides the usual facilities such as rest rooms and bathhouses, picnic sites and play areas, nature trails and a concession stand, but there's also a marina and eight remote rental cabins, each furnished in the best summer camp Spartan manner but equipped with cooking gear and linens, towels, and blankets, enough for seven people. Each also has a fireplace and such modern conveniences as private bathrooms, central air-conditioning, heating, plus a boardwalk to the bay.

The bay is one of the most productive in the world, home to a wealth of sea creatures inhabiting the vast tidal marshes and grass beds that are protected from the dinosaurs of development by the largest state government purchase of endangered lands in the country, supplemented by the largest Nature Conservancy rescue east of the Mississippi. The 200 miles of protected shoreline and interior wetlands is in reality Florida's last frontier.

To share in the private pleasures of this kind of virgin wilderness, drive from the Port St. Joe mainland area on State Road 30, and at Cape San Blas head north on 30E. For cabin and camping reservations and other park information, contact the St. Joseph Peninsula State Park, Star Route 1, Box 200, Port St. Joe, Florida 32456; 904-227-1327. For information on the area, contact Gulf County Chamber of Commerce, P.O. Box 964, Port St. Joe, Florida 32456; 904-227-1223.

◎ ◎ ◎

AMELIA ISLAND AND
FERNANDINA BEACH

The best way to approach Fernandina Beach on Amelia Island is from the south via A1A from Jacksonville Beach, crossing the mouth of the St. Johns River by ferryboat (*The Blackbeard* or *The Buccaneer*) from Mayport, a bustling fishing port that claims to be the oldest fishing village in the country. Flocks of pelicans perch on the pilings, watching the fleets of fishing boats and keeping a wary eye on the rows of warehouses where the seafood is processed. As you cross the St. Johns, you will see the massive Naval Station off to the left and the ocean to the right. Across the water, Little Talbot Island State Park beckons with its 5½ miles of beach, vegetated sand dunes, and tranquil untouched salt marshes, clumps of magnolia and holly, and coastal hammocks of live oak sheltering marsh rabbits, bobcats, and raccoons. Along the water are colonies of shorebirds, and under the water are redfish, sheepshead, flounder, and mullet.

The ferry lands at the continuation of A1A, which becomes the Buccaneer Trail, passing through an area of natural barrier island beaches. Then you go on to the 13½ miles of beachfront that make Amelia Island one of the premier waterfront wonders in the world. The southernmost section of sand, so fine and fully packed, is the Amelia Island Beach, boasting a full 23,500 feet of ocean and sound beaches with easy access via dune walkovers and overnight camping possibilities. Amelia Island Plantation takes over a large chunk of the shoreline, and the next public access to the ocean is at American

Beach, north of the resort, with its own fishing pier and access roads, at Julia and Lewis streets and Burney Avenue. To the north lies Amelia City Beach, with a couple of miles of good beach and accesses at Peters Point, Belle Glade, and Scott and Sadler roads. And finally there's Fernandina Beach itself, a laid-back collection of simple little cottages and shoreline structures that are anything but sky-scraping condominiums.

The broad expanse of white sand takes on a paler hue as you move north along A1A, traveling under canopies of giant trees and through canyons where the north Florida greenery is thick and lush. Peeking through the trees here and there are patches of greener-than-green golf course and well-manicured and inviting emerald islets, integral to the beauty of the Amelia Island Plantation. Buccaneer Trail, which leads to the still somnolent settlement of Fernandina Beach, is one of the loveliest drives in all of Florida. A1A becomes South Fletcher Avenue as it winds its way north to town, a sporadic assemblage of convenience stores, a Kmart and supermarket, some rental accommodations, motels, inns, and clumps of homes in a variety of architectural styles suggesting the kind of Florida familiar to travelers decades ago. In the center of town, at the Atlantic Avenue intersection, is the beach proper, a 325-foot segment of developed frontage with lifeguards, plenty of public parking, covered picnic tables, gazebos, and a miniature golf course.

Atlantic Avenue leads a mile inland to the heart of the main town, 30 blocks of which comprise a National Historic District. Also in town are a museum, the most impressive vintage Victorian courthouse in the state, and numerous restaurants and bars, many of them housed in historic buildings that date back to the glory days of this onetime key railroad and shipping center. North Fletcher Avenue, continuing along the beach at Atlantic, has a few accommodations, mixed in with an inventory of less-than-plush dwellings and handled by the rental agencies. The real appeal of this northern tip of Amelia Island, which juts into the Atlantic across from Georgia's barrier Cumberland Island, is Fort Clinch State Park, one of the first to be established in Florida's sensational state park system. In the mid-1930s the Civilian Conservation Corp (CCC) commenced development, laying out trails and walkways, and starting the restoration of the 1847 Gibraltar-like fort that was headquarters for occupying Yankee forces during the Civil War. Their life at the fort is vividly reenacted the first weekend of each month by the state park rangers and volunteers. What a wonderful way to absorb history while enjoying all the natural beauty in the surrounding 1,100 areas: the great dune and shoreline, the overwash plains and estuarine tidal marsh, the 45-minute trail that takes hikers into a coastal hammock hugging a freshwater pond. The bastions of this silent sentinel afford panoramic views of the ocean, whose waters provide ample opportunity for fishing, either from the surf or the 1,500-foot pier. The beach beckons swimmers, and there are picnic sites with grills, primitive camping areas for the more rugged park visitors, and campfire programs and guided tours—some by candlelight—conducted by park rangers (reservations required).

Where It Is

Fernandina Beach and Amelia Island are 32 miles north of Jacksonville via Interstate 95 or U.S. 17. Turn off east at Highway 200 and continue on it to State Road A1A. This takes you directly to Amelia Island and Fernandina Beach.

Where to Stay

AMELIA ISLAND PLANTATION
Resort/Amelia Island

This 1,250-acre spread, so reminiscent of the Hilton Head complexes, is a complete resort in every sense of the word—and a perfect vacation getaway for families. The 21 tennis courts are world-class; the championship golf courses have been cited by golf magazines as among the finest in the country. There are nature trails for hiking and lagoons for fishing, a Jacuzzi and swimming pools, and beaches seemingly without end. Programs for children of all ages include activities such as paddleboating, swimming, sand castle building, boogie boarding, and seining—fishing with a net. The fishing dock at Aury Island is open only to anglers under 12, and the same set can go crabbing at Walker's Landing, close to a 900-year-old Indian mound. Swings, a jungle gym, and a sunken forest provide other possibilities for keeping the young ones busy while parents are otherwise involved with golf clubs or tennis rackets. The accommodations are luxurious and range from hotel rooms and one- to four-bedroom villas to honeymoon havens with private pool. Convenience stores on the Plantation supply all the needs for do-it-yourself food preparation, and there are several shops that specialize in beach and action wear. Bars and lounges abound, and restaurants range from the snack bar by the pool to the Dune Side Club, whose top-flight kitchen prepares the kind of food not available elsewhere on the island. Only Plantation guests are allowed to eat there, or to play golf, tennis, or swim.

3000 First Coast Highway (A1A), Fernandina Beach 32084. 904-261-6161; toll-free: 1-800-874-6878. Expensive.

BEACHSIDE MOTEL INN
Motel/Fernandina Beach

Jerry and Joy Kight are the convivial owner-operators of this small, new, and very modern motel with a swimming pool. Each room has a private bath, a telephone, and cable television. Complimentary coffee and doughnuts are offered to all guests. Another plus is the pier alongside the property, perfect for fishing and boating.

3172 South Fletcher Avenue, Fernandina Beach 32034. 904-261-4236. Moderate.

THE PHOENIX NEST
Inn/Fernandina Beach

If ever a country inn reflected the personality and philosophy of its proprietor it is the Phoenix Nest, named for that mythical bird that rose from the ashes of death. This bird took wing in 1989 when a wonderful woman named Harriet Johnston Fortenberry opened this two-story, four-suite escape. As she explains, "Some years ago, I wanted a chance to be by the sea, to gather myself up, to be with others I enjoyed, and so designed a 'retreat' in a wonderful old house at the beach. And people came and left with more than they brought, most times more energy, more calm, more clarity." Across the road is that beach and behind the inn are a couple of hundred acres of untouched forest wilderness. The inn has a marvelous collection of books and magazines, including *The Scots Magazine* from 1745 and 1748, an 1863 issue of *Harpers,* copies of *Cosmopolitan* from 1899 and 1903, and numerous copies of the *Reader's Digest* from the Great Depression. "When you read about a problem of 1889," innkeeper Fortenberry explains, "no one could expect *you* to solve it. You can relax!" And you can relax listening to audio cassettes and watching videos from her highly stimulating collection. There's everything from *The Wizard of Oz* and Chaplin's *Gold Rush,* to meditations on Jung and songs of the eastern birds, from Lionel Ritchie, Maria Callas in concert, and Luciano Pavarotti to Beryl Markham's *African Memoir.* Again, to quote the innkeeper: "This is a good place to be still, deliberate, intentional as you while and wander our sandy beaches, witness the grace and glide of the pelican skimming the swells, feed the gulls from your fingertips, listen to the ancient, assuring, and splendid monotony of the surf."

619 South Fletcher Avenue, Fernandina Beach 32084. 904-277-2129. Moderate.

SEASIDE INN
Inn/Fernandina Beach

This beachfront blockhouse of informality is furnished summer camp plain, but each of the 20 rooms has a private bath and great views of the sandy surroundings. The staff is superfriendly, baskets of fresh fruit are provided for guests on arrival, and complimentary continental breakfasts are brought to the rooms with the morning newspaper. Those who want to mingle with other vacationers can have the fruit, croissants, and coffee served on the cozy veranda—or in the living room, where the fireplace blazes when there's a chill in the air. Afternoon tea is also a part of the daily ritual, as is a complimentary cordial at the end of the day. Other important extras are the ground-floor gift shop and Sliders Restaurant.

1998 South Fletcher Avenue, Fernandina Beach 32034. 904-261-0954. Moderate. Includes continental breakfast, tea, and cordials.

THE 1735 HOUSE
Inn/Fernandina Beach

This simple beachfront cottage was converted to a five-suite inn named for the year of that historic occasion when the English governor of Georgia, James Oglethorpe, first set foot on Amelia Island and named it for the daughter of his sovereign, King George II. The inn was built in 1928 as one of the many simple seashore homes that then dotted the white sandy beaches. It was converted to an inn in 1981. Each of the suites is nautical-style, with bunk beds making it possible to accommodate parties of six. Three of the suites—those facing the ocean—have a kitchenette and dining area, and all have a private bath and television. Included in the rates is a continental breakfast with fresh fruit and juice, delivered in a wicker basket with the morning paper.

584 South Fletcher Avenue (A1A), Fernandina Beach 32034. 904-261-5878. Moderate.

THE 1735 LODGING SYSTEM
Several condominium units and private homes, most of them beachfront, are available for longer-term rentals and are handled by this operation, located in a fake lighthouse next door to The 1735 House, with the same address but a different telephone number, 904-261-2148. Among their properties is our favorite, **The Captain's House,** a three-story, modern, soft gray-blue wooden oceanfront condominium with two-bedroom, two-bath apartment units, each with a large fully furnished kitchen, spacious living room with dining area, and patio or balcony facing the ocean. The master bedroom has a king-size bed and the other has twin beds. It's an ideal location for long-term vacations on the beach. Expensive.

Where to Eat

THE GREAT KHAN
Chinese/Fernandina Beach
Of course there's a Chinese restaurant on the island, next door to the Kmart at Island Walk. But this one features something more than moo goo gai pan and lemon chicken, and that means Mongolian barbecue, a variety of meats and vegetables prepared on tympani-size grills. The luncheon buffet is a real budget-stretcher.

1521 Sadler Road, Fernandina Beach. 904-261-5887. Inexpensive to moderate. Lunch buffet Sunday to Friday; dinner daily.

ISLAND BAR-B-Q
Barbecue/Fernandina Beach
The place on Amelia Island for finger-lickin' ribs, buns layered thickly with barbecue pork, and platters overflowing with chicken. Eat in or take out, it's all back-country gooooood.

2045 South Fletcher Avenue, Fernandina Beach. 904-277-3894. Inexpensive to moderate. Lunch and dinner daily.

JAD'S
American/Amelia Island
Cozy, quiet, two-story cottage newly built to look old and in the heart of a country-charming complex of shops, this little gem is proud of its "Low Country Cookery," inspired by the chefs of Charleston, Beaufort, Savannah, and St. Simons. That means she-crab soup, pan-fried crabcakes, shrimp-scallop curry served on rice, chicken breasts sautéed with a tart lemon-mushroom sauce, and toffee shortbread—plus such local favorites as walnut-freckled chicken salad, baked brie and fruit, garlic-spiked clams on linguine, and New York strip steak. A final bit of good news: the back room makes a sincere effort to reduce sodium and cholesterol in its cooking.

Palmetto Walk Shopping Village, 4802 Palmetto Walk, Amelia Island. 904-277-2350. Moderate. Lunch and dinner Monday to Saturday.

THE SANDBAR
American/Fernandina Beach
The landmark restaurant on the beach, The Sandbar has been in business since 1932, so it must be doing something right. It is the oldest family-owned restaurant in North Florida, and still features the same kind of fresh seafood, with shrimp prepared in a variety of ways the real headliner. But don't sell the chicken or steaks short. The place is not hard to find—just follow the red arrows that are all over the island and prepare to turn off A1A three miles

north of the Amelia Island Plantation entrance at the flashing caution light, then head west to the Intracoastal Waterway.

Intracoastal Waterway, Fernandina Beach. 904-261-4185. Moderate. Dinner daily.

SLIDERS
Seafood/Fernandina Beach

In the heart of Fernandina Beach at the Seaside Inn, this 150-seat restaurant is a casual oasis with live entertainment—for the lounge crowd that wants to party late into the night. But the food is worth some serious attention: sliders, otherwise known as oysters, prepared every which way but on the half-shell (oysters Nelson, "Rockefeller on a Personal Basis," are our favorite); shrimp by the bowlful; and deep-fried veggies, broiled snapper, dolphin, or whatever else came swimming into shore that day, such as grouper, treated to a breadcrumb-pecan coating. Don't worry about the calories. After dinner you can work them off on the dance floor, or you can walk the beach.

1998 South Fletcher Avenue, Fernandina Beach. 904-261-0954. Moderate. Lunch and dinner daily in summer season; dinner only in winter months.

SURF SEAFOOD RESTAURANT
Seafood/Fernandina Beach

A motel afterthought on the highway, informal and inexpensive but featuring superlative shrimp salad and stuffed flounder. The deviled crab is a standout, and we also like the cocktail hour buffets in the lounge, the bargain lunches, and the Friday-Saturday combination platters for two.

3199 South Feltcher Avenue, Fernandina Beach. 904-261-5711. Inexpensive. Breakfast, lunch, and dinner daily.

Where to Shop

Driftwood Sun & Surf, conveniently located at 87 South Fletcher Avenue at Main Beach, Fernandina Beach (904-261-4500), is a swimsuit center run by Billie Parkin and also stocks surfboards and skateboards and related gear, a variety of gifts, and souvenirs.

The **Palmetto Walk Shopping Village** on A1A, two and a half miles north of the entrance to Amelia Island Plantation, is one of those collections of shops housed in newly-built-to-look-old country cottages that are the delight of tourists in such places as Hilton Head, Naples, and Vero Beach. Undeniably upscale, the shops offer fine arrays of everything from golf and tennis apparel (**The Swing of Things**), beachwear (**Suits Me Fine**), books and cards (**Alexanders**), ladies' and men's resortwear (**Sugar Plum** and **Heron's Sportswear**), children's clothes and toys—lots of irresistibles for the grandparents to buy—(**Once Upon a Time** and **Mudpuddles**), and quality antiques and gifts (**The Plantation Shop**) to deli delights and booze (**The Pantry** and **Amelia Liquors**).

More Fun in the Sun

Island Falls, an 18-hole miniature golf course, is tucked into a setting of tunnels and wandering creeks with a clubhouse high, high atop a 20-foot waterfall. A video game room and snack shop adjoin. Find this at 1550 Sadler Road (across from Kmart), Fernandina Beach (904-261-7881).

Sea Horse Stable is at the southern end of Amelia Island, at the northern termination of the bridge from the mainland (904-261-4878). From here you can mount your steed for beach gallops or trail rides at one of the few stables in the northeast section of the state.

Where to Write

Amelia Island–Fernandina Beach–Yulee Chamber of Commerce, P.O. Box 472, Fernandina Beach, Florida 32034. 904-261-3248.

Fort Clinch State Park, 2601 Atlantic Avenue, Fernandina Beach, Florida 32034. 904-261-4212.

Little Talbot Island State Park, 12157 Heckscher Drive, Fort George, Florida 32226. 904-251-3231.

ST. AUGUSTINE BEACH

Peacefully removed from all the history and happenings in venerable St. Augustine is the beach, part of it named for our nation's oldest city, other parts of it known as Butler and Crescent beaches, and all of it part of the county's magnificent 43-mile stretch of sand "far away from the boisterous, busy beaches of south Florida," as local boosters never tire of pointing out.

St. Augustine Beach proper extends from Pope Road in the north down to St. Augustine-by-the-Sea. There are 32 different places for public access, a half dozen boat ramps, and numerous roads that allow beachgoers to drive their cars directly onto the sand, where the vehicles can serve as mobile headquarters or four-wheeled storage sheds for beach chairs, umbrellas, and other vacation paraphernalia. South from St. Augustine-by-the-Sea to Matanzas Inlet, the sands are all accessible for driving and parking.

The Greater St. Augustine beachfront is interrupted only by the St. Augustine Inlet, separating North and Vilano beaches from those to the south, the ones we like to wander and explore all the way down to Marineland, 15 miles of easy, breezy driving. Marineland, built in 1938, is on the National Register of Historic Places, and was the world's first water circus, originally designed as an underwater film studio (a Tolstoy and a Vanderbuilt were among the founders). During World War II shark repellent was developed on the site, and a few years later scientists here first learned about the dolphins' sonar skills. Today, you can watch the amazing creatures use those skills to soar skyward and dive deep during daily performances. Nearby you'll find penguins, sea lions, a giant oceanarium, and snack shops.

The dune line, already ancient when the first Spanish settlers sailed onto the shore, led by the legendary Ponce de Leon, runs all the way from Marineland to St. Augustine Beach—past acres and acres of wetlands and scattered settlements reflecting varied levels of affluence; past 298-acre Fort Matanzas National Monument, located on Rattlesnake Island where the Spanish built a strategic Moorish-style fortification to stand as solid sentinel against invaders from the south. You can reach the island by a boat that departs from the visitor center.

At the northern end of St. Augustine Beach, off A1A at State Road 3, is the Anastasia State Recreation Area, 1,750 acres of wilderness including 250 acres of wetlands, a lagoon ringed by tidal marshes, a hardwood forest of scraggly ancient oaks, and colonies of shorebirds—terns, gulls, sandpipers, and pelicans. Migrating northern songsters stop by during their annual migrations. A self-guided nature trail wanders through a coastal hammock, ending at the camping area and the park office, where information on local shorebirds is available. There are other camping areas close to the beginning of the trail and sufficiently inland to be protected from blowing sand and surf. Nearby are three picnic areas, within easy walking distance from the main road. The interior lagoon, Salt Run, is ideal for windsurfing, with lessons and equipment rentals available. Anglers can head for the surf—for bluefish, pompano, and whiting. The broad ocean beach is banked by dunes, which provide a beautiful backdrop for those who come to swim and sun or take their boards out to the waves.

The Anastasia State Recreation Area has what local enthusiasts regard as the best surfing on the beach—at its northern end—and the local press prints special surfing reports on tides, weather, water temperatures, and whether the waters are semiglassy or semichoppy. Each November there's a "Blowhole" surfing competition organized by the National Scholastic Surfing Association (NSSA).

Past the entrance to the Anastasia State Recreation Area beach, A1A swings off the sand by the black-and-white striped 1871 St. Augustine Lighthouse, with its restored lightkeeper's house and museum. Close by is the amphitheater where from the middle of June to the end of August Florida's official state play, *Cross and Sword,* is performed. The play depicts in epic swashbuckling fashion the Spanish settlement of St. Augustine by Don Pedro Menéndez de Aviles. Across the road at the St. Augustine Alligator Farm is a collection of those creatures whose ancestors were in residence here long before Menéndez and his conquistadors. Each of the farm's attractions has its own woodsy natural setting, the gators luxuriating on some 30 acres. Other critters include raccoons and ostriches, deer, sheep and goats, and turtles that are anything but teenage mutant Ninjas. For nearly a century visitors have been making the rounds of the farm, walking the elevated wooden boardwalk, watching the wildlife shows.

It's another few miles to the Bridge of Lions, which leads directly into Old Town and the wonders of St. Augustine proper, with its oldest everything. There is always some kind of festival or ceremony going on somewhere in town—along historic St. George Street, by the Yacht Club, at the County Fairgrounds, in the plaza, or at the massive Castillo de San Marcos, which dominates the city and Matanzas Bay.

The distinctive stone used to build much of that bastion was quarried out on the beach by masons and stonecutters who were housed in barracks at the southern end of what is now Old Beach Road, south of the Alligator Farm. The stone, called coquina, is actually a relatively soft, gray-white limestone formed of cohered fragments of coral and shells.

The best place to study coquina up close is at the oceanfront portion of the 340-acre Washington Oaks State Park, located south of St. Augustine Beach, two miles south of Marineland. Over the centuries the waves have washed away the sands, exposing outcroppings of coquina. There's no swimming at Washington Beach, but fishing is allowed and there is the possibility of finding a fine picnic spot. Tree-shaded sites are located across A1A in the groves and gardens surrounding the restored winter home of the late GE board chairman Owen Young. Situated on the banks of the Matanzas River, the house now serves as a mini-museum with displays of the flora and fauna of the area. Use the displays as prologue to a stroll on the nature trail shaded by cabbage palm and magnolia, live oak, and longleaf pine—northeast Florida's most commercially important tree, a source of pulp, resin, and turpentine.

Accommodations on the beach—a comfortable room or suite, maybe a full-scale condominium apartment complete with kitchen facilities—make for great base camps. What better way to spend a holiday than enjoying all the fascinations of the nation's oldest city, then retreating to the solace and solitude of the beach?

Where It Is

St. Augustine Beach is 52 miles north of Daytona Beach and 39 miles south of Jacksonville on State Road A1A. It can also be reached by taking the St. Augustine exit off Interstate 95 or following U.S. 1 to the city proper and crossing to the beach on the Bridge of Lions.

Where to Stay

BEACHER'S LODGE
Hotel/St. Augustine

This is a four-story low-rise spread across a fine section of dune and beach with an oceanfront pool. The 142 rooms include studios, and queen- and king-size suites, the royal designation meaning balconies and separate bedrooms. The rooms are motel functional, furnished in colors and accents harmonious with the setting, and all have kitchenettes. Strict rules forbid pets as well as anyone under the age of 21 not accompanied by "a responsible adult 21 or over, who is totally liable." There are daily and weekly rates, and special monthly rates in winter.

6970 A1A South, St. Augustine (Crescent Beach) 32086. 904-471-8849; toll-free (in Florida): 1-800-654-1450, (outside Florida): 1-800-527-8849. Moderate to expensive.

HOLIDAY INN—ON THE BEACH
Motel/St. Augustine Beach

This class motel-hotel act on the beach has easy access to the ocean past the giant pool and through the palm frond chickees and gazebo. The 150 rooms ringing the courtyard and pool have private balconies, many of them facing the Atlantic. The dining room, open for three meals a day, is far more attractive, in a spring-bright, orderly kind of way, than most motels can boast, and the Reflections Lounge is a magnet for adults of all ages. Music of the 1940s, 1950s, and 1960s is featured and there's a good-size dance floor. In season there are also special jazz and Dixieland evenings.

3250 Highway A1A South, St. Augustine Beach 32804. 904-471-2555; toll-free (in Florida): 1-800-6232, (outside Florida): 1-800-874-6135. Moderate.

HOWARD JOHNSON RESORT
Motel/St. Augustine Beach
Located at the big bend in A1A leading away from the beach and adjacent to St. John's County Park and Fishing Pier, this resort is fenced off from the water, which disappears under cement walls and piles of giant rocks, so there's no swimming along those edges of the property line, but the beautiful beaches begin again a few hundred yards to the north in the Anastasia State Park Recreation Area. Howard Johnson took over the property in early 1991 and immediately began thoroughly refurbishing the 144 rooms and sprucing up the surrounding landscape. Among the amenities are a swimming pool, a play area for the kids, and a lounge with live entertainment for the adults.

2500 A1A at Pope Road, St. Augustine Beach 32084. 904-471-2575; toll-free: 1-800-643-3970. Moderate.

LA FIESTA MOTOR LODGE
Motel/St. Augustine Beach
This is a real winner, neat as a pin, with spacious grounds and the Fiesta Falls miniature golf course as annex. Play the 18 holes or just sit in the Mountain Top Gazebo to enjoy the views of ocean, waterfalls, luxuriant landscaping, and even a Spanish galleon. The rooms are carefully maintained and have one or two beds and large picture windows. Some have a private oceanview balcony, and the bridal suite boasts a Roman tub. A large swimming pool, a play-ground, a shuffleboard court, and a game room complete the amenities, along

with a coffee shop open for breakfast and lunch during the season, otherwise for breakfast only. La Fiesta is a super place to siesta.

3050 A1A South, St. Augustine Beach 32084. 904-471-2220; toll-free: 1-800-852-6390. Moderate to expensive.

CONDOMINIUM RENTALS

There are many condominium units for rent, some on a daily as well as the more usual weekly and monthly basis. Rentals are handled by several realtors, among which we suggest: **THE OCEAN GALLERY**, 4600 A1A South, St. Augustine Beach 32084 (904-471-6663), and **RESORT SYSTEMS, INC.**, Crescent Beach Plaza, 6975 A1A South, St. Augustine 32086 (904-471-0774), who are agents for several of our favorite accommodations, including the oceanfront **SEYCHELLES,** designed by the same architect responsible for New Orleans's Superdome, and the **WINDJAMMER,** which has its own dock and fishing pier, a pool, and four tennis courts. Each of the 64 Windjammer units has a Jacuzzi whirlpool. Other condominium oceanfront properties we like are the 64-unit **PIER POINT SOUTH**, 2170 A1A South, St. Augustine Beach 32084 (904-471-3622), with pool and volleyball court; **PONCE LANDING**, 3100 South A1A, St. Augustine Beach, 32084 (904-471-1217), with the units flanking the supersize courtyard and a pair of pools. All accommodations are two-level town houses with two bedrooms and two baths, completely equipped, with kitchens, ground-floor patio and second-floor balcony, and—a real rarity on the beach—a private garage with washer and dryer. Weekly or monthly rentals only; **ST. AUGUSTINE OCEAN & RACQUET RESORT**, 3300 A1A South, St. Augustine Beach 32084 (904-471-0932; toll-free [outside Florida]: 1-800-448-0066), with swimming pool and Jacuzzi, tennis courts. All are two-bedroom, two-bath units with fully equipped kitchen. Rates for all but Pier Point South are expensive.

Where to Eat

CAP'S SEAFOOD RESTAURANT
Seafood/St. Augustine Beach

The local energizer who converted a clump of fish camp shacks into a water-front restaurant, complete with marina and fine outdoor deck for watching sunsets and fellow sailors glide past, sold out in 1986, but his spirit remains, as does the emphasis on fish freshly plucked from local waters and handled with care by the kitchen crew. The approach to the restaurant is unique: Go up A1A two and a half miles north of Vilano Beach Bridge, and turn off at Myrtle Street, a couple of hundred clam shells north of Compton's Restaurant. Immediately after the turnoff from A1A stop and wonder at that Castle Otttis, "An Original Sculpture Done in Remembrance of Jesus Christ."

Myrtle Street off A1A, St. Augustine Beach. 904-824-8794. Moderate. Lunch and dinner daily.

COMPTON'S
Seafood/St. Augustine Beach

Seafood by the sea, smack on the sand overlooking all that ocean, with the management dedicated to serving only the freshest fish local waters can produce, along with lobster, salmon, and beef imports. Among our favorite selections are Peg's West Indies salad with fresh lump blue crabmeat, the potato skins stuffed with crab and shrimp and crowned with cheddar, the macadamia shrimp salad, the grilled cobia with tarragon-tomato cream, the scallops and andouille cheddar mornay served on pasta, and the sensational crabcakes.

4100 Coastal Highway, A1A North Beach (2½ miles north of Vilano Beach Bridge). 904-824-8051. Moderate to expensive. Dinner nightly, Saturday lunch, and Sunday brunch.

CONCH HOUSE RESTAURANT & LOUNGE
Seafood/St. Augustine Beach

This touch of the tropics, all wood, rope, and palm fronds, overlooks Salt Run close to the beach and has the most intriguing cocktail lounge in the area, the Crow's Nest. Start there and then retire to a window table for one of the great noontime sandwiches such as the seafood-and-shrimp-stuffed pita pocket. For dinner, we always start with the peppery conch chowder and a few conch fritters before settling down to scallops Portofino, sautéed in a brandy-spiked cream sauce with garlic, mushrooms, scallions, and tomatoes; a steamed seafood platter, offering a rich harvest from the deep; the basil-impregnated breast of chicken, served on linguine; or the T-bone steak.

57 Comares Avenue, St. Augustine Beach. 904-829-8646. Moderate. Lunch and dinner daily.

JACK'S BAR-B-QUE
Barbecue/St. Augustine Beach

Simplest of shacks with outdoor stools for sunning while you work through a rack of ribs, or some heavenly barbecued chicken, pork, or beef, with all the trimmings. Eat in or take out.

2795 A1A South, St. Augustine Beach. 904-471-2055. Inexpensive. Lunch and dinner daily.

LA PARISIENNE CROISSANT SHOP
Bakery/Crescent Beach

The beach bakery of the superior La Parisienne restaurant at 60 Hypolita Street in town and featuring not only fresh-from-the-oven croissants, brioches, and those long loaves of French bread, but the best pastries to be found for miles and miles around.

Crescent Plaza Shopping Center, South A1A, Crescent Beach. 904-471-5914. Inexpensive. Open daily.

MEDITERRANEO
Italian/St. Augustine Beach
A family operation featuring both northern and southern Italian fare, finest in the area. That means superior pasta properly prepared al dente, excellent scampi and fine fowl, saltimbocca that's good enough to live up to its name, and the flair of tableside flame and flash by the Papa, who prepares a fine beef filet Don Carlo. For appropriate fiery finishers, what else but crepes Suzette?

604 A1A South, St. Augustine Beach. 904-471-6077. Moderate to expensive. Dinner Tuesday to Sunday.

THE OASIS
American/St. Augustine Beach
Popular spot for money-saving specials that really go back to the basics— meatloaf, spaghetti and meatballs, hot turkey sandwiches with cranberry sauce, and "hand-formed burgers." This is the best-value-for-the-money place on the beach, a no-frills setting featuring a simple dining room and one of the longest counters to be found anywhere in northeastern Florida.

A1A South and Ocean Trace Road, St. Augustine Beach. 904-471-3424. Inexpensive. Breakfast and lunch daily.

OUR PLACE
American/Crescent Beach
Budget-stretching breakfasts (starting at 6:00 A.M. for early risers) and lunches where the specialties are soup of the day and a half sandwich, Italian sausage and Philly cheese steak subs, and all kinds of cold and hot sandwiches, including a Coney Island hot dog with all the trimmings—chili, onions, and shredded cheddar.

6975 A1A South, Crescent Beach Plaza, Crescent Beach. 904-461-1720. Inexpensive. Breakfast and lunch Monday to Saturday.

PANAMA HATTIE'S
American/St. Augustine Beach

A roadside-tavern-from-the-past kind of place, with straightforward fare—sandwiches at noon, steaks and chicken at dinner. In the evening, there's live entertainment in a jumping lounge dominated by an oversize bar that never seems to lack for patrons. A deck affords views of a fishing pier and the ocean across the road. Typically, a package store adjoins.

2125 A1A South, St. Augustine Beach. 904-471-2255. Inexpensive to moderate. Lunch and dinner daily.

ROSENHOF
German/St. Augustine Beach

There's no way to miss this "gemütlich gasthaus" on the beach road, which in this instance could be renamed Romantischer Strasse, so evocative of something special—and historic—is this two-story gem that has absolutely nothing in common with anything else in this Spanish-swamped section of the state. The inside is as immaculate as the exterior, including the kitchen, on view through windows out back by the neat parking lot. The feeling, the ambience, the "stimmung" is gasthaus friendly, and there's a full inventory of solid German specials including sauerbraten, smoked pork, kraut and red cabbage, potato pancakes, and worst that is the best. Accordion music on the weekends.

1824 A1A South, St. Augustine Beach. 904-471-4340. Moderate. Dinner Tuesday to Sunday.

SALTWATER COWBOYS
Seafood/St. Augustine Beach

The road sign tells you the bad news: "You've just passed Saltwater Cowboys." So turn around and don't miss that turnoff to this rugged little shack surrounded by salt marshes and serving generous portions of good old-fashioned food at modest prices. The fried seafood is fabulous, the shrimp sensational, and the soft-shell crabs as good as any to be found this side of the Chesapeake. They're served with a zinger of a sauce called Rebel.

299 Dondanville Road, off A1A a half-mile south of the Best Western Ocean Inn, St. Augustine Beach. 904-471-2332. Moderate. Dinner daily. No reservations.

SUNSET GRILLE
American/St. Augustine Beach

Located a quarter mile south of the fishing pier, this is a fun place for all-day eating—breakfast early in the day en route to the beach or pier, burgers and fries at noon, and steaks and seafood at dinner. Live entertainment at night adds to the spirit.

2295 A1A South, St. Augustine Beach. 904-471-5555. Moderate. Breakfast, lunch, and dinner daily.

TONY'S PIZZA
Italian/Crescent Beach

When the pizza urge overwhelms, this is the place, whether for a modest 10-inch vegetarian supreme or an 18-inch super supreme with just about everything. They're New York style, so Chicago deep-dish devotees take note. Also available are pizza by the slice, budget-happy pasta dinners, and an array of hot and cold subs. Tony does not guarantee 30-minute delivery, but he does "Guarantee the Best Pizza in St. Augustine."

A1A South and State Road 206, Crescent Beach Plaza, Crescent Beach. 904-471-8660 and 904-471-9027. Inexpensive to moderate. Lunch and dinner daily.

Where to Shop

Blue Sky Surf Shop, 517 Anastasia Boulevard (904-824-2734), is head-quarters for all kinds of surfing gear plus repairs and rentals, sunglasses, sandals, action sportswear, and wet suits. For 'round-the-clock surf repairs, call the shop's special number, 904-824-9855.

Dr. Livingston I Presume (904-461-0282) and **The Hands of Man** (904-471-3125) are side by side in the minuscule Surf Plaza at 2837 A1A South, between B and C streets. The first shop features tropical outfits and swim and casual wear, while the second store has all kinds of wonderfully unique hand-crafted gifts and artifacts from around the world: pouches from Nepal, cotton blouses from Mexico, African batik clothing, Japanese jackets, Chinese figurines, Ethiopian carpets, Costa Rican hammocks, and some Indonesian shoes.

Tom's Fruits and Gifts and Shells, located at 1812 A1A South (904-471-2355), is the closest place to your beachfront accommodation to have citrus shipped to the folks back home, and to find that silly Sunshine State souvenir and all kinds of shells.

Stop, 6943 A1A South, across from the State Road 206 beach ramp, Crescent Beach (904-471-7748), offers beach and casual wear, along with souvenirs, jewelry, and such surfing essentials as boogie boards and floats, and umbrellas and beach chairs for sale or rent by the hour, day, or week.

Surf Stations I and II have surfing equipment to buy or rent, everything from boogie boards to "the hottest surfboards in town," and a full inventory of beachware from sunglasses to wetsuits. They also issue a 24-hour surf report (904-471-1122). Surf Station I is at 1020 Anastasia Boulevard, St. Augustine Beach (904-471-WIND). and Surf Station II at South A1A, Crescent Beach (904-471-TUBE).

More Fun in the Sun

Camachee Cove Charters (904-825-1971) and **Merc Charter** (1-800-448-MERC), at the Camachee Cove Marina, A1A South, provide fishing and powerboat charters and rentals. At the same marina is **Club Nautico** (904-825-4848; toll free [in Florida]: 1-800-BOATRENT, [outside Florida]: 1-800-NAUTICO), with runabouts, pontoons, center consoles, and cabin cruisers to rent for fishing, diving, waterskiing, or just cruising.

Note: Dial AM 1170 on your radio for sunrise-to-sunset broadcasts of "the

St. Augustine Story," detailed information on the sights and sites, weather and tides, and fishing reports as well as surfing conditions for all those waiting to grab their boards the minute they hear the magic words "Surf's up!"

Where to Write

Alligator Farm, A1A, St. Augustine Beach, Florida 32084. 904-829-0745.

Anastasia State Recreation Area, 1340C A1A South, St. Augustine, Florida 32084. 904-461-2033.

Cross and Sword, P.O. Box 1965, St. Augustine, Florida 32085. 904-471-1965.

Fort Matanzas National Monument, A1A South, St. Augustine, Florida 32086. 904-471-0116.

Lighthouse Museum, 81 Lighthouse Avenue, St. Augustine Beach, Florida 32084. 904-829-0745.

Marineland, 9805 Ocean Shore (A1A), Marineland, Florida 32086-9602. 904-471-1111.

St. Augustine and St. Johns County Chamber of Commerce, One Riberia Street, P.O. Drawer 0, St. Augustine, Florida 32084. 904-829-5681.

Washington Oaks State Gardens, Route 1, Box 1280A, St. Augustine, Florida 32084. 904-445-3161.

SOUTHWESTERN FLORIDA: TAMPA BAY TO FORT MYERS BEACH

CLEARWATER BEACH

Less than four miles long, Clearwater Beach is a busy, bustling family-oriented vacation destination with acres and acres of white sand and a rich variety of water-oriented fun and games. Fully equipped marinas are available for boat rentals and charters out into the Gulf of Mexico or to the more protected waters of Clearwater Bay.

For a painless way to explore and enjoy the commercial district of the beach, board the free Jolly Trolley, which makes regular runs from the main beach street, Gulfview Boulevard, every half hour. Then escape to the splendid isolation of the Sand Key County Park, a carefully landscaped facility with 2,100 feet of beach shielded by a rock barrier—good for trying your luck with rod and reel—at its southern end and featuring well-tended picnic sites, showers, and rest rooms.

The park is located south of Clearwater Pass, which leads into Clearwater Harbor. To the north is Caladesi Island State Park, one of the few remaining undisturbed barrier islands in Florida, with 1,400 acres of wilderness and two miles of developed beachfront complete with such facilities as picnic sites, a playground, rest rooms and showers, a snack bar, and lifeguard stations. Despite the development, the surroundings have been allowed to remain in their pristine state, as is obvious when you wander the nature trails, which you can do alone or with a park ranger as guide. A 60-foot-tall observation tower provides panoramic views of the area, the Gulf of Mexico, and the sheltered interior waterways. Access to the park is by boat, leaving from the Clearwater Marina or the marina in Dunedin, a few miles to the north.

On Clearwater Beach Island there's developed beachfront with lifeguards and full facilities. Access is off Eldorado and Mandalay avenues and Aurel, Avalon, Bohemia Circle, Cambridge, Gardenia, Glendale, Hellwood, Idlewild, Kendall, and Juniper streets.

Mandalay Park is a city-owned stretch of sand, 500 feet of it, with full facilities and lifeguards, three tennis courts, and a playground, and is located a half mile north of the Memorial Causeway, leading to the beach from the mainland.

At the southern end of the island is the Clearwater Beach Park, a half mile of developed beachfront with full facilities, including lifeguard stations.

Where It Is

Clearwater Beach is two and a half miles west of downtown Clearwater on State Road 60 and the Memorial Causeway that leads directly to the beach.

Where to Stay

ADAM'S MARK CARIBBEAN GULF RESORT
Hotel/Clearwater Beach
Originally built in the early 1970s and recently renovated, this Gulf-front hotel has a couple of hundred rooms and offers the usual water sports gear. It is close to the marina, where there are charter boats and cruise ships. The dining room, Calico Jack's, overlooks the beach and specializes in weekend all-you-can-eat seafood buffets. Out on the patio a Caribbean steel drum band performs, so you can sip a cool one, listen to that wonderful music, and watch the boat parade in Clearwater Pass.

430 South Gulfview Boulevard, Clearwater Beach 34630. 813-443-5714; toll-free: 1-800-231-5858. Moderate.

CLEARWATER BEACH HILTON
Hotel/Clearwater Beach
A ten-story tower and two lanai low-rises ring the white sands of the Gulf Beach, providing 210 rooms and suites furnished in tropical mod colors and

featuring private porches. Only a couple of dozen conch shells from the 1,000 feet of private beach is a spacious swimming pool along with a tropical bar and sunning deck. The strictly casual Barefoot Deli is where you can grab a pizza, sandwiches, some ice cream. The Cafe offers al fresco dining, and the main restaurant, Pippindale's, serves three meals a day.

715 South Gulfview Boulevard, Clearwater Beach 34630. 813-447-9566; toll-free (in Florida): 1-800-282-3566, (outside Florida): 1-800-248-1831. Moderate to expensive.

CLEARWATER BEACH HOTEL
Hotel/Clearwater Beach

Charm-charm-charm is captured with vigor in this crown jewel of historic beachfront hostelries, whose origins date back to the turn of the century. Beautifully restored in 1987, it has 58 rooms, 77 efficiencies, and 23 suites with fully equipped kitchens. The dining room, enclosed with beveled glass, is a dark-green-and-white triumph of subdued style, and has been designed so that the multilevel tables have fine views of the Gulf of Mexico. The menu sparkles: veal paillard with a sauce of Roquefort butter freckled with toasted walnuts, the freshest of lightly cooked vegetables, superior salads, and such finishers as creme caramel with a shot of Grand Marnier.

500 Mandalay Avenue, Clearwater Beach 34630. 813-441-2425; toll-free: 1-800-292-2295. Expensive.

ECONO LODGE
Hotel/Clearwater Beach

A beachfront money-saver with a pool and hot tub, and a small fitness center, but no food-service operations on the premises. That's no problem in this area—there are numerous restaurants nearby, many of them as kind to the family budget as this establishment.

625 South Gulfview Boulevard, Clearwater Beach 34630. 813-446-3400; toll-free: 1-800-444-1919. Inexpensive.

HOLIDAY INN GULFVIEW
Hotel/Clearwater Beach

The 288 rooms of this local link in the Holiday chain sit with a view of the Gulf and the constant boat traffic of Clearwater Pass. Enjoy its large pool and cabana area or get some exercise walking the beach before tackling the Currents Restaurant, with its views of the Gulf, seafood buffets, and such signature dishes as roast duckling in a ginger-spiked raspberry sauce, chicken breast stuffed with ham and Swiss cheese and served atop a bed of broccoli bathed in hollandaise. Another reason to linger a little—there's live entertainment in the lounge.

521 South Gulfview Boulevard, Clearwater Beach 34630. 813-447-6461; toll-free: 1-800-HOLIDAY. Inexpensive to moderate.

HOLIDAY INN SURFSIDE
Hotel/Clearwater Beach

The Gulfview Holiday Inn sits close to the center of activity directly on the beach, providing access to the acres of sand and surf and to the adjacent city marina, which affords numerous opportunities for viewing Florida's waterborne fleets and for chartering your own voyage in the Gulf. A poolside bar and a far-better-than-average Holiday Inn dining room, Reflections, are among the other amenities. Our favorite eats here are the snapper Pontchartrain garnished with garlic-sautéed crab, shrimp, scallops, mushrooms, and almonds.

400 Mandalay Avenue, Clearwater Beach 34630. 813-461-3222; toll-free: 1-800-HOLIDAY. Moderate.

RADISSON SUITE RESORT
Resort/Sand Key, Clearwater Beach

This crown jewel resort sits at the north end of Sand Key in one of the most exclusive sections of condominium real estate on Florida's west coast. The $40 million property opened in 1991 and offers 220 suites in a ten-story tower situated in the heart of a seven-and-a-half-acre complex of shops and restaurants. On the resort grounds are a free-form swimming pool complete with waterfalls and whirlpool, an athletic club, and a child-care center. A hotel tram makes nonstop round-trips to the beach. The suites overlook the harbor and each has a private balcony, a wet bar and fridge, plus a coffee maker. For those on expense accounts, there's a pair of executive suites and a pair of presidential suites, fully outfitted displays of affluence.

1201 Gulf Boulevard, Sand Key, Clearwater Beach 34630. 813-596-1100. Expensive.

SEA WAKE INN
Hotel/Clearwater Beach

This hotel, tucked in at the south end of the beach, has 110 rooms, each with a fridge. It's the anchor operation of the Sea Wake Resort Properties, which includes the Econo Lodge. Together, they sponsor daily complimentary children's programs, keeping your young ones busy with nature and marine science studies, beach scavenger hunts, shell bingo, and sand sculpture. A link in the Best Western chain, the six-story inn has a pool, a lounge, and a restaurant called Lenora's. Mesquite grill cookouts are held on the patio deck.

691 South Gulfview Boulevard, Clearwater Beach 34630. 813-443-7652; toll-free: 1-800-444-1919. Inexpensive to moderate.

SHERATON SAND KEY RESORT
Resort/Sand Key, Clearwater Beach

This 1975 vintage link in the Sheraton chain started a renovation program at the same time the Radisson Resort was going up across the boulevard. They upgraded their 390 rooms and 15 executive suites, and spruced up the surroundings of their seven acres of white sand, the palm-tree-encircled swimming pool and its string of chickee shelters and poolside bar, their tennis courts, and water sports gear for guests. There are three restaurants on the property.

1160 Gulf Boulevard, Sand Key, Clearwater Beach 34630. 813-595-1611; toll-free: 1-800-325-3535. Expensive.

Where to Eat

BEACH DINER
American/Clearwater

This neon-chrome reborn HoJo is located on the strip of asphalt joining beach and mainland and it's happy to boast "Famous Since 1990." Stretch your dining-out dollars on the pizzas with a bit of California pizzazz, the memorable onion rings, the steaks and burgers, or the pasta tangled with seafood. The place is a spirited copy of a vintage diner right down to the malts.

56 Causeway Boulevard, Clearwater. 813-446-4747. Inexpensive. Breakfast, lunch, and dinner daily.

COLUMBIA
Spanish/Sand Key, Clearwater Beach

The seventh spin-off from the landmark restaurant of the same name in Tampa's Ybor City and serving the same kind of Spanish-accented fare. Start your quick trip to Seville with some bean soup or shrimp-scallop ceviche and then order our favorite, the snapper Alicante, the fish baked with green peppers and sweet onions, garlic, and sauterne, and crowned with fried eggplant, bacon-wrapped jumbo shrimp, and a sprinkle of almonds.

1241 Gulf Boulevard, Clearwater Beach. 813-596-8400. Moderate to expensive. Lunch and dinner daily.

FRENCHY'S CAFE
American/Clearwater Beach

If the Florida Seafood Council ever doled out awards for the best smoked fish spread, Frenchy's would win it fins down. Also not to be missed are the other specialties—the lightly fried grouper cheeks, the grouper sandwiches that are arguably the biggest and best in the state, and the peanut butter fudge pie.

But if you can't squeeze through the crowds, go around the corner to Frenchy's Saltwater Cafe, at 419 Poinsetta Avenue (813-416-6295).

41 Baymont Drive, Clearwater Beach. 813-446-3607. Inexpensive to moderate. Lunch and dinner daily.

GONDOLIER
Italian/Clearwater Beach

Here's the place for food all day long, from 7:00 A.M. breakfasts through noontime salads and mouth-stretching sandwiches, to simple homemade Italian dinners, served until midnight—and pizza anytime in between.

674 Gulfview Boulevard, Clearwater Beach. 813-441-3353. Inexpensive. Breakfast, lunch, and dinner daily.

HEILMAN'S BEACHCOMBER
American/Clearwater Beach

Retro-trip to a bygone era when relish trays preceded all dinners, the bread was baked and the ice cream was churned out back, and there were back-to-the-farm dinners featuring fried chicken and mounds of mashed potatoes with lakes of rich brown gravy. It's all served here in a setting that gives us the feeling of stepping into a time machine, going back, back, back, while the piano tinkles merrily away.

447 Mandalay Avenue, Clearwater Beach. 813-442-4144. Moderate to expensive. Lunch and dinner daily.

ISLAND HOUSE
Greek/Clearwater Beach

Solidly in place since 1963, this popular landmark is a real find for families eager to stretch their dining-out dollars while having the fun of a sing-along piano bar. Greek specialties range from moussaka and garlicked lamb to salads loaded with shrimp and something the Houllis family in charge calls Greek spaghetti—sautéed onions and Romano cheese browned in butter make the difference. Among other offerings, our favorites are the roast leg of lamb, the open-face prime rib sandwich, and the pork loin with candied yams.

452 Mandalay Avenue, Clearwater Beach. 813-442-2373. Inexpensive. Dinner daily.

RAJAN'S
Seafood/Clearwater Beach

Super seafood by the seashore, starting with a fine raw bar selection and swimming on to excellent oysters Rockefeller, reliable fried soft-shell crabs, and good steamed stuff like shrimp and clams. We also recommend with enthusiasm the broiled shrimp or grouper stuffed with spiced crabmeat. This is a laid-back retreat with none of the overdone nautical nonsense decor that overwhelms other seafood shacks.

435 Mandalay Avenue, Clearwater Beach. 803-443-2100. Moderate. Lunch and dinner daily.

SEAFOOD & SUNSETS AT JULIE'S
Seafood/Clearwater Beach

Here's the place for the coldest beer on the beach, an ultracasual upper-deck, open-air bar that captures the spirit of Key West. The grouper sandwiches slathered with American cheese and slaw are great, and they also feature good salads and dinners built around shrimp, flounder, and scallops, plus Florida lobster and stone crab in season. The whole menu is available for take-out, and Julie will make special packages for those on the run, on land or sea.

351 South Gulfview Boulevard, Clearwater Beach. 813-441-2548. Inexpensive to moderate. Lunch and dinner daily.

Where to Shop

The most impressive string of shops is south of Clearwater Beach, on Sand Key. A bunch of boutiques comprise **The Shoppes of Sand Key,** adjacent to the Radisson Suite Resort at 1201 Gulf Boulevard, braced by a boardwalk facing Clearwater Harbor. You can find Hawaiian fashions, swim suits of every kind, and casual sports clothes, various gift items, Disney souvenirs, and specimen shells. There's also a full-service beauty salon for men and women plus a well-stocked food market that's open around the clock.

On Clearwater Beach itself, across from the Clearwater Beach Hotel, is **The Green Turtle Shell & Gift Shop,** at 499 Mandalay Avenue (813-461-0874). It has a full inventory of tropics-oriented gifts and keepsakes, including lots of jewelry made from mother-of-pearl, and beach needs such as sunglasses, towels, and rafts. Across from the Holiday Inn Surfside is the **Swim & Play** shop, 407 Mandalay Avenue (813-461-4499), with one of the country's largest collections of swim and sportswear and all kinds of coverups. It's one of five outlets on the string of Gulf beaches, including another in Clearwater Beach, in the Bay Bazaar Shopping Center, at 780 South Gulfview Boulevard (813-461-5535). **Way Cool** also has two outlets for beachwear and T-shirts, at 468 Mandalay Avenue (813-446-7293) and 201 South Gulfview Boulevard (813-442-7558).

To develop your beach photographs go to the **One Hour Photo** shops at 333 South Gulfview Boulevard and 25 Causeway Boulevard at the Clearwater Beach Marina.

Your dry cleaning and laundry can be taken care of at the **Laundromat** at 604 Mandalay.

More Fun in the Sun

For runabout rentals in the bay—not the Gulf of Mexico—check into the **Beach Motor Boat Rentals** (813-446-5503) at slips 5 and 6 at the Clearwater Beach Marina. If you want someone else to do the driving, buy a ticket for harbor cruises aboard the *Admiral* at the same marina (813-462-2628; toll-free: 1-800-444-4814), for noontime bird-feeding and sight-seeing cruises, or dine-and-dance evening cruises.

Fisherfolk eager to try their luck can walk out on **Pier 60,** at the termination of State Road 60, and take advantage of the artificial reefs built by the city in 1986, magnets for blackdrum, flounder, redfish, and snook. The pier is open daily and rental rods are available at the tackle shop. If you really want to get serious about central casting, climb aboard one of the **Queen Fleet** fishing boats at the east end of the Clearwater marina (813-446-7666). They offer half-day and full-day deep-sea fishing excursions, and the boats have enclosed lounges and lunch bars. Tackle is available for rent and they furnish the bait.

For viewing underwater life, take a short trip over the Memorial Causeway to the Aquarium Museum, part of the **Clearwater Marine Science Center,** devoted to coastal research and the rescue and rehabilitation of stranded sea mammals. Featured are tanks of live fish; mounted wall replicas of Gulf underwater residents; and Big Mo, a giant sea turtle, and Sunset Sam, a rehabilitated bottlenose dolphin rescued from Florida waters in 1984.

If you want some exercise rent a ten-speed or tandem touring bike at the **Transportation Station,** 63 Baymont Street (813-443-3188). They're open 24 hours a day, and also have balloon beach bikes and motor scooters.

Volleyballers can pick up gear, along with sand castle molds and buckets, sunglasses, and even bikinis and beach chairs, at **Hidden Treasures,** 444 Mandalay (813-443-4209). There's more of the same, and the best selection of kites on the beach, at **The Sunshine House,** 28 Papaya Street (813-446-3989), just off the main Mandalay drag—on the north side of Holiday Inn Surfside.

Land-locked fun can be found at **Captain Bligh's Landing** (813-443-6348), a miniature golf course across from the Econo Lodge on Gulfview, at the foot of the Clearwater Pass Bridge.

Where to Write

Greater Clearwater Beach Chamber of Commerce, 40 Causeway Boulevard, Clearwater Beach, Florida 34630. 813-446-2424.

◎   ◎   ◎

ST. PETERSBURG BEACH
AND FORT DESOTO PARK

On the sandy side of Pinellas County, west of the city of St. Petersburg, there are two of the most distinctly different beaches in the state. Fort DeSoto Park is set in a natural wilderness, devoid of commercial development, and St. Petersburg Beach offers the visitor a terrific variety of hotels, motels, resorts, restaurants, recreational facilities, shops, and snack bars.

Although both beaches are completely surrounded by water, there is easy access by bridge and highway via U.S. 19 and Interstate 275, which leads to the Bayway ending at the Don CeSar, a pink 1920s Mediterranean-style hotel that dominates this part of the beach.

South of the Don CeSar is Pass-A-Grille, a quaint, tranquil village thirty-one blocks long and one to two blocks wide, bordered by the Gulf of Mexico, and listed in the National Register of Historic Places. The area doesn't have the "classic" National Register look—no old forts or rows of impressive buildings—but is instead an architectural hodgepodge with its own kind of charm and, like Key West, an end-of-the-road mentality, a laid-back, offbeat lifestyle.

Pass-A-Grille was the earliest settlement on this necklace of St. Petersburg's barrier islands. As early as World War I, Sunday excursion boats brought as many as 1,500 beachgoers to the 5,200-foot Gulf front. Today the tourists come to get away from the canyons of condominiums, the noise and bustle of the city. They come to swim and sun and stroll the easy-to-walk-on sand, to fish off the sea wall, or merely to loaf, finding soulmates in the open-air watering holes of Gulf Way, maybe renting houses or apartments from local realtors, or vacationing in one of the cottages at Island's End Resort. Between 15th and 16th avenues on Gulf Way is the Colonel Frank T. Hurley Park, with protected picnic tables, showers, a playground, a baseball diamond, and a basketball court.

Fort DeSoto Park is a half mile farther south, at the end of another road, Route 693. It's a place of remote scenic beauty—boasting an animal and bird sanctuary (361 documented sightings), peaceful recreational pursuits, and a fascinating history—comprising five islands: Mullet Key, Bonne Fortune Key, Madelaine Key, St. Jean Key, and St. Christopher Key, totaling 900 acres. That means seven miles of waterfront and three miles of fine beaches for swimming. Park hours are daybreak to dark. East Beach has 270 parking spaces and North Beach has 1,620 spots. Parking is free.

At the northern tip of Mullet Key, the largest island, there's a beautiful picnic area shaded by gnarled old oak trees. A profusion of pines, palms, and other tropical vegetation adds to the beauty, as does the lagoon, where Indians once camped. Fort DeSoto stands on the southwestern tip of Mullet Key and is open to the public. It was built during the Spanish-American War and armed with 12-inch mortars, but they were never fired at an enemy.

St. Christopher and St. Jean are used solely for camping. The 233 sites, most of them facing the waters of Tampa Bay, are tucked into the natural foliage to maximize the feeling of privacy. Electric and water hookups are available for trailers, and the rest rooms are large and modern. Household pets are not permitted in the camping or beach areas, and they must be kept on leashes in other sections of the park. Campers have 24-hour access to the 500- and 1,000-foot fishing piers, but other visitors can try their luck only from dawn to dusk.

Where It Is

Pass-A-Grille, Fort DeSoto Park, and St. Petersburg Beach are at the southern tip of the Pinellas County peninsula. They are adjacent to the city of St. Petersburg on Florida's west coast. They can be reached by car via Interstate 75 and are about 45 minutes by car from Tampa International Airport.

Where to Stay

THE BRECKENRIDGE RESORT HOTEL
Hotel/St. Petersburg Beach
Directly on the Gulf, this seven-story hotel offers 200 rooms, all with kitch-enettes and some with balconies overlooking the beach. For recreation, there's an on-site lighted tennis court and a heated, beachside swimming pool.

5700 Gulf Boulevard, St. Petersburg Beach 33706. 813-360-1833; toll-free (in Florida): 1-800-391-5700, (nationwide): 1-800-828-3371. Moderate to expensive.

DOLPHIN BEACH RESORT
Hotel/St. Petersburg Beach
Situated on the beach, this 21-acre property has 174 spacious rooms, includ-ing 70 efficiencies; a heated swimming pool on a landscaped patio; a dining room overlooking the beach; a pool bar; and the 50-store Dolphin Village Shopping Center across the street. There are sailboats, parasailing and shuf-fleboard courts on the premises.

4900 Gulf Boulevard, St. Petersburg Beach 33706. 813-360-7011; toll-free nationwide: 1-800-237-8916. Moderate.

THE DON CESAR—A REGISTRY RESORT
Resort/St. Petersburg Beach
Affectionately called "The Don," this ornate pink palace holds court in a prime beach location at the foot of the Bayway. F. Scott Fitzgerald called it "a hotel in an island wilderness" when he hung out there with wife Zelda in the 1930s. Recent expansion has brought the facilities up to 227 Gulf-view rooms, including 51 suites and a pair of penthouses. The hotel offers a children's program, fitness clinics, a swimming pool, an on-site tennis court, and golf privileges, as well as a wide variety of water sports and recreational activities. The ground-floor seaside café has been decorated in Key West style

and renamed Zelda's. Two other restaurants, one of them the King Charles Room (see page 231), are on the premises.

3400 Gulf Boulevard, St. Petersburg Beach 33706. 813-360-1881; toll-free: 1-800-247-9810. Expensive.

THE HILTON ON ST. PETERSBURG BEACH
Hotel/St. Petersburg Beach

It's no wonder this hotel's ads say "relax and unwind"—the 11-story larger-than-a-lighthouse hotel is round. Its 152 newly decorated rooms are crowned by the revolving rooftop Bali-Hi Lounge, great for sunset-watching. Its beach is a recreational center with parasailing, Hobie Cats, fishing, and most everything you can play with in the water.

5250 Gulf Boulevard, St. Petersburg Beach 33706. 813-360-1811; toll-free: 1-800-HILTONS. Moderate to expensive.

THE INN ON THE BEACH
Inn/St. Petersburg Beach

Built in three stages starting back in the 1920s, the inn was recently reno-vated to house ten efficiency and two one-bedroom beachfront apartments with full kitchens. This comfortable inn has bicycles for exploring, and fish-ing poles for finding some fin n' gill to cook on any of its barbecue grills.

1401 Gulf Way, St. Petersburg Beach 33706. 813-360-8844. Moderate to expensive.

ISLAND'S END
Houses/St. Petersburg Beach

Located at the southernmost tip of St. Petersburg Beach, where the Gulf and bay waters mingle, this group of gray-weathered guest houses is a throwback to the early rustic charm of Pass-A-Grille. Five one-bedroom cottages and a three-bedroom cedar house with private pool have a distinctive old-timey Florida feeling yet provide all the comfort of modern conveniences: phones, kitchens, televisions, private baths. The water on three sides of the land, the natural wood fences and walkways augmented by creative landscaping, together create an island ambience. The view from this six-cottage compound includes a stark apartment house to the west, but look at the Gulf instead and that stunning view of the Sunshine Skyway—the new bridge spanning Tampa Bay that rises like a sculpture from the sea.

One Pass-A-Grille Way, St. Petersburg Beach 33706. 813-360-5023; toll-free fax: 1-800-367-7890. Moderate to expensive.

SANDPIPER BEACH RESORT
Resort/St. Petersburg Beach
One of our favorite dependable hotels, the Sandpiper offers suites, motel-type rooms, and penthouses in a massive Y-shaped six-story building directly on a wide strip of beach. Choose from a full range of recreational opportunities: a beachfront pool, an enclosed pool, a racquetball court, a tennis court, and sailboats.

6000 Gulf Boulevard, St. Petersburg Beach 33706. 813-360-5551; toll-free: 1-800-237-0707. Moderate.

TRADEWINDS
Resort/St. Petersburg Beach
This ambitious resort used considerable imagination to set itself apart from the pack—you reach your room via one of the gondolas winding through the man-made canals, and wander the beach over catwalks and bridges to find

solitude at strategically placed white gazebos. There are also pedal boats for those waterways, along with four swimming pools; a putting green; a sauna and health center; croquet, racquetball, and tennis courts; and an active children's program. The hotel rooms are efficiencies with sinks, refrigerators, coffee makers, and toasters; suites have complete kitchens.

5500 Gulf Boulevard, St. Petersburg Beach. 813-367-6461; toll-free (in Florida): 1-800-282-5553, (nationwide): 1-800-237-0707. Moderate to expensive.

Where to Eat

BILL NAGY'S RESTAURANT ON THE BEACH
American/St. Petersburg Beach

This is a hotel setting for an upscale breakfast. At lunchtime we like the pâté plate and spinach salad; for dinner, the seafood tureen. A children's menu is available.

5390 Gulf Boulevard, St. Petersburg Beach. 813-367-4455. Moderate. Breakfast, lunch, and dinner daily.

BROWN DERBY
American/St. Petersburg Beach

Here's *beef* on the beach. Serving wait-in-line customers for years, this place specializes in steaks but also has lobster, seafood, and prime rib. Avoid peak hours and the delays. There's live entertainment in the lounge.

6000 Gulf Boulevard, St. Petersburg Beach. 813-360-2388. Moderate. Lunch and dinner daily.

BRUNELLO TRATTORIA
Italian/St. Petersburg Beach

This quiet and romantic spot has brought northern Italian cuisine to the beach in high style. We love its rich soups for starters, followed by any of the nightly risottos and an elegant array of entrees such as tri-colored angel hair pasta with salmon-and-dill cream sauce, grilled fish, or any of the pastas with wild mushrooms.

3861 Gulf Boulevard, St. Petersburg Beach. 813-367-1851. Expensive. Dinner Tuesday to Sunday. Reservations suggested.

BURGEE'S GRILLE AND BOAT BAR
American/St. Petersburg Beach

This two-story, open-air spot features Tampa Bay's ethnic mix on the menu—everything from Cuban sandwiches and smoked fish to black beans and rice. Boat slips are available.

677 75th Avenue, St. Petersburg Beach. 813-367-5986. Inexpensive. Lunch and dinner daily.

DOE-AL SOUTHERN COOKING
American/St. Petersburg Beach

A Southern institution on the beach, right down to lovable lumps in the mashed potatoes. The fried chicken, catfish, pork, cornbread, and a bevy of outstanding garden vegetables—greens, succotash, and squash—all of it at very reasonable prices, help the family stretch the beach vacation budget.

85 Corey Avenue, St. Petersburg Beach. 813-360-7976. Inexpensive. Lunch Monday to Saturday, dinner daily.

GOOD TIMES
Continental/Tierra Verde

This outpost of continental cuisine, incongruously hugging a convenience store, has been packing in locals for over ten years. And it has never run an ad. Beach visitors learn of it by word-of-mouth (and our reviews). Featuring Eastern European cuisine with a full continental menu, it specializes in fresh seafood, superb steaks, and whatever the chef-owner decides will be nightly delights.

1130 Pinellas Bayway, Tierra Verde (just over the Bayway Bridge from St. Petersburg Beach, take the turn toward Fort DeSoto Park). 813-867-0774. Moderate. Dinner Tuesday to Saturday. Reservations suggested.

HARP AND THISTLE
Irish/St. Petersburg Beach

A good-time Irish bar that forms a walking-distance triumvirate of nightlife with Woody's and Burgee's in this corner of the beach. Irish pub grub, lots of beer, and rousing Irish folksingers are the feature attractions.

650 Corey Avenue, St. Petersburg Beach. 813-360-4104. Inexpensive. Lunch and dinner daily.

HURRICANE SEAFOOD RESTAURANT
Seafood/St. Petersburg Beach

For 15 years the Hurricane has been a seafood institution. In the heart of Pass-A-Grille's beach, on the corner of Gulf Way and Ninth Avenue, this open-air oasis has been transformed by recent renovation into a three-story Victorian marvel but it still serves one of the area's best grouper sandwiches and good burger platters. In the evening, in the cooling Gulf breezes, locals join the tourists eating or drinking on the outdoor deck for great views of the sunset. Later in the evening the lounge becomes one of the best jazz rooms in town.

807 Gulf Way, St. Petersburg Beach. 813-360-9558. Inexpensive to moderate. Breakfast, lunch, and dinner daily.

KING CHARLES ROOM
Continental/St. Petersburg Beach
This elegant room has superb waterfront views with windows on three sides—and some of the highest prices in town. It's great when appropriate, but for everyday beach vacationers, we recommend it only if you are celebrating one of life's great events and have packed your best clothes. More reasonable is the Sunday brunch, the best on the beach. It's so popular that guests pack the place and adjoining nooks and crannies on the fifth floor. Dress then can be more casual—even shorts.

3400 Gulf Boulevard, St. Petersburg Beach. 813-360-1881. Expensive. Dinner Tuesday to Saturday; Sunday brunch. Reservations suggested.

KINJO RESTAURANT
Japanese/St. Petersburg Beach
When the mercury rises and we've been too long in the sun, we want something cool, fresh, and light. We want sushi. This Japanese restaurant in the Dolphin Village Shopping Center offers a full range of Japanese dinners, but we enjoy the sushi bar the most. The chefs are particularly entertaining, the imported beer is cold, and the fish is impeccably fresh. Tuna and salmon are standbys, but don't leave until you've downed a Tampa roll, with its delicious crunch of fried grouper.

4615 Gulf Boulevard, St. Petersburg Beach. 813-367-6762. Moderate. Dinner Monday to Sunday.

LEVEROCK'S SEAFOOD HOUSE
Seafood/St. Petersburg Beach
Started by local fisherman Johnny Leverock in 1948, and now a chain of eateries under new owners, Leverock's specializes in red snapper, grouper, salmon, lobster tails, and filet mignon. It is one of the area's most popular seafood houses, with a pleasant setting, reasonable prices, and consistent quality. This one is on the waterfront with free dockage.

10 Corey Avenue, St. Petersburg Beach. 813-367-4588. Moderate. Lunch and dinner daily; Sunday brunch.

LUCKY FISHERMAN SEAFOOD HOUSE
Seafood/St. Petersburg Beach

This is a place designed for tourists—but don't be deterred. Here you can catch fresh seafood, a great view of the Gulf of Mexico, and moderate prices. For starters, try the scallops on the half-shell or the smoked mackerel spiced with a peppery glaze. Then, for your main course, choose from salmon, grouper, or swordfish prepared in a variety of ways. A reasonable wine list and a good key lime pie round out the offerings. They have tables and serve from an appetizer menu in the roomy bar. An outside deck by the bar has half a dozen tables for those who want to enjoy their drinks and the sunset together.

5100 Gulf Boulevard, St. Petersburg Beach. 813-360-5448. Moderate. Dinner daily.

PEP'S SEA GRILL
Seafood/St. Petersburg Beach

Pep's has successfully refined the art of creating a no-nonsense fish restaurant emphasizing cleanliness, freshness, and healthful food. Look for a large selection of daily catches priced under $10—and long lines out front. We like the salmon, snow crab, or mahi mahi accompanied by rice pilaf and finished off with apple pie. There are three locations in the Tampa Bay area, including this one on the beach.

5895 Gulf Boulevard, St. Petersburg Beach. 813-367-3550. Moderate. Dinner daily.

THE SEA HORSE
American/St. Petersburg Beach

This Pass-A-Grille landmark is famous for its good breakfasts, beautiful burgers, and friendly service. It's the local coffee stop for fisherfolk, boat crews, repair workers, and anyone else in shorts.

800 Pass-A-Grille Way, St. Petersburg Beach. 813-360-1734. Inexpensive. Breakfast, lunch, and dinner Wednesday to Monday. No credit cards. No reservations.

TED PETERS FAMOUS SMOKED FISH
American/South Pasadena

A beach institution serving Florida smoked mullet to crowds who enjoy the indoor-outdoor picnic tables. The waitresses are all veterans. What to eat? That's the hardest decision to make if you are limited to only one trip. The smoked fish spread is the best around, so start your table with an appetizer portion. Chowder lovers can zero in on the sweet Manhattan version, then move on to the smoked mullet platter, a Florida tradition, with a side of the warm German Potato Salad a must. The irony of all this is that this place serves a great burger, with a slice of Bermuda onion on *top* of the bun. Its iced tea is great, but it also features root beer in iced mugs. Watch out for the nontraditional Tuesday closing!

1350 Pasadena Avenue South, South Pasadena. 813-381-7931. Inexpensive. Lunch and dinner Wednesday to Monday. No credit cards.

WOODY'S WATERFRONT
American/St. Petersburg Beach

This is the atmosphere you came to Florida to find! An old-fashioned, open-air beach bar with burgers, beer, grouper sandwiches, and a great breeze. Mellow, acoustical music some nights and Sunday afternoons. The souvenir hat is our favorite.

7306 Sunset Way, St. Petersburg Beach. 813-360-9165. Inexpensive. Lunch and dinner daily.

Where to Shop

Dolphin Village Shopping Center, on the 4700 block of Gulf Boulevard, is the retail center for necessities at that end of the beaches. You can't miss this stylish pink center traced with blue neon. It has all the main stores you'll need: **Publix Supermarket, Eckerd Drugs & Pharmacy, T.G. & Y.,** the beach five-and-dime, a laundry and dry cleaner, a beauty salon and barbershop, a bank, a bookstore, a rapid photo processing shop, a card store, and an assortment of other shops to sell you suntan oil, beach floats, swimwear, and a variety of vacation necessities.

To get away from the high-tech T-shirt shops, look for **Wood Citrus Shop,** 6400 Gulf Boulevard (813-360-7421). The outside neon sign announces: BULK FRUIT, TROPICAL GIFTS, CITRUS SHIPPING, but this fruit shipper has evolved into a marvelous hodgepodge of goodies: it has the largest assortment we've seen of those round squat jars of tropical jellies and marmalades, with flavors from tangelo to guava to lime to jalapeño pepper; an eclectic selection of tropical fruit; sand castle molds; salt and pepper shakers; Florida ballpoint pens, erasers, and key chains; and freshly squeezed orange juice (available in pints and quarts).

The **Sanders & Markoe Gallery,** 3112 Pass-A-Grille Way (813-360-0729), is a showplace of fine hand-made pottery, jewelry, and other handicrafts by local artists.

Evander Preston Contemporary Jewelry Design, 106 Eighth Avenue, Pass-A-Grille (813-367-7894), is a plush gallery for custom jewelry and eccentric trinkets in the surroundings of African art and contemporary art prints. If not on traveling display, the solid-gold N-gauge train may be up and running. With an international reputation, this gallery draws worldwide customers for the gold items custom-made by Preston himself.

If you want to keep up on the homefront, the best selection of out-of-town newspapers is at **Scottie's News Stand,** 310 Corey Avenue, St. Petersburg Beach (813-360-6700). You'll also find a great selection of magazines, European newspapers, the latest paperback best-sellers, and dog track programs.

More Fun in the Sun

Nestled between towering condos and resorts is the **Suncoast Seabird Sanctuary,** 18328 Gulf Boulevard, Indian Shores (813-391-6211), the largest bird hospital in the United States. Its one and a half acres are dedicated to the rescue, treatment, rehabilitation, and release of wild birds. More than 50 species call the sanctuary home. Open from 9:00 A.M. to dark seven days a week, the sanctuary conducts hourlong tours every Tuesday at 2:00 P.M. Two-hour lectures are given the first Sunday of every month. Admission is free.

Beaches provide excellent places for kite-flying adventures, so when someone tells you to go fly a kite, hurry over to **Crystal Reflections,** 7390 Gulf Boulevard, St. Petersburg Beach (813-367-5383), or farther north on the

Gulf beaches to **Kitesville USA,** 405 Gulf Boulevard, Indian Rocks Beach (813-596-3431), for fine selections of all kinds of kites.

If you want to send more than a kite in the air, call Captain Mike at **St. Pete Parasails.** He has two St. Petersburg Beach locations: Colonial Gateway Inn at 6300 Gulf Boulevard (813-360-1998) and Dolphin Beach Resort at 4900 Gulf Boulevard (813-367-2921). From 8:00 A.M. to 5:00 P.M. daily he'll take you out soaring 400 feet or more above the waters of the beach.

What we love about deep-sea fishing from aboard *Miss Pass-A-Grille* is that the boat looks like one that Humphrey Bogart or Spencer Tracy would have chosen—not one of those sleek, modern cruisers, but a wooden, high-beamed, tar-roofed old-timer with the proper captain's cabin midships. Choose from full-day, three-quarter-day, or half-day trips departing from the **Dolphin Landings,** 4737 Gulf Boulevard, St. Petersburg Beach (813-360-2082; toll-free: 1-800-537-3429), directly behind the Dolphin Village Shopping Center. Just show up with money; they provide rod, tackle, bait, and on-the-spot instructions.

If Pass-A-Grille isn't remote enough, go to **Merry Pier,** 801 Pass-A-Grille Way, St. Petersburg Beach, and get on the *Shell Island Shuttle* (813-360-6606), a 35-foot covered pontoon boat that takes you to the three barrier islands off Pass-A-Grille. On the islands, you can spend the day shelling, sunbathing, fishing, swimming, or snorkeling. There are daily departures every two hours from 10:00 A.M. to 6:00 P.M., and a 90-minute sunset cruise departing at 7:00 P.M.

The original *Captain Anderson Dinner Boat,* a cruising boat in the Mississippi paddle-wheel style, offers dinner and luncheon cruises up and down the Intracoastal Waterway. Departures are from its docks at St. Petersburg Beach Causeway. For information call 813-367-7804; toll-free: 1-800-533-2288.

When you feel like puttering around, find one of those overdesigned miniature golf courses. The **Ruins of El Dorado,** 5301 Gulf Boulevard (813-367-7396), offers a golfing adventure above the traditional putt-putt. Two 18-hole courses are fashioned among ancient Spanish gold-mining structures, streams, and tumbling waterfalls. At **Paradise Golf,** 155 Corey Avenue (813-360-1862), you'll find a tropical setting with more shade, but plenty of water holes and rocky obstacles.

The tiki god at **Polynesian Putter,** 4999 Gulf Boulevard (813-360-9678), has towered over tourists for more than 25 years and offers classic mini-golf at its best.

For some fun in the dark, you can travel back to a simpler time, when movie theaters had only one screen, and enjoy a film at the **Beach Theater,** 315 Corey Avenue, St. Petersburg Beach (813-360-6697). The Beach, the oldest independent cinema in the county, turned 50 in 1990 and still has a loyal following. It seats 248 for its showings of foreign films and quality second-run movies.

Where to Write

Fort DeSoto Park, Box 3, Tierra Verde, Florida 33715. 813-866-2662. Tent and trailer reservations, no more than 30 days in advance, must be made in person—not by mail or phone. Two-day minimum stay. Fourteen-day maximum.

St. Petersburg Beach Area Chamber of Commerce, 6990 Gulf Boulevard, St. Petersburg Beach, Florida 33706. 813-360-6957.

◎ ◎ ◎

LONGBOAT KEY AND LIDO BEACH

Longboat Key and Lido Beach are on some of the priciest real estate in Florida—and some of the most rigidly zoned. Commercial development is at a minimum and there are no strip stores and mini-malls to deface the landscape. Instead, there's a splendid combination of superluxe resorts, some rustic vacation retreats, neatly laid-out condominiums, and lushly landscaped private homes. No billboards, no hard sell, no shouting, but liberal doses of understated elegance, a significant sense of place, and a few reminders of the flamboyance of Sarasota's premier developer, John Ringling North, who put a Ritz Carlton out on Longboat Key, only to see it flounder and perish during the Great Depression.

On Lido—a name loved by Ringling, who had a weakness for all things Venetian—located a few blocks from St. Armands Key, there are three public beaches, with North Lido having more than 3,000 feet of soft powdery sand on the west side of West Way Drive. It is connected to the 3,000-foot Lido Beach (with year-round lifeguards), which leads to South Lido Beach, 1,000 feet long and with lifeguards only from Memorial Day to Labor Day.

The total Lido shoreline is one and two-tenths miles, nine-tenths of it patrolled by lifeguards operating out of some of the best towers in the South, controlled by a 30-foot command center that posts the daily temperatures and water conditions. Close by is a modern pavilion with changing rooms and rest rooms, showers, a snack bar, a beach shop, meeting rooms, two volleyball courts, and a 25-meter freshwater swimming pool with a 3-meter diving board and provisions for the handicapped. In the North Beach area a wooded zone provides the chance to see a wilder part of Florida—even in this highly, and expensively, developed corner of the state.

Where It Is

By car from Atlanta, Georgia, and Tallahassee, Florida, Interstate 75 leads directly to Sarasota. From downtown Sarasota, the John Ringling Causeway, State Road 789, crosses Sarasota Bay to St. Armands Key. Lido Beach is at the south end of St. Armands Key and Longboat Key is north of it. From Miami, Alligator Alley and Interstate 75 cross the Everglades and turn north at Naples, going north to Sarasota. Longboat Key is approximately seven miles from the Sarasota-Bradenton Airport.

Where to Stay

AZURE TIDES RESORT
Resort/Sarasota

Close to the jut of land leading from Lido Key into the infinity of water, with the Gulf of Mexico at one flank and Sarasota Bay at the other, this 34-suite stunner has 160 feet of beach embraced by a boardwalk, a swimming pool, and sunning decks, all framed by low-rise buildings with modern, high-ceilinged suites, ranging in size from single-bedroom to two-bedroom, two-bath. Kitchens include microwaves and icemakers, and there are VCRs in the living rooms, with a VCR library conveniently located in the lobby. An ideal place for families of all ages.

1330 Ben Franklin Drive, Lido Key, Sarasota 34236. 813-388-2101; toll-free: 1-800-872-5848. Expensive.

THE COLONY BEACH AND TENNIS RESORT
Resort/Longboat Key

The Colony is a complete resort with a beach, a swimming pool, and sailing and windsurfing instruction at the Watersports Center. For the tennis enthusiast, the Colony offers 21 courts (10 soft) and a team of professionals for instruction and assistance in finding a partner or a match at your own playing level. There's a state-of-the-art fitness center, plus daily aerobics classes. Accommodations range from standard hotel rooms to bungalow suites and individual beachfront houses with two and three bedrooms. The restaurant is an award-winner for both the food and the wine list, the wine list being one of the best in the country. And if you wish to "eat in," Tastebuds, an on-premise mini-grocery, offers everything from bread and milk to elaborate deli concoctions. For the younger set, supervised children's programs run year-round, and for the youngest set, those under six, there's Tiny Tots tennis.

1620 Gulf of Mexico Drive, Longboat Key 34228. 813-383-6464; toll-free (in Florida): 1-800-282-1138, (United States and Canada): 1-800-237-9443. Expensive.

THE HARLEY SANDCASTLE
Hotel/Sarasota
Like most sand castles, you'll find this one right on the beach—600 feet of private Lido beachfront, one mile from the shopping and entertainment center of St. Armands Circle. There are four different views for the 179 guest rooms. To avoid disappointment, specify your preference of gulfside, poolside, courtyard, or northside when reserving. The on-site staff gives sailing lessons, and Hobie Cats and Windsurfers are available for rental. Bicycles are also available for exploring the island and St. Armands Circle.

1540 Ben Franklin Drive, Sarasota 34236. 813-388-2181; toll-free (nationwide): 1-800-321-2323. Expensive.

HOLIDAY INN LIDO BEACH
Hotel/Lido Beach

Located across the street from all the action on the Lido beaches, this is a terrific spot for body-bronzers and bikini-watchers. Built in 1970 and completely renovated and revitalized in 1989, this 130-room link in the Holiday chain affords sensational views of beach and Gulf, St. Armands Circle, and the distant skyline of Sarasota across the bay. The setting is tropical, in the guest rooms as well as in the restaurant and the pair of lounges, and the woodsy surroundings, surprising for this section of Sarasota, help create a feeling of escape from the workaday world.

233 Ben Franklin Drive, Lido Beach 32436. 813-288-3941; toll-free: 1-800-HOLIDAY. Moderate to expensive.

THE RESORT OF LONGBOAT KEY CLUB
Resort/Longboat Key

This 1,000-acre resort is, in fact, a club, but nonmembers can stay as hotel guests and enjoy all the privileges. And there are quite a few—including miles of white-sand beach on Longboat Key, 18 tennis courts (6 lighted), an 18-hole championship golf course, a swimming pool and Jacuzzi spa, bicycle rentals, and charter boats for fishing and cruising. Accommodations are definitely on the superluxe side, with a variety of rooms, primarily suites, most of which are beachfront. All guest rooms have twin beds, a dressing area, a balcony, and a refrigerator equipped with the all-important icemaker. Suites have king-size beds and large kitchens, and the larger suites have separate dining areas. This club is perfect for a family not overly concerned about sticking to a budget, or for anyone who puts a premium on space.

301 Gulf of Mexico Drive, Longboat Key 34228. 813-383-8821; toll-free (in Florida): 1-800-282-0113, (United States and Canada): 1-800-237-8821. Expensive.

Where to Eat

BUCCANEER INN
American/Longboat Key

One of the leftovers from Florida's pirate-theme days, this landmark has an all-American menu featuring charbroiled prime rib, barbecue baby-back ribs, roast duck, and seafood specialties. We like the slabs of beef at night and the noontime light fare poolside at the Peg Leg Patio.

595 Dream Island Road, Longboat Key. 813-383-1101. Moderate to expensive. Lunch and dinner daily.

CAFE LA SCALA
Italian/Longboat Key

Superb northern Italian cuisine expertly prepared by Chef Joe Mele. We start with anything farinaceous and then proceed to the delicacy of such veal variations as francaise or piccata.

Center shopping area, 5350 Gulf of Mexico Drive, Longboat Key. 813-383-3744. Moderate to expensive. Dinner Tuesday to Sunday.

CAFE L'EUROPE
Continental/St. Armands Circle

The perfect café for sophisticated St. Armands, with its circle of conservative shops, and perfect for indulging in the classics—hors d'oeuvres, soups, salads, and entrees—few new or daring but all faultlessly prepared and served with European élan. For starters, we're fans of the goose liver pâté presented with chopped nuts. We move on to such rich creamy soups as lobster and then the rack of lamb in mustard sauce or the medallions of tenderloin topped with peppercorns and a brandy cream sauce, saluting the performance with one of the wines from a fine list.

411 Harding Circle, St. Armands Circle. 813-388-4415. Expensive. Lunch Monday to Saturday; dinner daily.

CHARLEY'S CRAB
Seafood/St. Armands Key

Take a breather from shopping at this sidewalk café, where you can watch the wealthy go by. Have a luncheon built around tuna melt or seafood spinach salad and plan to come back at night for a meal in one of the well-appointed rooms. Fillets of fresh fish are the specialty.

420 Harding Circle, St. Armands Key. 813-388-3964. Moderate to expensive. Lunch and dinner daily.

THE COLONY RESTAURANT
American/Longboat Key

Tall windows on three sides of the teal-and-peach dining room provide spectacular views of the Gulf of Mexico. Hanging ferns, paddle fans, and island accents lend a plush, tropical resort atmosphere for relaxed meals. We like to start with the lump crabmeat ravioli in beurre blanc sauce, the salad of duck breast and spinach, or the escargot Bordelaise with a great garlic sauce. For entrees, we favor the tender tarragon-seasoned roast rack of lamb. The 18 entrees include something for everyone—beef, lamb, pork, veal, and six to ten fish selections daily. For dessert order the key lime pie, with its proper balance of sweet and tang, or the rich and moist white flourless cake. The wine list is a national award winner, and the selection of after-dinner coffees and liqueurs provides the proper grand finale to the evening.

1620 Gulf of Mexico Drive, Longboat Key. 813-383-5558. Expensive. Breakfast, lunch, and dinner daily; Sunday brunch.

EUPHEMIA HAYE
American/Longboat Key

Euphemia charms with the quaintness of its surroundings and the inventiveness of its kitchen. Each of the three small dining rooms is ornately cluttered with a collection of plants, historic prints, and antiques harking back to the days of Euphemia, grandmother of the original chef-owner. Consider seriously the classic Caesar salad or one of the daily appetizer specials. Homemade pasta comes in full or half servings—that pasta with shrimp poached in white wine, garlic, and basil is our favorite. Anyone who gets weak-kneed over fowl should try the roast duckling, with either sweet pepper or strawberry-almond sauce. And for the seafood, the kitchen challenges convention with inventive sauces and chutneys that are hard to resist.

5540 Gulf of Mexico Drive, Longboat Key. 813-383-3633. Expensive. Dinner daily.

HARRY'S CONTINENTAL KITCHENS
Continental/Longboat Key

Harry's can be what you want it to be, but its motto is: "Deliberately different." You can get take-out or eat in the tiny dining room with the garden patio decor. If you sit, start with the salmon timbale, a creamy salmon mousse cradled in a shell of salmon slivers; the grilled shrimp; or the roasted garlic. Entrees favor seafood—crab, scallops, salmon, grouper, pompano, and dolphin—but there are ample choices for landlubbers, too, including chicken, veal, lamb, and filet mignon. But save room for the peanut butter pie, a delectable concoction topped with hot fudge sauce.

525 St. Judes Drive, Longboat Key. 813-383-0777. Moderate to expensive. Lunch, dinner, and take-out daily.

L'AUBERGE DU BON VIVANT
French/Longboat Key

In this country inn setting you'll feel comfortably transported to a provincial restaurant in France where the kitchen has avoided the nouvelle trend. Cream and liqueurs flavor the sauces of the country-style French menu—we like the pepper steak topped with a cognac cream sauce. Other specialties are the sweetbreads, frog legs Provençal, tarragon chicken, fish stew, and poached salmon. To finish, try les Crepes Georgettes, bananas and strawberries nestled in a paper-thin crepe crowned with creme of cassis.

7003 Gulf of Mexico Drive (at the north end of Longboat Key at Broadway Street), Longboat Key. 813-383-2421. Moderate to expensive. Dinner Monday to Saturday.

MOORE'S STONE CRAB
Seafood/Longboat Key
When stone crabs are in season—October 15 to May 15—there's no finer place on Florida's west coast to have them than here. Set at the northern end of Longboat Key, the rambling dining rooms are properly rustic. Begin your meal with Moore's chowder, and then roll up your sleeves and start cracking and picking the crab claws. Year-round offerings from the Moore fishing fleet are shrimp, Florida lobster, flounder, snapper, and grouper.

80 Broadway Street, Longboat Key 813-383-1748. Moderate. Lunch and dinner daily.

THE PLAZA
Continental/Longboat Key
One of the most beautifully appointed restaurants in the greater Sarasota area, offering a fine menu of eclectic cuisine. We like to start with the chilled melon soup, spiked with dark rum, or the sherry lobster bisque with a puff pastry dome. Then comes Jamaican chicken, saffron ravioli with a shellfish mousse, or grilled swordfish enhanced by avocado and red pepper–tomato coulis.

525 Bay Isles Parkway, Longboat Key. 813-383-8844. Moderate. Dinner Tuesday to Sunday.

SCHENKEL'S
American/Longboat Key
With more than 30 years serving Longboat Key, Shenkel's has become an institution—and a must stop for breakfast, when they'll dish up anything from soup to sirloin to omelets. For lunch, don't miss the chicken pot pie or one of their award-winning sandwich combinations.

3454 Gulf of Mexico Drive, Longboat Key. 813-383-2500. Moderate. Breakfast, lunch, and dinner Tuesday to Saturday; breakfast only on Sunday.

Where to Shop

John Ringling had big dreams, aspiring to be "The Greatest Showman on Earth," and when, in 1925, he announced plans to create an exclusive shopping district to cater to residents of his John Ringling Estates, he had only the finest shops in mind. The Florida land bust of the 1920s and the Great Depression crushed that dream. But in the early 1950s the dream, known today as **St. Armands Circle,** became a reality in a splendid variety of shops set in a unique boutique village.

St. Armands has some 100 shops, including 34 featuring the latest fashions, 20 specialty and gift shops, and 5 galleries, along with 4 shoe stores, 7 jewelers, and 20 assorted restaurants, delis, and food specialty shops. There are too many for us to mention in detail, except for a few special favorites— **Aussie, Ltd.,** with its exclusive Australian fashions; **The Square on the Circle,** specializing in linens and accessories for bed, bath, and table; and **Sock It to Me,** selling every variety of—you guessed it—socks.

For day-to-day necessities, **Town Plaza,** at the north end of Longboat Key, has the traditional shopping center offerings, including a **Publix Supermarket, Eckerd's Drugstore,** a card shop, a travel agency, a laundry and dry cleaner, a post office, and several banks.

More Fun in the Sun

Mote Marine Laboratory, 1600 Thompson Parkway (813-388-4441), is a nonprofit operation specializing in environmental and marine research and education that makes for the perfect rainy day adventure. It's great for children as well as a treat for adults to wander through the scores of exhibits. In fact, if it doesn't rain, find time to visit anyway. Founded in 1955 and opened in its present location at City Island at the north end of Longboat Key in 1978, the laboratory features 22 aquaria ranging in size from 30 to 800 gallons and housing over 200 varieties of fish and invertebrate sea creatures, including sea horses, octopi, sea turtles, sponges, coral, and starfish. A 1,000-gallon touch tank provides an opportunity to interact with marine life, and the aquarium's centerpiece, the 135,000-gallon shark tank, features several species of sharks measuring more than 8 feet. The gift shop has a wide selection of environmentally oriented gifts such as educational books and games, plus T-shirts, jewelry, more games, and postcards.

For deep-sea fishing go north of Longboat Key and over the bridge to the fishing village of Cortez, where on the Intracoastal Waterway, you'll find the **Miss Cortez fleet,** State Road 684 (813-794-1223), with four-, six-, and nine-hour fishing trips available. They also offer a tropical island cruise three days a week to uninhabited Egmont Key, where you can walk through old military ruins, explore the tropical growth, collect shells, snorkel, and swim.

Where to Write

Longboat Key Chamber of Commerce, 5390 Gulf of Mexico Drive, Longboat Key, Florida 34228. 813-383-2466.

Sarasota Convention and Visitors Bureau, 655 North Tamiami Trail, Sarasota, Florida 34236. 813-957-1877; toll-free: 1-800-522-9799.

SANIBEL AND CAPTIVA ISLANDS

The sign at the entrance to the largest of all the barrier islands necklaced across the bay bordering Fort Myers and Lee County sets the proper tone: WELCOME TO OUR SANCTUARY ISLAND.

There are actually two islands, Sanibel and Captiva, but almost half of their total acreage has been placed in a perpetual-care bank of wildlife preserve. The J. N. "Ding" Darling Wildlife Refuge, named for an early environmentalist and Pulitzer Prize–winning cartoonist for the *New York Herald Tribune*, is a 4,900-acre safe haven on Sanibel Island for alligators, birds—40 permanent species and some 55 winter visitors—and all kinds of four-legged critters. The six miles of hiking and nature trails and the five-mile drive are very popular, with upward of 750,000 people a year making the pilgrimage. Our favorite trail, called Indigo, starts at the boardwalk by the visitor center (open daily, and with a slide show) and wanders for two miles past such resident feathered friends as egrets, herons, moorhens, and anhingas.

Other walking trails we like are the one-and-three-quarter-mile path in the Bailey Tract on Tarpon Bay Road, which circles a freshwater pond with more gators and birds, and the four miles weaving through the 240 acres of wilderness surrounding the Sanibel-Captiva Conservation Foundation (813-472-2329), at 3333 Sanibel-Captiva Road, known to the locals as the San-Cap Road. These four miles of well-tended trails provide easy-to-read identification markers in front of the various grasses, plants, and trees, and at a strategic point, an observation tower affords a splendid panoramic view of the total holdings of the foundation, some 1,200 acres, most of it wetlands along the Sanibel River, but scattered in various parcels around the island. There's a visitor center with a fine shell collection, a nursery with native plants, and meeting rooms where the foundation, funded in the main by donations and aided mightily by close to 200 volunteers, actively engages in promoting the cause of conservation. Their efforts have made these two islands world famous as models of intelligent and persistent environmental planning and controlled development. What other community has a vegetation committee, one with the power to cite a trucker for backing into a buckthorn tree or a golf course for not providing sufficient water to recently planted trees along the Sun-Cap Road?

You can do your own part in preservation by not picking sea oats or sea grapes, as tempting as it might be to take some home. No dogs, fires, camping, or vehicles are allowed on the beaches, and the Florida State Department of Natural Resources strictly enforces Marine Fisheries Conservation Rule, Chapter 46–26, limiting the taking of live shells of any species to only two per person. Violators are subject to a $500 fine and 60 days in jail. And that's for a first offense!

Not to worry. There's an abundance of dead shells. The 14 miles of beaches are the finest shelling area on the continent, and the third best in the world. Whelks and drills, snails, cones, and periwinkles are in plentiful supply—as are fighting conch, banded tulip, lion's paw, coquina, fan and ark shells, turkey wings, and sunray Venus. The several shell shops on Sanibel can define all those names, and they show and sell samples as well as guidebooks. But if you want the ultimate in conchology, plan to be on the islands the first week in March for the Sanibel Shell Fair, an annual happening since 1938. Sanibel hosts several annual events, including an arts-and-crafts show and a Taste of the Islands festival in April, and Jazz on the Green in October, but the Shell Fair is the biggie. Serious shell collectors and artists working with shells congregate from around the world to meet their fellow conchologists, to display and sell their wares and buy more, and to compete for the trophies and ribbons awarded in such categories as Best Shell in Show, Best Exhibits, Best Flower Arrangement, or Best Christmas Theme Decoration. The public is invited to all events, including the awards banquet held at Mulligan's Restaurant in the Dunes Golf & Tennis Club (813-936-6044)—reservations required.

Where can you do your own shelling? A few feet from your home-away-from-home, or outside the door of your resort suite, motel room, inn court-yard, or cottage gate. The best locations for practicing your own "Sanibel Stoop" are at Bowman's Beach on the Gulf, an emerged sandbar on the north end of Sanibel with a pretty good picnic area, and at Blind Pass, beneath the bridge that joins Sanibel and Captiva. The current is rather strong there and it drives in the shells from the large plateau that extends from the island out into the Gulf. During the January and February storms, particularly the "nor' easters," the shells can come to shore by the thousands.

North of Blind Pass are the 3 acres of developed Turner Beach on the southern tip of Captiva. At the opposite end of the islands are the Tarpon Bay Road Beach and Gulfside City Park Beach, 30 acres of developed beachfront with access at the end of Southwinds Drive East. Lighthouse Park, with its 1884 lighthouse, lies at the tip of Sanibel and has 5 acres of undeveloped beach with parking for some 100 cars in a rustic setting reminiscent of Florida beaches half a century ago.

Maps and other useful information—lots of it—identifying the beaches and pointing out everything you've ever wanted to know about Sanibel-Captiva are available at the Chamber of Commerce Welcome Center at the entrance to the islands from the Sanibel Causeway. And what a wonderful drive from the mainland it is, the best of approaches to a beach holiday. Water on both sides and numerous pull-off spaces for parking with plenty of shaded picnic tables and fishing spots, adding greatly to one's sense of anticipation of what's ahead. But there's really no adequate preparation for the pleasures to come, the leisurely drives along heavily shaded roads leading past wildnerness areas and an array of architectural styles—churches harmoniously tucked into the trees, Victorian and Cape Cod cottages, some shacks here and there confronted by modern blockhouses, many of them hidden behind lush growths of tropical greenery. But watch for signs warning of gator crossings ahead!

Where It Is

Sanibel and Captiva islands are reached by the Sanibel Causeway and Bridge (toll), which is a three-mile extension of State Road 876, 15 miles southwest of Fort Myers.

Where to Stay

CASA YBEL RESORT
Resort/Sanibel

You can really step back into Sanibel history at this Gulf-front spread of affluent comfort, covering the site where the island's first inn, the House of Isabel, was built just after the turn of the century. The core of the complex is Thistle Lodge, carefully designed to re-create the home of one of Sanibel's first settlers, and housing the superior Truffles restaurant (see page 260). Handsomely furnished one- and two-bedroom condominium units surround the lodge, the heated Olympic-size pool with waterslide and an adjacent pond for the kids, a spa, and a bar. Off to the side are a half dozen laykold tennis courts with a resident pro, shuffleboard and volleyball courts, and on the beach, cabanas and sailboat rentals. The resident recreation staff does its best to put more fun in the sun for the younger set. Preschoolers enroll in a Tiny Tots program of toy boat racing, Care Bear cookouts, face painting, puppet making, and storybook reading; preteens engage in supervised pool activities and bicycle outings, fishing, hiking, tennis, and shell crafts; and teenage programs include a tennis clinic, windsurfing, sand sculpture, shelling tours, and fright-night movies.

2255 West Gulf Drive, P.O. Box 167, Sanibel 33957. 813-481-3636; toll-free: 1-800-237-8906. Expensive.

THE CASTAWAYS
Cottages/Sanibel

It's the perfect name for these cottages, which give every appearance of being built by marooned sailors and colonists who wanted some order in their enforced island existence. Shaded by lots of trees and comfortably spaced, the accommodations range from fairly standard motel-style rooms and studio efficiencies with kitchenettes to duplexes and one-, two-, and three-bedroom cottages, which are located bayside or beachside. The complex includes a solar-heated swimming pool, a fishing pier, private docks, and beachside tiki huts with barbecue grills. This is a fine place for families who are not looking for all the fuss of a resort with organized recreation programs.

6460 Sanibel-Captiva Road, Sanibel 33957. 813-472-1252. Inexpensive to moderate.

CONDOMINIUM AND COTTAGE RENTALS

Available are many apartment, chalet, and cottage rentals, some by the day, many for a one-week minimum. Several organizations on the islands handle such accommodations, among them the **Sanibel Resort Group** (813-472-1833 and 813-472-1001) and the **Vacation Shoppe** (813-454-1400).

GALLERY MOTEL

Motel/Sanibel

Neatly laid out and very well maintained motel rooms, efficiencies, cottages, and apartments on the beach blended quietly into the landscape with a center-court swimming pool shaded by graceful palms. Each of the rooms has a balcony. Jack and Betty Reed are in charge, and that means direct contact with one of the island's Coast Guard–licensed guides—Captain Betty at the helm of *Piece A Cake*, which is available for shelling, sight-seeing, and luncheon cruises. Check with her at the motel, or dial 813-472-4575 for your special adventure on the water.

541 East Gulf Drive, Sanibel 33957. 813-472-1400. Moderate to expensive.

HILTON INN

Inn/Sanibel

There's no lovelier landscaping on the island. Trees, bushes, and bright plantings beautifully frame the seven two-story low-rise buildings painted in muted shades of blue and gray. The awnings are a particularly nice touch. A swimming pool, a bar, and three putting greens are in the center courtyard facing the rental boats, cabanas, and beach chairs, and on Gulf Drive is a pair of tennis courts. Close by is the Brass Elephant, a fine restaurant open for breakfast, lunch, and dinner, and featuring special savings at sunset with entrees as varied as prime rib and shrimp fettuccine Alfredo, chicken divan, and baby-back ribs. The Sunday brunch buffets are virtual groaning boards, offering salads and crudités, smoked salmon and shrimp, made-to-order omelets and waffles, egg dishes and prime rib, plus complimentary champagne.

The 97 guest rooms, crisply decorated in tropical colors and patterns, have service bars, small fridges, and screened lanais; the suites also have separate living areas and kitchenettes; and the one- and two-bedroom villas boast full-size kitchens and washers and dryers.

937 Gulf Drive, Sanibel 33957. 813-472-3181; toll-free (in Florida): 1-800-282-2240, (outside Florida): 1-800-237-1491. Expensive.

ISLAND INN
Cottages/Sanibel

An ole-timey kind of destination with comfortably homey furnishings in lodges and cottages overlooking the Gulf of Mexico. Some accommodations have single beds, others double and king-size beds; all have a refrigerator, temperature control, a telephone, and cable TV. Cottage units (a one-week stay is minimum) have sofa beds and fully furnished kitchens. The Matthews Lodge units have screened porches, as do the Spoonbill North and South duplex cottages. During the winter season, a modified American plan is in effect, which means breakfast and dinner are included. In the summer the dining room is closed.

Corner of West Gulf Drive and Island Inn Road, Sanibel 33957. 813-472-1561. Moderate.

SEAHORSE COTTAGES
Cottages/Sanibel

On the eastern tip of the island close to the lighthouse, one block from the Gulf and 200 feet from San Carlos Bay, this clump of cottages behind Seahorse Shops is an appealing off-the-beaten-path retreat. Each of the one- and two-bedroom accommodations has a complete kitchen, cable TV, temperature control, double beds, a sofa bed, and a sun deck overlooking the swimmi g pool sheltered by lush tropical plants. Each cottage is individually decorated, but all have antique oak furnishings and white lace window curtains—a nice touch of class.

1223 Buttonwood Lane, Sanibel 33957. 813-472-4262. Moderate.

SOUTH SEAS PLANTATION
Resort/Captiva

Three hundred and thirty acres, with 22 tennis courts, 17 swimming pools, a 9-hole executive golf course, and a marina with rentals and charters of anything and everything waterborne, make this the *ne plus ultra* of Florida's family resorts. Chadwick's, the King's Crown, Cap'n Al's Pub, and snack bars do the feeding in a variety of settings ranging from poolside bathing suit casual to gussied-up semiformal. There's a similar diversity in the accommodations, which include fairly standard motel-style guest rooms, handsomely furnished one- and two-bedroom villas, and full-fledged beachfront homes with four bedrooms and fully equipped kitchens. Children are cared for by very active programs: the 3-to-5 set participates in finger painting, sing-alongs, and coconut crafts; ages 6 to 8 graduate to inner tube relays and nature and seashell study; ages 9 to 12 engage in lawn and beach sports; and teenagers enroll in courses for snorkeling, shelling, canoeing, water volleyball, jetskiing, and treasure hunting. The whole family can enroll in weeklong learn-to-sail programs or take shorter island cruises or indulge in organized nature walks or scavenger hunts.

P.O. Box 194, Captiva 33924. 813-472-5111; toll-free (in Florida): 1-800-282-3402, (outside Florida): 1-800-237-3102. Expensive.

SUNDIAL BEACH & TENNIS RESORT
Resort/Sanibel

This Gulf-front winner has been newly refurbished and revitalized by a talented team of professionals who seek perfection in all aspects of their operation. It offers an overstocked inventory of appealing features, including seven laykold and six Har-Tru tennis courts (the only clay courts on Sanibel), five heated swimming pools, bike and boat rentals, and instructors to give whatever lessons are required. There's also a very active program for youngsters with a full-time recreation staff supervising such activities as shell crafts, shelling tours (pail and shovel are included with the fee), and bike hikes. Pelican Pete's Children's Camp is in session every day except Saturday (when they gather for Kids, Pizza, and Movie Night), and it revolves around pool games, island excursions, scavenger hunts, and sand sculpture. The 225 one- and two-bedroom suites, all with fully equipped kitchens and most with screened balconies overlooking the Gulf or pool, are attractively furnished in tropical tones. The main building houses a lounge, a well-stocked deli, and Windows on the Water, an aptly named oasis of innovative new American cuisine. To check out that claim, order a confit of duck with stir-fried vegetables and buckwheat noodles, or seafood sausage with mustard sauce, or some authentic Louisiana gumbo, then move on to snapper with blue crab and béarnaise sauce, grilled chicken with pineapple salsa, or tuna au poivre.

1451 Middle Gulf Drive, Sanibel. 813-472-4151; toll free: 1-800-237-4184. Expensive.

'TWEEN WATERS INN
Resort/Captiva

Since 1931 this wonderful island escape has been seducing visitors from all over the world, initially the Charles Lindbergs and then the famed cartoonist of the 1930s, John W. "Ding" Darling, pioneer environmentalist and apparently the first to characterize the shell collectors' "Sanibel Stoop." His Sanibel sketches are part of the decor of this 13-acre ramble of accommodations old and new (but none pretentiously tropical or too-too modern) between the Gulf and Pine Island Sound, with its 'Tween Waters Marina. Three tennis courts, a game room, a swimming pool and boat ramp, and bocce and shuffleboard courts are the on-site activities. And the staff is always willing and able to advise guests on activities in other parts of the island. The Inn offers a variety of eating experiences. The Captiva Canoe Club, with an observation deck overlooking the marina, is a fun place for pizza, burgers, and other light fare. Breakfasts are served from 7:30 to 11:00 A.M. Monday to Saturday. On Sunday the Old Captiva House is the place to be for a bountiful brunch. On Friday the tables are spread with a sensational seafood buffet. Dinners are served nightly and there's a pianist in place to provide proper background music. Next door, the Crow's Nest lounge with its time-honored bar offers live jazz, blues, and soft rock in the evenings. Noon and night it serves a good array of sandwiches and fresh seafood. For shopping, there's the Pelican's Roost by the marina, where you can rent bicycles and charter boats for shelling and fishing.

P.O. Box 249, Captiva 33924. 813-472-5161; toll free (in Florida): 1-800-282-7560, (outside Florida): 1-800-223-5865. Moderate to expensive.

Where to Eat

BANGKOK HOUSE
Thai/Sanibel
When you really want to Thai one on, and dig into some Goong Tod, Gai Tom Kha, Mee Grob, Pad Khing, or just a bit of Larb, this is the place, the first Thai restaurant in southwest Florida. Over the years it has converted legions of loyal fans to the special stir-fried, deep-fried, steamed, and grilled wonders of the land of *The King and I.* Our meals here usually begin with spring rolls (infinitely better than the flavors and textures that name usually evokes); do-it-yourself chicken satay, with its distinctive peanut sauce and counterbalancing cucumber salad; or some of the Mee Grob, crispy rice noodles tangled with shrimp, scallions, and bean sprouts in a tamarind sauce. Next comes anything with coconut milk and Thai curry—the red, green, or yellow—but on several occasions we've enjoyed the frog legs sautéed with chili paste and bay leaves or the squid mingled with a harvest of fresh vegetables.

1547 Periwinkle Way, Sanibel. 813-472-4622. Moderate. Dinner daily.

THE BUBBLE ROOM
American/Captiva
No restaurant on the islands—and for many a mile on the mainland—can boast this kind of setting, a unique gathering of authentic antiques, performing puppets, and the namesake bubbling Christmas tree ornaments. But it's not all stage setting: the staff (in Scout uniforms) performs to perfection, and the kitchen cranks out reliably fresh seafood, great steaks, and one of the thickest slabs of prime rib to be found. Save space for the king-size desserts.

Captiva Road and Andy Rosse Lane, Captiva. 813-472-5558. Expensive. Lunch and dinner daily. No reservations accepted.

CAPTIVA INN
Continental/Sanibel
Chef-owner Evan Snyderman is the main man in this cozy little hidden treasure with just 40 chairs and one seating—at 7:30 P.M. Reservations at least one day in advance are necessary. Snyderman telephones his guests the day before they're due to offer a choice of a half dozen entrees, predicated on the vagaries of the marketplace and his own whims. Dinner commences with complimentary champagne and a sensational seafood appetizer followed by brewed-out-back soup, salads freshly assembled with delicious dressing, some hot garlic bread, and a sorbet palate-cleanser, then moves to the main action, which ranges from freshly caught grouper, salmon, or snapper to veal marsala, rack of lamb, Long Island duckling, and beef tenderloin. The setting is intimately charming and the table appointments are far more formal than you'd expect to find on a barrier island.

11509 Andy Rosse Lane, Captiva. 813-472-9129. Expensive. Dinner Tuesday to Saturday.

CHADWICK'S
American/Captiva
Chadwick's holds down an important corner of the entrance to the South Seas Plantation complex, and honors the name of the pioneer family that first tried

to tame the northern tip of Captiva. The Chadwicks owned a coconut and key lime plantation on the site of South Seas, and their family portraits and other memorabilia can now be found in this restaurant. It's open for three meals a day, but we like it most for the Sunday brunch and the Friday seafood buffet with chefs performing before your very eyes. There's live entertainment in the lounge, which has a good-size dance floor for working off the calories from the impossible-to-resist desserts.

Entrance to South Seas Plantation, Captiva. 813-472-5111. Expensive. Breakfast, lunch, and dinner daily.

IGGY & PAUL'S LOBSTER HOUSE
Seafood/Sanibel
This is the place for the pride of Maine waters, prepared 17 different ways. It also has a seemingly endless variety of shrimp selections along with farm-raised, beer-battered catfish, baby-back barbecue ribs, and broiled mahimahi served with garlic butter and red bliss potatoes. There are early-bird savings, a children's menu, and the Schooner Lounge, where free hors d'oeuvres are offered at the cocktail hour.

Corner of Periwinkle Way and Tarpon Bay Road, Sanibel. 813-472-1366. Moderate to expensive. Lunch and dinner daily.

ISABELLA'S
Italian/Sanibel
Pizza is just one of the Italo-American treats Isabella will deliver to your table or to your home-away-from-home. There's also a good selection of the kind of veal and pasta dishes—lasagna and gnocchi, ravioli and manicotti—you've learned to expect, but not always respect, from pizzerias of this type.

1528 Periwinkle Way, Sanibel. 813-472-0044. Inexpensive. Lunch and dinner Monday to Saturday; limited menu Sunday afternoon and evening.

THE JACARANDA
Seafood/Sanibel

A jamming place on Sunday nights, with rock 'n roll, rhythm 'n blues, and jazz, but there's live entertainment and dancing every night from 8:30 to 12:30 P.M. From 4:00 P.M. until midnight the lounge provides a good selection of snack stuff—chicken wings, oysters and clams, snow crabs, and peel-'em-yourself shrimp. The offerings in the dining room are more ambitious, with crabmeat-stuffed grouper, prime rib and steaks cut from Angus beef, butter-sautéed crabcakes, snapper en papillote, and blacktip shark, climaxed by turtle pie, a nutty fudge ice cream finish with a flourish.

1223 Periwinkle Way, Sanibel. 813-472-1771. Moderate. Dinner daily.

JEAN-PAUL'S FRENCH CORNER
French/Sanibel

The Corner is indeed French, with glorious Gallic music hall posters on simple wooden walls and aromas familiar to anyone who has traveled the provinces. The intoxicating smells are proof positive that owner-chef Jean-Paul Cavanie is hard at work producing the evening meal: chilled soup made with fresh fruit and/or vegetables, escargot en cassolette, rough-textured pâtés, soft-shell crabs Provençale, and some favorite entrees—sole filled with salmon mousse, breast of chicken with lemon sauce, roast duckling in a variety of fruit sauces, veal medallions with mushrooms in a cream sauce, and filet mignon with a green peppercorn sauce. It's a small menu, but one that Jean-Paul has perfected, and he's stocked wines that admirably complement his achievements. For proper finishers try his own version of pecan pie and the orange-infused creme caramel.

Tarpon Bay Road, Sanibel. 813-472-1493. Expensive. Dinner Monday to Saturday.

THE MUCKY DUCK
Continental/Captiva

An english pub setting serving Whitbread ale and Foster's lager and a good selection of pub grub—Scottish meat pies, fish 'n chips, steak-and-sausage pie, and such headliners as barbecue shrimp and bacon, Florida lobster tails, Polynesian chicken, New York strip steak, and of course, duckling. A great place too for sunset-watching.

Andy Rosse Lane, Captiva. 813-472-3434. Moderate to expensive. Lunch and dinner daily. No credit cards.

PALM RIDGE CAFE
American/Sanibel
Partners Skeeter Crossley and Jeff Bundy, refugees from Skaneateles, New York, where they own the Old Stone Mill Restaurant, are responsible for this newcomer to the island provinces. Their new operation is not in quite as historic a setting, but it's informal and laid-back, with a menu built around grilled swordfish and veal Oscar, sautéed scallops and shrimp scampi, mixed seafood grill and steak Madagascar.

Palm Ridge Plaza, 2330 Palm Ridge Place, Sanibel. 813-395-2300. Expensive. Dinner daily.

THE TIMBERS RESTAURANT & FISH MARKET
American/Sanibel
An island spin-off from the highly successful Prawnbroker restaurants and fish markets found in Fort Myers, Bradenton, Marco Island, and Stuart, and driven by uncompromising insistence on freshness and quality, living up to its pledge: "We Serve It Fresh . . . Or We Don't Serve It At All!" On the seafood side of the menu that means everything from oysters Florentine and Romanoff to grouper, red snapper, pompano, cobia, dolphin, salmon, and scrod, as well as monkfish, triggerfish, and tripletail—either simply broiled with lemon butter and light seasoning, charbroiled with garlic butter, or blackened. On the landlocked side of the menu is beef, and there are no better steaks to be found on the islands.

975 Rabbit Road, Sanibel. 813-472-3128. Moderate to expensive. Dinner daily. (The fish market is open daily from noon until 10:00 P.M.)

TIMMY'S NOOK
American/Captiva

Captiva's oldest restaurant, which clutches a side cove of sand at the big bend in the road leading to South Seas Plantation, this aptly named roadside seafood shack has walls that talk—of the good old days before the bridge and causeway brought the invasion from the mainland, when everything was real easy. From the city of the Big Easy—New Orleans—Timmy has brought all the spices of the back bayous, and he serves Cajun-blackened fish, shrimp, and steak; grouper imperial; and seafood Vera Cruz. Saturday is prime rib night.

15183 Captiva Drive, Captiva. 813-472-9444. Moderate. Lunch and dinner daily except Wednesday.

TRUFFLES
American/Sanibel

A super spin-off from the bistro of the same name in Naples, Florida, and just as exciting when it comes to superior service, good wines, beautiful baked goods (on display by the entrance), and the imaginative but not excessive performance in the kitchen. At noontime there are pizzettas of the day along with such departures as Cajun chicken with onions and peppers, fried-oyster or grilled-andouille "Pore Boys," and fried chicken sandwiches with lettuce and tomatoes plus cheddar, guacamole, or salsa. Our favorite fare for dinner includes starters of shrimp-and-veggie egg rolls or fried cashew chicken fingers, followed by crispy fish, grilled Gulf shrimp or Norwegian salmon, eggplant lasagna, stir-fried vegetables, grilled lamb loin, or Jamaican-spiced pork loin. The view of Gulf and green out the wall of windows is terrific.

Casa Ybel, 2255 West Gulf Drive, Sanibel. 813-472-9200. Expensive. Lunch and dinner daily.

Where to Shop

For swimwear, cover-ups, sweats, aqua socks, and sport sandals, check out **Beach Stuff** (813-472-3544) and its neighbor **More Stuff**, two-tenths of a mile from the entrance to South Sea Plantation in Captiva. Directly across from that entrance is the **Plantation View Shopping Center,** with the **Surf and Sport Store,** next door to a grocery and liquor store.

Sanibel Surf Shop (813-472-8185) in Jerry's Shopping Center, at 1700 Periwinkle Way, advertises "Everything for the Beach"; **Spoil Me,** at Tahitian Gardens, 2017 Periwinkle Way, Sanibel (813-472-0999), stocks a good selection of designer swimwear; and **Teasers of Sanibel,** 33 Periwinkle Place, Sanibel (813-472-2616), has a solid array of casual resortwear for men, women, and children.

Three Crafty Ladies, 1446 Periwinkle Way (813-472-2893), features wearable art, unique jewelry, painted shirts, beads, baskets, art supplies, and how-to crafts demonstrations.

If you want to ship five pounds or more of shrimp, check into **The Real Eel,** at 1723 Periwinkle Way (813-472-2674), a seafood shop and the headquarters of **Carolyn's Custom Catering,** which offers a wonderfully extensive menu of some 60 hot and cold hors d'oeuvres, 30 entrees, salads, soups, side dishes, and such decadent desserts as chocolate mile-high mousse pie, Scotch shortbread, white chocolate tartlets, English plum pudding with hard sauce, and killer brownies.

Next door is **Ron's Photo Finish** (813-392-0040), with one-hour rush processing, and around the corner at 1711 Periwinkle is **A Touch of Class** (813-472-5500), a dry cleaner that also does repairs and alterations.

As you might suspect, there is no lack of shell shops on Sanibel. Start with **She Sells Sea Shells,** at 1157 Periwinkle Way (813-472-6991); or **Showcase Shells** (813-472-1971) and **Shell World of Sanibel** (813-472-9411) at 1614 and 2407 Periwinkle Way, respectively.

Book shops number three: **MacIntosh,** 2365 Periwinkle Way (813-472-1447) is the oldest (opened in 1960) and is well stocked with books about the islands; as are **Island Book Nook,** 2440 Palm Ridge Road (813-472-6777), and **Sanibel Island Bookshop,** 975 Rabbit Road (813-472-5223).

More Fun in the Sun

Sanibel and Captiva are perfect for pedaling, and scooter and moped riding, and there are several outlets for rental of the equipment, including bicycles built for two, jitneys with the fringe on top, and the new buddy bike (with side-by-side seating), ideal for newlyweds. There are 22 miles of paved nature paths and 58 miles of paved and shell-packed roads. Rental shops such as

Island Moped, 1470 Periwinkle Way (813-472-5249), have do-it-yourself guides covering the sights to be seen and the places to snack and feast along the way. Moped renters must have a valid driver's license or permit and must wear helmets. Other bike rental agencies include **The Bike Rental,** 2330 Palm Ridge Road, Sanibel (813-472-2241); **Finnimore's Cycle Shop,** Jacaranda Plaza, 1223 Periwinkle Way, Sanibel (813-472-5577); and **Jim's Bike and Scooter Rental,** 11534 Andy Rosse Lane, Captiva (813-472-1296), which also has waverunners for rent.

Billy's Beach Service, with eight Gulf-front locations, four of them in hotels—the Hilton, Sundial, 'Tween Waters, and West Wind—and close to 20 years of experience in the business, has the right to call itself "Your Fun in the Sun Expert." It rents sailboards, Hobie Cats, and Sunfish, giving lessons right on the beach, and also has bikes, beach chairs, cabanas, and umbrellas.

Windsurfing of Sanibel, 1554 Periwinkle Way (813-472-0123), has a teaching school and guarantees you'll learn how to windsurf. It also sells sports clothes and swimwear. Scuba divers can take lessons and rent all the necessary equipment at the **Pieces of Eight Dive Center** in South Seas Plantation (813-472-9424), which also organizes half-day snorkel trips for all ages, with the snorkeling done in two-to-five-foot depths off the ledge of Caya Costa State Park.

Those who want to cruise on the surface of the water can make reservations on Nancy and Dick Barnes's 32-foot custom Downeaster, the *Lady,* docked at the 'Tween Waters Marina on Captiva, 15951 Captiva Road (813-994-1922), behind the 'Tween Waters Inn. The *Lady* offers narrated trips to the outer islands, lunch and dinner cruises to Upper Captiva or Cabbage Key (the former home of mystery writer Mary Roberts Rinehart), and cruises to isolated spots for picnics or out into the Gulf for the nightly ritual of sunset-watching.

Other charter boat captains, rental boats, and water taxis can be found at other marinas; namely, **Jensen's Twin Palms,** 15107 Captiva Drive, Captiva (813-472-5800); **Sanibel Harbor Marina,** 15051 Punta Rassa Road, Sanibel Causeway (813-454-0141); and **Sanibel Marina,** 634 North Yachtsman Drive, Sanibel (813-472-2723). In addition to shelling and sight-seeing excursions, the boats go on fishing trips, and the guide recommended to make sure you find the mackerel, redfish, and trout is **Captain John Fussell** (813-267-6444). Recommended by whom or what, you might ask. By **The Bait**

Shop, 1041 Periwinkle Way, Sanibel (813-472-1618); the local fisherman's headquarters, with a full line of equipment: tackle (rental as well as purchase), protective clothing, and frozen and live bait—they catch their own.

To learn more about the marine life of Sanibel's beaches, tidal grass flats, and mangrove forests, **Aqua Trak** (813-472-8689) organizes half-day trips. Shoreline beach life is caught by seine and studied, and the tour terminates at an oceanarium where there are hands-on encounters with live shells, sea urchins, crabs, and other residents of local waters.

Canoeist who don't bring their own craft can find rentals at the **Tarpon Bay Recreation Area** off Tarpon Bay Road, and also at the **'Tween Waters Marina**. Among the most interesting routes to explore are the **Buck Key Canoe Trail** and the waters of Pine Island and San Carlos Bay that lap the jagged shorelines of the **J. N. "Ding" Darling Wildlife Refuge Area**. **Canoe Adventures** (813-472-5218) conducts naturalist tours of the refuge.

If you're worried about where to leave the wee ones when planning an excursion on the high seas, contact the **Rabbit Road Center for Children**, 975 Rabbit Road, Sanibel (813-472-8687). It takes infants and preschoolers.

Where to Write

The Sanibel-Captiva Islands Chamber of Commerce, P.O. Box 166, Sanibel Island, Florida 33957. 813-472-1080.

◎　　◎　　◎

FORT MYERS BEACH

Fort Myers Beach is in fact Estero Island, a low-lying barrier island across Matanzas Pass and Estero Bay between the Gulf of Mexico and the mainland. This eight-mile-long, crescent-shaped home to 14,000 residents is the most popular recreational area in the county, with more than 40,000 visitors arriving each year, many of them during the high season (mid-December to mid-April). That's the time when the traffic on Estero Boulevard, the main artery of the island and originally a hard-packed sand thoroughfare, gets a bit backed up, so consider using Molly the Trolley. A fleet of the conveyances covers the island from one end to the other during the high season, and daily and monthly tickets are available—with reduced fares for senior citizens.

Why drive the boulevard if you're comfortably settled into one or another of the many accommodations? To shop and snack, of course; to visit the marinas and shrimp docks where the commercial fishermen hang out under that magnificent Sky Bridge; to get your exercise at a golf course or tennis court; or to check out Carl E. Johnson Park, a county facility past the southern tip of Estero. Drive across the bridge over Big Carlos Pass and on to the Bonita–Fort Myers Beach Causeway to the park entrance, clearly marked and with ample parking out front. After paying the entrance fee and picking up a small flyer explaining the coastal ecosystem—"one of the most productive biological factories in the world—the Mangrove Estuarine Bay System"— walk the marked trail to the beach. Or take the trackless tram, which winds to the water over the wetlands on the islets of Black Island, Inner Key, and Lover's Key, where the tram unloads its passengers at a developed beach with rest rooms, changing rooms, picnic sites, and showers. Fishing is permitted (no license required) throughout the park unless specifically posted, and there is a series of ten numbered posts corresponding to the flyer explanations. The flyer provides a painless way to learn about the birth and growth of a barrier island, and the important role played by those arching stiltlike roots of the red mangrove, festooned in many sections with tiny "coon oysters," a staple of the raccoon diet. Algae, small crabs, mussels, barnacles, and their cousins find safe shelter under those mangrove roots—safe, that is, from all predators except ravenous fish and the larger varieties of crab. Whether walking or tramming, be on the lookout for the bird life in the area: the black-and-white osprey and the cormorant, two of nature's most effective fishermen, and the dive-bombing pelican. There are also egrets and herons and the ubiquitous screeching gulls.

Lover's Key is the nearest departure point for a mile-long waterborne trip—in your own shallow-draft boat or with a tour group—to Florida's first capital, 149-acre Mound Key, chief city of the Calusa Indians who once ruled those shores and the territory that on a contemporary map stretches as far north as Sarasota, east all the way over to Cape Canaveral, and south to the keys. From 1200 B.C. to A.D. 1600 the Calusa were the most powerful of the local native societies, repulsing Ponce de Leon in his early attempts to colonize their territory and attracting the homage of no less a personage than Pedro Menéndez de Aviles, the mighty Spanish admiral who founded St. Augustine. The year after he arrived there he made a pilgrimage to Mound Key to marry the sister of the Calusa chief, and to forge an alliance with the politically sophisticated Indians. A State Archaeological Site, this highest of all mounds in Florida was created by the thousands and thousands of shells tossed there by the Indians after removing the life-sustaining meat from the mollusks and crustaceans. Shell fragments are very much in evidence today, as are bits and pieces of native pottery, visible underfoot and alongside the paths, where they lie under snake plants and the foliage dropped from wild orange trees, royal poincianas, guavas, and palms. Look but do not touch—and do not remove anything from the protected site. The guides (contact information is listed in "More Fun in the Sun") will emphasize this point while providing a good deal of stimulating and speculative commentary to trigger your own imagination.

For a different kind of stimulation, consider spending some time on the fishing pier jutting out into the Gulf; there's no charge. Right alongside the pier is the Lynn Hall Memorial Park, with plenty of parking, rest rooms, picnic tables, and barbecue grills. It's the headquarters for various beach happenings and festivals, including the annual mid-November sand sculpture contest, sure to fascinate children of all ages. Also perfect for children is Fort Myers Beach; in fact, it's touted by local boosters as "the world's safest beach," thanks to a double sandbar and very gradually sloping shorelines.

Where It Is

Fort Myers Beach is 14 miles south of Forth Myers on State Road 867, MacGregor Boulevard, which leads to State Road 865, San Carlos Boulevard, which continues to and across the beach south as Estero Boulevard.

Where to Stay

CONDOMINIUM RENTALS

There are numerous condominium units available on the beach, most of them in high-rise structures with elevators and apartment-style accommodations—a fully furnished kitchen, one or two bedrooms, one or two baths, a large living room, a balcony overlooking the Gulf, and a washer-dryer. Some buildings have swimming pools and other recreational facilities. Rentals are seldom available on a daily basis, and some units require a two-week minimum rental. Several realtors on the island handle these rentals, including such firms as **Kathy Nesbit Vacations, Inc.**, 7205 Estero Boulevard, Fort Myers Beach, Florida 33931 (813-463-4253).

HOLIDAY INN
Motel/Fort Myers Beach

A brightly shining link in the nationwide chain that enjoys one of the best of all locations—just a few feet from the Gulf. There's a splendid tropical courtyard with a pool at center stage surrounded by palm frond chickees that are shaded by tall palms and lush plantings. Guest rooms and suites are on the uppermost scale of Holiday Inn upscale, and there's a very popular restaurant, Heron's, with Sunday breakfast buffets, stir-fry nights plus all-you-can-eat fish frys, shrimp boils, and Italian feasts. The sports bar packs in the fans during special events, and the Heron's Nest poolside bar features light lunches, cocktail hour savings with free hors d'oeuvres, and live entertainment Wednesday to Saturday.

6890 Estero Boulevard, Fort Myers Beach 33931. 813-463-5711; toll free: 1-800-HOLIDAY. Moderate.

LANA KAI
Hotel/Fort Myers Beach

There's a top-floor sun deck, a ground-floor lounge with live (as in lively and loud) entertainment, the Casablanca piano bar and Gulf View restaurant, and functionally modern rooms, furnished in a style more or less in keeping with the Polynesian name. Each of the 100 rooms has a private balcony and a refrigerator, plus other amenities. The free-form pool is heated, and there are gas-fired barbecue grills and tables out on the patio for do-it-yourself feeding. The six-story hotel is the parasailing headquarters on the beach and can also arrange Jet Ski and other boat rentals.

1400 Estero Boulevard, Fort Myers Beach 33931. 813-463-3111, 463-5332; toll-free: 1-800-237-6133. Moderate to expensive.

LAUGHING GULL COTTAGES
Cottages/Fort Myers Beach

There are many clumps of cottages on and off the beach that run the gamut from primitive to near posh. Our favorites are in this complex hanging on to the sands between the boulevard and the Gulf of Mexico, just as the earliest cottage built has been doing since 1937. The 11 units are painted with inviting shades of blue and gray and remind us of what Florida beaches used to look like before the arrival of the motels and high-rises. The stilt-supported wooden cottages have porches or patios, and include efficiencies and one- and two-bedroom units, all with kitchenettes, air-conditioning, and cable television. Cottages 6A, 6B, 8, and 9 are closest to the Gulf.

2890 Estero Boulevard, Fort Myers Beach 33931. 813-463-1346. Moderate to expensive.

NEPTUNE INN
Motel/Fort Myers Beach
A two-wing unit flanking a pair of swimming pools on some 300 feet of Gulf front, with kitchenette-equipped efficiency units, each with twin or double beds and balconies. The larger of the 64 accommodations are in the north wing and contain sofa beds, making this inn/motel a comfortable family place on the beach and close to all the action on the boulevard.

2310 Estero Boulevard, Fort Myers Beach 33931. 813-463-6141. Moderate.

OUTRIGGER BEACH RESORT
Motel/Fort Myers Beach
Another sandy shore sentinel, this one on 350 feet of one of the safest beaches in the world. The 144 units, all bright, clean, and uncluttered, range from standard single or double rooms to efficiencies large and small, with kitchenettes and sofa beds. In addition to a center-court swimming pool with a tiki bar and chickee-dotted sun deck, there's a small coffee shop that serves breakfast and light lunches and a guest activities center that organizes stretch and exercise sessions in and out of the pool, volleyball and shuffleboard competitions, hot dog and hamburger barbecues, fashion shows, bingo games, and shelling seminars.

6200 Estero Boulevard, P.O. Box 271, Fort Myers Beach 33931-1281. 813-463-3131; toll-free: 1-800-749-3131. Moderate to expensive.

PINK SHELL
Cottages/Fort Myers Beach
The largest collection of cottages and apartment-motel accommodations on Fort Myers Beach. Located on 12 acres at the northern tip of the island, with 1,500 feet of beach for one border and the deep waters of Estero Bay for the other, this water-surrounded property is perfect for families of all sizes. Accommodations range from standard motel rooms to a three-bedroom, two-and-a-half-bath penthouse with kitchen, living room, large screened porch,

and sun deck. There are also conference rooms, convenience stores, a pair of Har-Tru tennis courts, swimming and wading pools, and 200 feet of private fishing pier and boat slips on the bay. The level of maintenance, the condition of the rooms, and the combination of designer colors in the fabrics and furnishings are on a par with those found at South Seas Plantation out on Captiva Island and other properties of the Mariner Corporation. Pink Shell (and it is very definitely pink) is in the same corporate portfolio. Rentals of water sports gear—waverunners, sailboats, beach chairs, and umbrellas—are available at the on-site Holiday Shop (813-765-4FUN). Their services are also available to non-hotel residents.

275 Estero Boulevard, Fort Myers Beach 33931. 813-463-6181; toll-free (in Florida): 1-800-282-0485, (outside Florida): 1-800-237-5786. Moderate to expensive.

SANDPIPER GULF RESORT
Resort/Fort Myers Beach

A two- and three-story spread of 63 apartments facing the ocean or embracing the courtyard. Palm trees frame the pool and the shuffleboard courts—the assembly station in the morning, when complimentary coffee is served—and the gentle surf rolls right up to the edge of the property. The rooms are functional modern, immaculate in overall appearance, and practical for families and couples, each room having two double beds, a dressing room and bath, and a fully stocked full-size kitchen. There are electronic games for the kids in the lobby.

5550 Estero Boulevard, Fort Myers Beach. 813-463-5721. Moderate to expensive.

Where to Eat

THE FISH MONGER
Seafood/Fort Myers Beach
The best-value-for-the-money seafood shack in the area, with a series of surprises such as seafood gumbo; roasted garlic; barbecue baby-back ribs; escargot in mushroom caps; seafood lasagna made with shrimp, scallops, fish, and cheeses; pan-sautéed rock shrimp scampi, served on linguine; a simmering, steaming, mussel-scallop-shrimp-marinara stew; lightly breaded and fried mullet; shrimp etouffee; and chicken breasts baked with Monterey Jack, spinach, and a touch of jalapeño. There's also a five-item children's menu.

883 San Carlos Boulevard, Fort Myers Beach. 813-765-5544. Inexpensive to moderate. Dinner daily.

GALLO'S RISTORANTE D'ITALIA
Italian/Fort Myers Beach
When the pasta urge gets too great, or the need for osso buco becomes overwhelming, go over Sky Bridge to this outpost of many good things Italian; as soon as you reach the mainland look to the right and dock your gondola. The veal dishes—all the usual—are excellent and the pasta selection is seemingly endless. The wine list is adequate to the challenges of the food, and there are seasonal savings along the lines of early-bird specials.

19051 San Carlos Boulevard, Fort Myers Beach. 813-463-4400. Moderate. Dinner daily.

GOLDEN DRAGON
Chinese/Fort Myers Beach
You have to cross the Sky Bridge and go a few hundred yards to reach this Oriental restaurant, which features all the familiar Cantonese creations—from moo goo gai pan to sweet-and-sour pork—but also Sichuan specialties utilizing those devilishly hot little red peppers and having a lot more zing than you'll find in egg foo yung. There's a fully stocked bar and lounge plus the

Dragon Room Club, with live entertainment and dancing on the weekends. Take-out is available of course.

Summerlin Square, 17105 San Carlos Boulevard, Fort Myers Beach. 813-466-7077. Moderate. Lunch and dinner daily.

GULF SHORE
American/Fort Myers Beach

A sensational shoreline setting with walls of windows for early morning blinking and late afternoon sunset-watching. Start your day with eggs Benedict, Alaskan (with king crab, fried eggs, and sauce choron), or Caliente (a flour tortilla with fried eggs, refried beans, a blanket of spicy salsa, and melted cheddar), the first served with a Bloody Mary, the second with a Screwdriver, and the South of the Border special with Red Beer. We usually order the Gulf Shore Scrambler, eggs tangled with ham, mushrooms, and spinach and crowned with cheese—served on an English muffin and accompanied by skins-on fries. At noontime we stick to the steak sandwiches, the honey-dipped shrimp, or grilled chicken melt; and at dinner we order a broiled seafood platter or whatever fish is listed as catch of the day.

1270 Estero Boulevard, Fort Myers Beach. 813-463-9551. Inexpensive to moderate. Breakfast, lunch, and dinner daily.

THE MUCKY DUCK
Continental/Fort Myers Beach

A near clone of the duckie on Captiva Island and with the same kind of English pub setting and polyglot menu, offering everything from smoked salmon and gazpacho to honey-glazed fried chicken, crabcakes, beer-battered shrimp, fish and chips, duckling à l'orange, and filet mignon. When available, there are also Florida lobster, salmon, swordfish, and tuna, all fresh off the grill. And from the hours of five to six there are early-bird savings on a quartet of dishes.

2500 Estero Boulevard, Fort Myers Beach. 813-463-5519. Moderate to expensive. Dinner daily.

NICK AND STELLA'S BEACH DINER AND PIZZERIA
Italian/Fort Myers Beach

Order a 14-inch or 16-inch pizza for devouring on the spot or delivery to your home-away-from-home. Or have some subs sent over, or maybe something Greek like a salad with feta or skewered souvlaki. There's a variety of budget-stretching dinners built around the likes of chicken Parmesan, veal marsala, and spaghetti with meatballs.

1165 Estero Boulevard, Fort Myers Beach. 813-463-2060. Inexpensive to moderate. Lunch and dinner daily.

PATE'S AT THE BRIDGE
Seafood/Fort Myers Beach

A familiar name in these parts—and as far afield as Naples—and in a great location, the Gulf Star Marina under the Sky Bridge. Killer seafood is what they boast, but they are also proud of their prime rib, strip sirloin, and porterhouse—all of it prime and prepared in the same manner as it was when they started out four decades ago with the opening of Cape Cod's first charcoal steak-pit and seafood house. Seafood in this southern outpost is spelled fresh grouper and snapper, and lobster and salmon from the frigid waters of Maine and Norway. At noontime order a deep-fried fresh fish of the day on a bun, one of the platters built around grouper, or a thickly stacked "Ultimate Club," featuring char-broiled chicken, Swiss cheese, and avocado in addition to the usual ingredients. They even assemble some pretty good fajitas platters.

708 Fisherman's Wharf, Fort Myers Beach. 813-765-0050. Moderate to expensive. Lunch and dinner daily.

PLAKA
Greek/Fort Myers Beach

The place in all of Fort Myers to find spinakopita, moussaka, baklava, and all the other standbys of the Greek taverna, as well as the Americanized gyros. Strictly informal and close to all the action near the Big Bend, the place where Estero Boulevard makes its swing south after crossing the Sky Bridge.

1001 Estero Boulevard, Fort Myers Beach. 813-463-4707. Inexpensive.
Lunch and dinner daily.

REESE'S
American/Fort Myers Beach
Since 1979 this simple coffee shop has been pleasing beachgoers who really like to sleep in—it serves breakfast all day. A few of the reasons for checking into this spot next door to the post office are the blueberry, strawberry, and pecan-freckled pancakes and Belgian waffles; the vegetarian and corned beef hash omelets; and the thickest of French toast. Lunch starts at eleven, and that means chicken fingers or fried ravioli, Greek salad, homemade chili, and a fine assortment of sandwiches.

Key Estero Shops, 1661 Estero Boulevard, Fort Myers Beach. 813-463-3933. Inexpensive. Breakfast and lunch daily.

THE SKIPPER'S GALLEY
American/Fort Myers Beach
A relative newcomer to the beach, occupying the sands where the landmark Pelican Inn stood for over half a century, this mission to the south from Anthony's on Cape Cod is a real winner. There's a shipboard design and atmosphere, with the cheerful, concerned wait staff in nautical garb, and seafood as the specialty—from seafood gumbo and New England clam chowder to oysters Rockefeller and clams casino, from baked and fried scallops to pompano in parchment, snapper with almonds, and sensational garlic shrimp. There are also landlocked entrees to choose from: baby-back barbecue ribs, chicken, New York strip steak, filet mignon, and a trio of veal treats, including francese and marsala and something called Madagascar, which is a bit of overkill—Swiss cheese–spinach stuffing with a crown of mushrooms and a splash of brandy in the brown sauce. The portions are huge, the desserts eye-popping.

3040 Estero Boulevard, Fort Myers Beach. 813-463-6139. Moderate to expensive. Dinner daily.

SNUG HARBOR
Seafood/Fort Myers Beach

Snug is the right word for this nifty little dockside hideaway tucked under the Sky Bridge and serving excellent seafood. For lunch that means crab-a-mato (crabmeat *on* the tomato, not *in* it), steamed shrimp in the shell, a basket of fried oysters, crabcakes or crab-stuffed potato skins, burgers, and a fillet of fresh garlic-infused grouper layered with mushrooms and Parmesan—which earns it the right to be called New Orleans. Our dinners here start with oysters casino or Rockefeller, move on to a steamed Florida lobster tail or shrimp scampi, fresh grouper steamed with spinach (and called Popeye, of course), or the broiled platter "Supreme," which means just about everything from the deep. The herbed rice is good, the bread is baked on the premises, and the desserts are excellent.

645 San Carlos Boulevard, Fort Myers Beach. 813-463-4343. Moderate. Lunch and dinner daily.

Where to Shop

For shipping citrus to your vitamin C–starved friends back home, check into the **Gulf View Shops**, 2943 Estero Boulevard (813-463-9252). They have a variety of packings, some including extras of pecans and other nuts, honey, and marmalades, in champagne hampers and flamingo-decorated tins.

The **Silver Witch**, 1270 Estero Boulevard (813-463-5155), sells an interesting variety of sterling silver including enough trolls to fill a forest. **Tropical Treasures**, 1901 Estero Boulevard (813-765-4868), next door to the bike rentals at **Pelican Plaza**, outfits the younger set with baby and junior-size beach wear.

For men's and women's beach and resort wear, go to **Villa Santini Plaza**, on the south end of the island, and check into **Leani's** (813-463-2838) or **Mulberry Street** (813-463-4537) for more of the same plus a variety of soft summery cottons and the latest for golf and tennis. The **Paper Basket**, 1113 Estero Boulevard (813-463-6212), has totes, sweats, and cover-ups, plus shirts hand-embroidered with Fort Myers Beach logos.

At the northern end of Estero Boulevard, near the Big Bend where Estero Boulevard swings south after Sky Bridge, there's a string of shops with beach and resort wear and equipment, namely, **Wings, C. Dreams, West Coast**

Surf Shop, Flamingo Cay Traders, Mango Bay, Sand Dollar, and T-Shirt Depot. To get your car and your clothes washed, check into **Mid-Island Car Wash and Laundry and Dry Cleaning** (which even does alterations), 5689 Estero Boulevard on the corner of Lazy Way.

More Fun in the Sun

Island Water Tours sails into the sunset with *Ragtime*, a 50-foot sloop departing from the dock at the **Pink Shell Resort**, 275 Estero Boulevard (813-463-6181 ext. 246). Other voyages on other boats run by Island Water Tours including hourlong trips into the back bays and luncheon-dinner cruises with a stop at a restaurant, leaving from the same dock. For charter fishing trips, contact the **Getaway Marina** (813-466-3600) for half-day, all-day, and overnight expeditions, or **Deebold's** (813-466-3525) or the **Gulf Star** (813-765-1500) marinas located at the docks underneath the Sky Bridge. **Beach House Marina** (813-466-7400) is at 18900 San Carlos Boulevard, at the foot of the Little Bridge. The *Class Act* fishing boat (813-463-7800) takes larger groups out for half-day trips or full-day trips from 6:00 A.M. or 8:00 A.M. to 5:00 P.M., departing from 416 Crescent Street, under the Sky Bridge.

Half-day and full-day trips to Mound Key via canoe, kayak, or pontoon boat can be arranged through the **Nature Center of Lee County** (813-939-3678), **Estero River Boat Tours** (813-992-1223), or the Naples branch of the **Nature Conservancy** (813-262-0304).

Located at the southern end of the island, the **Bay Beach Golf Club**, 7401 Estero Boulevard (813-463-2064), is an 18-hole par-61 executive course with a driving range, rental clubs, and lessons—and it's the only course on the beach open to the public. The **Bay Beach Racquet Club**, 120 Lenell Street, behind the Villa Santini Plaza (813-463-4473), with Har-Tru lighted courts and a resident teaching pro, is also open to the public.

Rental bikes and scooters are available at the **Pelican Plaza** (813-463-8844), a two-shop mini-mall at 1901 Estero Boulevard—riders of vehicles must have a valid operator's license.

Miniature golf can be played at the **SeaBreeze**, 7295 Estero Boulevard (813-463-PUTT), at the south end of the island. Its Patio Grill has terrific burgers.

Where to Write

The Lee County Visitor and Convention Bureau, 2180 West First Street, #100; P.O. Box 2445, Fort Myers, Florida 33902-2445. 813-335-2631; toll-free (in Florida): 1-800-533-7433, (outside Florida): 1-800-237-6444.

INDEX

ACCOMMODATIONS

Abbott Realty Services, Inc., Destin, 156
Acapulco Inn, Daytona Beach Shores, 127
Adam's Mark Caribbean Gulf Resort, Clearwater Beach, 214
Aku Tiki Inn, Daytona Beach Shores, 128
Aloha Village, Fort Walton Beach, 155
Amelia Island Plantation, Amelia Island, 190–91
Azure Tides Resort, Sarasota, 238

Bahia Cabana Beach Resort, Fort Lauderdale, 75
Bahia Mar Resort and Yachting Center, Fort Lauderdale, 75
Barbary Coast Motel, Pensacola Beach, 143
Barefoot Beach Inn, Panama City Beach, 174
Barnacle, The, Big Pine Key, 39
Beacher's Lodge, St. Augustine, 200
Beach Hut, Daytona Beach Shores, 128

Beachside Motel Inn, Fernandina Beach, 191
Beacon, Miami Beach, 6–7
Bentley, The, Miami Beach, 7
Bermuda Inn, Delray Beach, 88
Best Western Key Ambassador Resort Inn, Key West, 47
Betsy Ross Hotel, The, Miami Beach, 7
Blue Horizon, Fort Walton Beach, 156
Boca Raton Resort and Club, Boca Raton, 88–89
Breakwater/Edison, Miami Beach, 8
Breckenridge Resort Hotel, The, St. Petersburg Beach, 225
Bridge Hotel, The, Boca Raton, 89
Buccaneer Lodge, Marathon, 39–40

Camino Real Holiday Inn, Delray Beach, 90
Captain's House, The, Fernandina Beach, 193
Cardozo, The, Miami Beach, 8
Carlyle, The, Miami Beach, 8–9
Carousel Beach Resort, Fort Walton Beach, 156
Casa Ybel Resort, Sanibel, 250
Castaways, The, Sanibel, 250
Cavalier Hotel and Cabana Club, Miami Beach, 9

Chateau, Panama City Beach, 172
Cheeca Lodge, Islamorada, 40
Chesapeake of Whale Harbor Resort, Islamorada, 41
Clearwater Beach Hilton, Clearwater Beach, 214–15
Clearwater Beach Hotel, Clearwater Beach, 215
Clevelander, Miami Beach, 9
Cocoa Beach Hilton & Tower, Cocoa Beach, 114
Colony Beach and Tennis Resort, The, Longboat Key, 238–39
Comfort Inn, Navarre, 143
Comfort Inn, Pensacola, 144
Condominium and cottage rentals, Sanibel, 251
Condominium rentals, Destin, 156
Condominium rentals, Fort Myers Beach, 266
Condominium rentals, St. Augustine Beach, 202
Condominum rentals, Okaloosa and Walton counties, 156
Curry Mansion Inn, Key West, 47

Days Hotel, Vero Beach, 102
Days Hotel Gulfstream Beach Resort, Hollywood Beach, 62
Days Inn–Lauderdale Surf Hotel, Fort Lauderdale, 76
Days Inn Oceanfront, Cocoa Beach, 114
Daytona Beach Hilton, Daytona Beach, 128–29
Daytona Beach Marriott, Daytona Beach, 129
Dolphin Beach Resort, St. Petersburg Beach, 225
Don CeSar–A Registry Resort, The, St. Petersburg Beach, 223, 225–26
Dover House, Delray Beach, 90
Driftwood on the Ocean, Hollywood Beach, 62
Driftwood Resort, Vero Beach, 103
Dunes, The, Pensacola Beach, 144

Econo Lodge, Clearwater Beach, 215
Edgewater Beach Resort, Panama City Beach, 172

Fairmont, Miami Beach, 12
Five Flags Motel, Pensacola Beach, 144
Flamingo, Panama City Beach, 172–73

Gallery Motel, Sanibel, 251
Greenbriar Apartment/Motel, Hollywood Beach, 62–63
Guest Quarters, Vero Beach, 103
Gulfcrest, Panama City Beach, 173
Gulfside Miracle Mile Inn, Panama City Beach, 174
Gulfview Inn, Sunnyside, 173

Harbor House, Delray Beach, 90–91
Harley Sandcastle, The, Sarasota, 239
Hawk's Cay Resort and Marina, Duck Key, 41–42
Hilton Inn, Sanibel, 251–52
Hilton on St. Petersburg Beach, The, St. Petersburg Beach, 226
Holiday Inn, Fort Myers Beach, 266–67
Holiday Inn, Fort Walton Beach, 156–57
Holiday Inn, Highland Beach, 91

Holiday Inn, Key West, 46
Holiday Inn, Pensacola Beach, 145
Holiday Inn Beachside, Key West, 47
Holiday Inn Cocoa Beach Resort, Cocoa Beach, 115
Holiday Inn Gulfview, Clearwater Beach, 216
Holiday Inn Lido Beach, Lido Beach, 240
Holiday Inn Oceanside, Vero Beach, 104
Holiday Inn—On the Beach, St. Augustine Beach, 200–201
Holiday Inn Surfside, Clearwater Beach, 216
Holiday Isle Resorts & Marina, Islamorada, 42–43
Hollywood Beach Hilton, Hollywood Beach, 63
Howard Johnson Hollywood Beach Resort Inn, Hollywood Beach, 63
Howard Johnson Oceans Edge Resort, Fort Lauderdale, 76
Howard Johnson Plaza-Hotel, Cocoa Beach, 115
Howard Johnson Resort, St. Augustine Beach, 201
Howard Johnson's Oceanfront, Daytona Beach, 129
Hyatt Key West, Key West, 46, 48

Inn at Cocoa Beach, The, Cocoa Beach, 116
Inn on the Beach, The, St. Petersburg Beach, 226
Ireland's Inn, Fort Lauderdale, 76
Islander Motel, The, Vero Beach, 104
Island Inn, Sanibel, 252

Island's End, St. Petersburg Beach, 224, 226–27

Jamaica Joe's Islander, Fort Walton Beach, 157
Jules' Undersea Lodge, Key Largo, 31

Kathy Nesbit Vacations, Inc., Fort Myers Beach, 266
Key Largo Holiday Inn Resort and Marina, Key Largo, 32

La Fiesta Motor Lodge, St. Augustine Beach, 201–2
Lago Mar, Fort Lauderdale, 77
Lana Kai, Fort Myers Beach, 267
Laughing Gull Cottages, Fort Myers Beach, 267
Little Palm Island Resort, Little Torch Key, 48–49

Marina del Mar Bayside, Key Largo, 32
Marina del Mar Resort and Marina, Key Largo, 32–33
Marlin Apartments, Cocoa Beach, 116
Marriott Bay Point Resort, Bay Point–Panama City Beach, 174
Marriott's Casa Marina Resort, Key West, 46, 49
Marriott's Harbor Beach Resort, Fort Lauderdale, 77
Miracle Mile Resort, Panama City Beach, 174

Neptune Inn, Fort Myers Beach, 268
New Leonard Beach Hotel, The, Miami Beach, 9–10

Ocean Gallery, The, St. Augustine Beach, 202

Ocean Key House Suite Resort & Marina, Key West, 50

Ocean Lodge, Boca Raton, 91

Ocean Suite Hotel, Cocoa Beach, 116

Outrigger Beach Resort, Fort Myers Beach, 268

Park Central, Miami Beach, 10

Perdido Sun, Pensacola, 145

Phoenix Nest, The, Fernandina Beach, 191–92

Pier House, Key West, 46, 50

Pier Point South, St. Augustine Beach, 202

Pink Shell, Fort Myers Beach, 268–69

Ponce Landing, St. Augustine Beach, 202

Porters Court, Panama City Beach, 175

Radisson Suite Resort, Sand Key, Clearwater Beach, 216–17

Ramada Beach Resort, Fort Walton Beach, 157

Ramada Oceanfront Resort, Satellite Beach, 117

Reach, The, Key West, 51

Reef, The, Panama City Beach, 175

Registry, Key West, 46

Resort of Longboat Key Club, The, Longboat Key, 240

Resort Systems, Inc., St. Augustine Beach, 202

Ruffy's Intracoastal Waterway Resort, Hollywood Beach, 64

St. Augustine Ocean & Racquet Resort, St. Augustine Beach, 202

Sandestin Beach Hilton, Destin, 158

Sandestin Beach Resort, Destin, 158

Sandpiper Beach Resort, St. Petersburg Beach, 227

Sandpiper Gulf Resort, Fort Myers Beach, 269

Sands Inn, Panama City Beach, 174

Sanibel Resort Group, Sanibel, 251

Sea Aire Motel, Cocoa Beach, 117

Seagate Hotel and Beach Club, The, Delray Beach, 92

Seahorse Cottages, Sanibel, 252–53

Sea Lodge, Panama City Beach, 175

Seaside Inn, Fernandina Beach, 192

Seaside Resort, Santa Rosa Beach, 159

Sea Wake Inn, Clearwater Beach, 217

1735 House, The, Fernandina Beach, 192–93

1735 Lodging System, The, Fernandina Beach, 193

Seychelles, St. Augustine Beach, 202

Shalimar Plaza, Panama City Beach, 165

Sheldon Ocean Resort, Hollywood Beach, 64

Sheraton Coronado Beach Resort, Fort Walton Beach, 159

Sheraton Inn, Daytona Beach Shores, 130

Sheraton Key Largo Resort, Key Largo, 33

Sheraton Miracle Mile Inn, Panama City Beach, 174

Sheraton Royal Biscayne Beach Re-

sort & Racquet Club, Key Bis-
cayne, 21
Sheraton Sand Key Resort, Sand
Key, Clearwater Beach,
217
Sheraton Yankee Clipper Beach
Resort, Fort Lauderdale,
78
Sheraton Yankee Trader Beach
Resort, Fort Lauderdale,
78
Shore Edge, Boca Raton, 92
Shore View Apartments, Hollywood
Beach, 64–65
Silver Sands Motel, Key Biscayne,
21
Sonesta Beach Hotel, Key Biscayne,
22
South Seas Plantation, Captiva, 253
Spindrift Tropical Resort, Key
West, 51
Sugar Sands Motel, Panama City
Beach, 165
Sundial Beach & Tennis Resort,
Sanibel, 254
Sunset Cove Motel, Key Largo, 33
Sun Tower Motor Hotel, Fort Lau-
derdale, 78
Sun Viking Lodge, Daytona Beach,
130

Tops'l Beach and Racquet Club,
Destin, 160
Tradewinds, St. Petersburg Beach,
228
Tristan Towers, Pensacola Beach,
146
'Tween Waters Inn, Captiva,
254–55

Vacation Shoppe, Sanibel, 251

Wakulla Motel, Cocoa Beach, 117
Windjammer, St. Augustine Beach,
202
Wright-by-the-Sea, Delray Beach, 92

BEACHES

Amelia City Beach, 189
Amelia Island Beach, 188
American Beach, 188–89
Anastasia State Recreation Area,
198
Atlantic Dunes Park, 87

Bahia Honda State Recreation Area,
38–39
Bay County Pier and Park, 171
Beach Highlands, 154
Bill Baggs Cape Florida State Rec-
reation Area, 19–20
Biltmore Beach, 171
Blind Pass, 249
Bowman's Beach, 249
Burney Henderson Beach State Rec-
reation Area, 155
Butler Beach, 197

Caladesi Island State Park, 213
Casino Beach, 142
Charnow Park, 60
Clarence Higgs Memorial Beach, 46
Clearwater Beach Park, 214
Conn Beach, 101
Crandon Park, 20
Crescent Beach, 197

Dania Beach, 61
Daytona Beach, 125–26
Dune Allen Beach, 154

East Beach, 224

Fernandina Beach, 189
Fort Clinch State Park, 189–90
Fort DeSoto Park, 223, 224
Fort Lauderdale Beach, 73–74
Fort Pickens, 141–42
Four Mile Village Beach, 154

Government Tracking Station, 101
Grayton Beach, 154
Grayton Beach State Recreation
    Area, 154
Gulf Breeze, 141
Gulf Islands National Seashore, 141,
    142
Gulfside City Park Beach, 249

Harry Harris County Park, 38
Haulover Park, 3
Highland Beach, 86
Hollywood North Beach Park, 59,
    60–61
Humiston Beach Park, 101

Indian River Shores Walkway, 101

Jaycee Park, 101
John C. Beasley Park, 155
John Pennekamp Coral Reef State
    Park, 30–31
Johnson Beach, 142

Langdon Beach, 142
Lido Beach, 237–38, 240
Lighthouse Park, 249
Little Duck Key County Park, 38
Little Talbot Island State Park, 188
Long Key State Recreation Area, 38
Lori Wilson Park, 114
Lummus Park, 5

Mandalay Park, 214
Miramar Beach, 154–55

National Seashore on Santa Rosa, 141
Navarre Beach, 142
Newman Bracklin Wayside Park,
    155
North Beach, Fort DeSoto Park,
    224
North Beach, St. Augustine, 197
North Beach Park, 59
North Lido Beach, 237

Panama City Beach, 170–71
Pensacola Beach, 142
Pepper State Park and Visitor's
    Center, 100–101
Perdido Key State Preserve, 142
Pier Park, 4

Quietwater Beach, 142

Red Reef Park, 88
Ross Marler Park, 155

St. Andrews State Recreation Area,
    171
St. Joseph Peninsula State Park, 187
Sand Key County Park, 213
Seagrove Beach, 154
Shell Island, 171
Sheppard Park, 113–14
Sidney Fischer Park, 114
Silver Beach Wayside Park, 155
Smathers Beach, 46
South Beach, Key West, 46
South Beach, Miami Beach, 3, 6
South Beach Park, Boca Raton, 87
South Lido Beach, 237
Spanish River Park, 87
Switlick County Park, 38

Tarpon Bay Road Beach, 249
Turner Beach, 249

Unnamed Beach, 142

Vero Beach, 101
Vilano Beach, 197
Virginia Key Beach, 20

Washington Beach, 199
Washington Oaks State Park, 199

CITIES / TOWNS

Amelia Island, 188–96

Bay Point, 174
Big Pine Key, 39
Boca Raton, 86–99
Bonne Fortune Key, 224

Captiva Island, 247–63
Clearwater, 213–22
Clearwater Beach Island, 214
Cocoa Beach, 113–24
Crescent Beach, 204, 205, 207

Daytona Beach, 125–37
Delray Beach, 86–99
Destin, 156, 158, 160, 161, 162–
    63, 164
Dog Island, 184–86
Duck Key, 41

Fernandina Beach, 188–96
Flagler Beach, 135
Fort DeSoto, 223–36
Fort Lauderdale, 73–85
Fort Myers Beach, 264–76

Fort Walton Beach, 155–57, 159,
    160–61, 165
Freeport, 165

Grayton Beach, 163
Gulf Breeze, 147

Hollywood Beach, 59–72

Indialantic, 118
Islamorada, 40, 41, 42, 43

Key Biscayne, 19–28
Key Largo, 30–37
Key West, 46–58

Little St. George Island, 186
Little Torch Key, 48–49
Longboat Key, 237–46
Lover's Key, 264–65

Madelaine Key, 224
Marathon, 38, 39, 43
Merritt Island, 120
Miami Beach, 3–18
Mullet Key, 224

Navarre, 143

Panama City, 170–83
Pass-A-Grille, 223–24
Pensacola, 141–53
Perdido Key, 142
Ponce Inlet, 131
Port Orange, 131, 132

St. Armands Circle, 241
St. Augustine, 200
St. Augustine Beach, 197–209
St. Christopher Key, 224
St. George Island, 186

St. Jean Key, 224
St. Petersburg Beach, 223–36
St. Vincent Island, 186
Sand Key, 216, 217, 218
Sanibel Island, 247–63
Santa Rosa Beach, 159, 161, 162,
    163–65
Santa Rosa Island, 142
Sarasota, 238, 239
Satellite Beach, 117
Seaside, 162
South Pasadena, 233
Stock Island, 55
Sunnyside, 173

Tavernier, 38
Tierra Verde, 230

Upper Matecumbe Key, 38

Vero Beach, 100–110

R E S T A U R A N T S

A-aaah At'sa Pizza, Daytona Beach,
    130–31
Adventure Island, Marathon, 43
Al Amir, Miami Beach, 10–11
Alma's Italian Restaurant, Cocoa
    Beach, 118
A Mano, Miami Beach, 7, 11
Angelo's Steak Pit, Panama City
    Beach, 176
Antonia's Restaurant, Key West, 51
Aunt Catfish's, Port Orange, 131
Aunt Rose's, Key West, 52

Babe's Seafood House, Destin, 158
Back Porch, The, Destin, 160

Bananas, Hollywood Beach, 62
Bangkok House, Sanibel, 255
Barefoot Deli, Clearwater Beach, 215
Barocco Beach, Miami Beach, 10,
    11
Bay Cafe, Fort Walton Beach,
    160–61
Bayou Bill's, Santa Rosa Beach,
    161
Beach Club Grill, Destin, 158
Beach Diner, Clearwater, 218
Beachside Cafe and Bar, The, Des-
    tin, 161
Bernard's Surf, Cocoa Beach, 118
Bill Nagy's Restaurant on the
    Beach, St. Petersburg Beach,
    228
Bill's Key West Fish Market & Res-
    taurant, Key West, 52
Billy's Oyster Bar I & II, Panama
    City Beach, 177
Bishop's Gulf Family Buffet, Pan-
    ama City Beach, 177
BJ's Bar-b-que, Key Largo, 34
Black Pearl, The, Vero Beach,
    104–5
Blueberry Muffin, Indialantic, 118
Boar's Head, Panama City Beach,
    178
Bobby's, Vero Beach, 105
Bostons, Delray Beach, 93
Boy on a Dolphin, Pensacola Beach,
    146
Brass Elephant, Sanibel, 251
Brown Derby, St. Petersburg Beach,
    228
Brunello Trattoria, St. Petersburg
    Beach, 229
Bubble Room, The, Captiva, 256
Buccaneer Inn, Longboat Key, 241
Bud & Alley's, Seaside, 159, 162

Burgee's Grille and Boat Bar, St. Petersburg Beach, 229

Buttery, The, Key West, 52

Cabana Café, Fort Lauderdale, 75

Cafe, The, Clearwater Beach, 215

Cafe, Fort Walton Beach, 157

Cafe des Artiste, Key West, 52–53

Cafe Key Largo, Key Largo, 33

Cafe la Scala, Longboat Key, 241

Cafe l'Europe, St. Armands Circle, 241

Calico Jack's, Clearwater Beach, 214

Cantina, The, Duck Key, 42

Capone's Flicker Lite, Hollywood Beach, 65

Cap's Seafood Restaurant, St. Augustine Beach, 203

Captain Anderson's, Panama City Beach, 178

Captain Davis Dockside Restaurant, Panama City Beach, 178–79

Captiva Canoe Club, Captiva, 255

Captiva Inn, Sanibel, 256

Caribbean Room, Duck Key, 42

Caribbean Room, Key Biscayne, 21, 22

Carlyle Grill, Miami Beach, 12

Carlyle's, Cocoa Beach, 115

Casino, Pensacola Beach, 145

Chadwick's, Captiva, 256–57

Charley's Crab, St. Armands Key, 242

Chez Marcel, Boca Raton, 93

Chez Yannick, Vero Beach, 105

Christina's, Key Largo, 33

Ciao, Delray Beach, 94

Cirolla's, Santa Rosa Beach, 162

Coconuts, Fort Lauderdale, 79

Coconuts, Key Largo, 33

Colony Restaurant, Longboat Key, 242

Columbia, Sand Key, Clearwater, 218

Compton's, St. Augustine Beach, 203

Conch House Restaurant & Lounge, St. Augustine Beach, 204

Crawdaddy's, Miami Beach, 12

Criolla's, Santa Rosa Beach, 162

Currents Restaurant, Clearwater Beach, 216

D.J.'s Raw Bar, Key West, 50

Dockside, Hollywood Beach, 65

Doc's Galley Restaurant, Key Largo, 33

Doe-Al Southern Cooking, St. Petersburg Beach, 229

Down the Hatch, Ponce Inlet, 126, 131

Duke Snider's Restaurant and Bar, Vero Beach, 102, 106

Dune Side Club, Amelia Island, 191

Eatery, Key West, 46

Elephant's Walk, Destin, 158

El Siboney, Key West, 53

Emma's Seafare, Key West, 51

English Pub, Key Biscayne, 23

Erny's, Delray Beach, 94

Euphemia Haye, Longboat Key, 242–43

Fairmont Gardens Bar & Grille, Miami Beach, 12–13

Fiddler's Green, Panama City Beach, 179

Fiesta, Daytona Beach Shores, 127

Fish House Restaurant and Fish Market, The, Key Largo, 34

Fish Monger, The, Fort Myers Beach, 270

Flamingo Cafe, Destin, 162–63

Flounder's Chowder & Ale House, Pensacola Beach, 146–47

Frank and Mario's Pizzeria, Hollywood Beach, 66

Frenchy's Cafe, Clearwater Beach, 218–19

Gallo's Ristorante D'Italia, Fort Myers Beach, 270

Gatsby's Dockside Eatery, Cocoa Beach, 119

Golden China, Gulf Breeze, 147

Golden Dragon, Fort Myers Beach, 270–71

Gondolier, Clearwater Beach, 219

Good Times, Tierra Verde, 230

Grayton Corner Cafe, Grayton Beach, 163

Great Khan, The, Fernandina Beach, 193

Gulf Shore, Fort Myers Beach, 271

Half-Shell Raw Bar, Key West, 53

Harbor Bar, Islamorada, 41

Harbor Docks, Destin, 163

Harbour View Cafe, Key West, 50

Harp and Thistle, St. Petersburg Beach, 230

Harriette's Restaurant, Key Largo, 34

Harry's Continental Kitchens, Longboat Key, 243

Harry T's, Destin, 158

Heidelberg Restaurant, Cocoa Beach, 119

Heilman's Beachcomber, Clearwater Beach, 219

Hemingway, Key West, 47

Henry's, Key West, 49

Herbie K's, Cocoa Beach, 115

Heron's, Fort Myers Beach, 266

Heron's Nest, Fort Myers Beach, 266

Hog Heaven, Daytona Beach, 132

HoJo, Fort Lauderdale, 76

HoJo, Hollywood Beach, 63

Hunky Dory's, Hollywood Beach, 66

Hurricane Seafood Restaurant, St. Petersburg Beach, 230

Ice Cream Delights, Hollywood Beach, 66

Iggy & Paul's Lobster House, Sanibel, 257

Il Paparazzi, Miami Beach, 13

Incredible Edibles, Delray Beach, 94–95

Isabella's, Sanibel, 257

Island Bar-b-q, Fernandina Beach, 194

Island House, Clearwater Beach, 219–20

Italian Courtyard, The, Cocoa Beach, 119

Italian Fisherman, Key Largo, 35

Jacaranda, The, Sanibel, 258

Jack Baker's Lobster Shanty, Cocoa Beach, 120

Jack's Bar-b-que, St. Augustine Beach, 204

Jad's, Amelia Island, 194

J.C.'s Oyster Deck, Port Orange, 132

Jean-Paul's French Corner, Sanibel, 258

Joe Sonken's Gold Coast Restaurant, Hollywood Beach, 67

Joe's Stone Crab, Miami Beach, 13
J.P.'s Restaurant, Fort Walton
    Beach, 157
Jubilee Restaurant & Oyster Bar,
    Pensacola Beach, 148
Jungle Jim's, Merritt Island, 120

King Charles Room, St. Petersburg
    Beach, 226, 231
Kinjo Restaurant, St. Petersburg
    Beach, 231

La Choza, Key Biscayne, 23
La Concha Beach Club, Hollywood
    Beach, 67
Lake Place, The, Santa Rosa Beach,
    163
La Parisienne Croissant Shop, Cres-
    cent Beach, 204
L'Auberge du Bon Vivant, Longboat
    Key, 243
La Vielle Maison, Boca Raton, 95
LeBleu's Cajun Kitchen, Santa Rosa
    Beach, 164
Lenora's, Clearwater Beach, 217
Leverock's Seafood House, St. Pe-
    tersburg Beach, 231
Little Italy on the Beach, Fort Lau-
    derdale, 79
Lobster House, Fort Walton Beach,
    157
Lorelei Restaurant, Islamorada, 43
Louie's Backyard, Key West, 54
Lucky Fisherman Seafood House, St.
    Petersburg Beach, 232
Lulu's, Miami Beach, 14

Maison de Pepe, Key West, 54
Mangia Mangia, Key West, 54
Mango Tree, The, Cocoa Beach, 120
Margaritaville Cafe, Key West, 55

Marina Cafe, Destin, 164
Martha's on the Intracoastal, Holly-
    wood Beach, 68
McGowan's, Hollywood Beach, 68
Mediterraneo, St. Augustine Beach,
    205
Melting Pot, The, Panama City
    Beach, 179
Menu, The, Vero Beach, 107
Mezzanotte, Miami Beach, 14
Mikato Japanese Steakhouse, Pan-
    ama City Beach, 180
Mike's Italian Restaurant & Pizze-
    ria, Fort Lauderdale, 79
Montego Bay Seafood House & Oys-
    ter Bar, Panama City Beach,
    180
Moore's Stone Crab, Longboat Key,
    244
Moorings, The, Pensacola Beach,
    148
Mucky Duck, The, Captiva, 258–59
Mucky Duck, The, Fort Myers
    Beach, 271

Nena's, Santa Rosa Beach, 164–65
Nero's, Pensacola Beach, 149
News Cafe, Miami Beach, 14
New York Pizza, Key Biscayne, 23
Nick and Stella's Beach Diner and
    Pizzeria, Fort Myers Beach,
    272
Nick's, Freeport and Santa Rosa
    Beach, 165
Nick's Bar & Grill, Hollywood
    Beach, 68–69

Oasis, The, St. Augustine Beach,
    205
Ocean Grill, Vero Beach, 107–8
Ocean Room, Fort Lauderdale, 80

Oceans Eleven, Hollywood Beach, 69
Old Captiva House, Captiva, 255
Old Fisherman's Wharf, Cocoa Beach, 121
Our Place, Crescent Beach, 205

Palm Ridge Cafe, Sanibel, 259
Panama Hattie's, St. Augustine Beach, 206
Park's, Daytona Beach, 132
Pate's at the Bridge, Fort Myers Beach, 272
Patio Bar and Cafe, Boca Raton, 89
Peg Leg Pete's, Pensacola Beach, 149
Pelican's Roost, Fort Walton Beach, 157
Pep's Sea Grill, St. Petersburg Beach, 232
Pier House Restaurant, Key West, 50
Pier House Restaurant, The, Cocoa Beach, 121
Pippindale's, Clearwater Beach, 215
Place on the Beach, The, Hollywood Beach, 69
Plaka, Fort Myers Beach, 272–73
Plaza, The, Longboat Key, 244

Quay Restaurant, The, Key Largo, 35

Rajan's, Clearwater Beach, 220
Rattlesnake Jake's, Deerfield Beach, 95
Red Snapper, Daytona Beach Shores, 133
Reese's, Fort Myers Beach, 273
Rib Room, Key Biscayne, 22

Rib Room Terrace, Key Biscayne, 22
R.J.'s Landing, Fort Lauderdale, 80
Roof Restaurant, Daytona Beach, 128
Rosenhof, St. Augustine Beach, 206
Ruffy's, Hollywood Beach, 64, 70
Rusty Anchor Restaurant and Fishery, Stock Island, 55
Rusty Pelican, Key Biscayne, 24
Rusty's Raw Bar, Cocoa Beach, 121

Sahara International, Hollywood Beach, 70
St. Regis Hotel, Daytona Beach, 133
Saltwater Cowboys, St. Augustine Beach, 206–7
Salty Sally's, Fort Lauderdale, 80–81
Sandbar, The, Fernandina Beach, 194–95
Sandbar, The, Key Biscayne, 21, 24
Sandcastles Restaurant, Destin, 158
Sandshaker Sandwich Shop and Lounge, Pensacola Beach, 149
Sandwiches by the Sea, Delray Beach, 96
Sapporo Japanese Steak House, Daytona Beach Shores, 134
Schenkel's, Longboat Key, 244
Seacrest, Delray Beach, 90, 96
Seafood & Sunsets at Julie's, Clearwater Beach, 220
Sea Horse, The, St. Petersburg Beach, 232
Ships Galley, Duck Key, 42
Sinbads, Port Orange, 134
Skipper's Galley, The, Fort Myers Beach, 273
Sliders, Fernandina Beach, 195

Snook's Bayside Club, Key Largo, 35

Snug Harbor, Fort Myers Beach, 274

Sound, The, Fort Walton Beach, 165

Spinnaker's, Cocoa Beach, 122

Stars and Stripes, Miami Beach, 7, 15

Stefano's, Key Biscayne, 24

Stuart's at the Cardozo, Miami Beach, 15

Sundays on the Bay, Key Biscayne, 25

Sundeck, The, Pensacola Beach, 150

Sundowners, Key Largo, 36

Sun Ray Taco Shop, Pensacola Beach, 149–50

Sunset Cafe, Marathon, 40

Sunset Grille, St. Augustine Beach, 207

Surf Seafood Restaurant, Fernandina Beach, 195

Surfside Cafe, Fort Lauderdale, 81

T.C.'s Top Dog, Daytona Beach, 134–35

Ted Peters Famous Smoked Fish, South Pasadena, 233

Thai Toni, Miami Beach, 15

Theo's, Panama City Beach, 180

Tijuana Joe's, Miami Beach, 16

Timbers Restaurant & Fish Market, The, Sanibel, 259

Timmy's Nook, Captiva, 260

Toni's, Miami Beach, 16

Tony's Beach Pizza Shack, Fort Lauderdale, 81

Tony's Pizza, Crescent Beach, 207

Topaz Cafe, Flagler Beach, 135

Top of Daytona, Daytona Beach Shores, 135

Top of the Bridge, Boca Raton, 89

Top of the Tower, Boca Raton, 89

Tower of Pizza, Key Largo, 36

Tristan Towers, Pensacola Beach, 146

Tropics International, Miami Beach, 8, 16–17

Truffles, Sanibel, 250, 260

Two Dragons, Key Biscayne, 22

Ventana's Restaurant on the Green, Key Biscayne, 25

Village South, Vero Beach, 108–9

Waldo's, Vero Beach, 108–9

Wednesdays on the Beach, Fort Lauderdale, 82

Whale Rib's Atlantic Whaler, Delray Beach, 97

Whale's Rib, Deerfield Beach, 96

Windows on the Water, Sanibel, 254

Woody's Waterfront, St. Petersburg Beach, 233

Zelda's, St. Petersburg Beach, 226